An Introduction to the UK Hospitality Industry

A comparative approach

**Edited by
Bob Brotherton**

BUTTERWORTH
HEINEMANN

OXFORD AUCKLAND BOSTON JOHANNESBURG MELBOURNE NEW DELHI

Butterworth-Heinemann
Linacre House, Jordan Hill, Oxford OX2 8DP
225 Wildwood Avenue, Woburn, MA 01801-2041
A division of Reed Educational and Professional Publishing Ltd

☟ A member of the Reed Elsevier plc group

First published 2000

Collection © Bob Brotherton 2000
Individual chapters © Reed Educational and Professional
Publishing Ltd 2000

British Library Cataloguing in Publication Data
A catalogue record for this book is available from
the British Library

ISBN 0 7506 4711 6

Composition by Genesis Typesetting, Rochester, Kent
Printed and bound in Great Britain

FOR EVERY TITLE THAT WE PUBLISH, BUTTERWORTH-HEINEMANN
WILL PAY FOR BTCV TO PLANT AND CARE FOR A TREE.

An Introduction to the ...dustry

...pproach

For Paul

A son to be proud of
and a braver teacher than me

Contents

Contributors

Mike Boella is a Principal Lecturer at the University of Brighton Business School where he teaches law, human resource management and international management. He is a *professor invité* at the University of Perpignan in France and teaches regularly at the Ecole Hotelière de Lausanne. He trained for the hotel and catering industry at Portsmouth, later specializing in personnel management, working for Forte, Bass and as a consultant with Price Waterhouse. He has a masters degree from Sussex University. Mike is the author of a number of books including *Human Resource Management in the Hospitality Industry*, now in its seventh edition, and co-author with Professor Alan Pannett of *Principles of Hospitality Law*.

Bob Brotherton is a Principal Lecturer and Director of postgraduate programmes in Hospitality and Tourism Management at the Manchester Metropolitan University. He teaches comparative hospitality studies, research methods and operational management. Bob has been involved in hospitality management education for nearly twenty years and has undertaken a number of consultancy assignments in the UK and overseas during this period. He has published a wide range of conference and academic journal papers, book chapters and edited two books. He is currently undertaking research concerned with the 'nature' of hospitality and the critical success factors associated with various types of hospitality operation.

Cathy Burgess qualified in Hospitality Management at Leeds Polytechnic (now Leeds Metropolitan University) and then spent thirteen years in various operational and financial management positions within the hotel and catering industry. Her later appointments were as a financial controller with Marriott Corporation and Thistle Hotels. In 1989 she was appointed Senior Lecturer in Accounting at Oxford Brookes University, teaching financial management to degree and masters level students, and gained her MPhil in 1993. She maintains close links with industry through research and consultancy and as a Council member of the British Association of Hospitality Accountants. Her current research interests include the role of the hotel financial controller.

Andrew J. Frew is a Reader in Applied Information Management and Director of the Institute for Tourism Research (ITR) at Napier University, Edinburgh, and has developed a range of applied IT teaching programmes and directed extensive PhD work in the field. Since 1979 he has specialized in hospitality and tourism information technology with research covering international reservations networks, intelligent software agents and global electronic distribution. He is a chair of HITA Europe, is a regular contributor to international journals, conferences and forums and is currently on the Advisory Boards for EURHOTEC and HOSTEC. He retains strong industry contacts, between 1988–1991 ran the Scottish arm of Innsite Hotel Services Ltd and has been active in many consultancy and contract research projects in the last ten years, embracing information systems construction, and also holds a range of advisory and non-executive director roles within industry software houses. As principal researcher and project director, he has completed one of the largest tourism economic modelling projects undertaken in recent years and is currently engaged in a number of European-wide tourism IT projects in research and education.

Hadyn Ingram is a third-generation publican, having been the licensee of a large west London pub for fifteen years after training in hotel management. He is currently Director of Corporate Development and Professor at International Management Centres Association, responsible for a number of MBA courses. Hadyn held lecturing posts at the Universities of Bournemouth and Surrey, where he still teaches on hospitality management programmes. He owns a hotel in the city of Salisbury, but finds time to write books and articles on operations, strategy and properties management for the hospitality industry. To date, he has written three books, eight book chapters and more than thirty articles and conference papers.

Keith Johnson is a Professor of Management at Trinity and All Saints College, University of Leeds, where he is responsible for management research and postgraduate programmes. He has considerable experience as an external examiner for hospitality management programmes, ranging from sub-degree to post-graduate level. He has written extensively on a variety of general management and human resource issues as they relate to the hospitality industry. He continues to be involved in the supervision of a number of research projects in this field. On a personal level, he is currently researching the use of humour within management.

Peter Jones holds the Forte Chair of Hotel Management at the University of Surrey and is responsible for the Centre for Hospitality Industry Productivity Research. He is the author or editor of nine textbooks and over thirty journal articles, and has presented at conferences in eleven countries on five continents. He is currently researching a number of topics related to chain operations, including hotel yield management performance.

Clare Kelliher is a Senior Lecturer in Strategic Human Resource Management in the School of Management Studies for the Service Sector at the University of Surrey. Her research interests are in HRM and industrial relations in the service industries. She was formerly at the Surrey European Management School.

David Litteljohn has been publishing in hospitality for over fifteen years. His work spans strategic and economic aspects of the industry, with an orientation to the larger business side of hotel operations. He is also interested in policy as it affects the hotel industry and the dynamics of the Scottish hotel and tourism industry. He is in the Department of Hospitality, Tourism and Leisure Management at Glasgow Caledonian University and, in addition, holds the post of Director of Research and Scholarship for the Faculty of Business. David graduated from Strathclyde University and has a Masters degree from the University of Manchester, Institute of Science and Technology. In the 1970s he worked in tourism development with the government funded Highlands and Islands Development Board. He has taught in the new university sector: Huddersfield and Napier (Edinburgh) and now at his current post in Glasgow.

Andrew Lockwood is Professor of Hospitality Management in the School of Management Studies for the Service Sector at the University of Surrey, where he teaches undergraduate and postgraduate courses in international hospitality management, operations management and operations analysis. He has developed and taught short courses for the hospitality industry in the UK, Bali, Bulgaria, Crete, Cyprus, Ireland and Mauritius. His industrial experience includes working for international hotel companies both in London and the provinces in a range of managerial positions, before running his own hotel. He has extensive experience of hospitality education having taught from craft level to masters degree and supervised numerous PhD students. He has written or edited seven books and over 100 articles, chapters and conference papers on the management of hospitality operations. His longstanding research interests lie in the fields of quality management, hospitality education and managerial activity in the hospitality industry.

Rosemary Lucas is a Professor of Employment Relations and Director of *the* Centre for Hospitality Employment Research (CHER) at *the* Manchester Metropolitan University. Her most recent research has been on the introduction of the National Minimum Wage (NMW), and she has produced two reports commissioned by the Low Pay Commission on the impact of the NMW in the hospitality industry. She is currently working on data from the Workplace Employee Relations Survey 1998 in order to write a sequel to her book *Managing Employee Relations in the Hotel and Catering Industry*.

Josef Ransley has been involved in the design and development of international hotel leisure projects since 1973. In 1983 he established, and is the Chairman of, the Ransley Group, which is dedicated to this sector. Recent major projects include the Stuttgart International Centre, Germany and the Royal Garden Hotel, Kensington, London. He is currently Chairman of the Interiors Group for the Chartered Society of Designers and a Visiting Fellow at the University of Surrey. He has been involved since 1996 in designing and delivering undergraduate and postgraduate courses for the hospitality industry. He has published widely in industry and academic journals and contributed chapters to seven books.

Roy Wood holds the Chair of Hospitality Management at The Scottish Hotel School, University of Strathclyde. He has researched and written extensively on human resource management and employee relations in the hospitality industry and is the author or co-author of seven books and numerous academic articles.

Figures

Tables

Editor's preface

This text aims to provide an introduction to the hospitality industry for first or second-year students on Hospitality Management HND or degree courses. It is also a book which more advanced undergraduates may find useful for final year dissertation or project work that is comparative in nature. The approach used is rather different from the 'traditional' sector-by-sector structure adopted in other 'introduction to the industry' type books that have been produced in the past. Here the hospitality industry is illuminated and explored through a series of its key aspects, as indicated in the chapter titles. Thus, the structure of the book is more thematic than sectoral in nature, and the approach taken within each of these themes is overtly comparative rather than descriptive.

This, of course, begs the question; why is this change in approach required? First, it has the value of focusing attention on the key aspect of the industry dealt with in each chapter and provides an approach which should encourage you to analyse and evaluate these aspects across the sectors of the industry in a comparative manner. Second, it is more realistic in relation to the contemporary structure and operational nature of the hospitality industry for a number of reasons. The boundaries between the traditional sectors of the industry are becoming increasingly blurred as hospitality companies engage in a wider range of activities that cut across such sectors and, in some cases, industries. This is evidenced, at least in part, by companies that would previously have been categorized as public house, pub restaurant, or catering/restaurant companies now describing themselves as hospitality/leisure retailing, multiple licensed retailing or leisure catering companies.

Hospitality managers also move between the sectors as they pursue their careers. A significant number of hospitality companies are now international, if not global, enterprises operating in many different countries and markets. Many of tomorrow's hospitality managers will have a range of jobs across the traditional sectors of the industry, and a significant number will move from country to country as hospitality businesses become more international in their outlook. For example, who would have thought twenty years ago that Harry Ramsdens' would become an international business by the end of the twentieth century?

Third, there is great value in future managers taking a wider perspective. Even those who do not move around from sector to sector, or country to country, need to be more aware of the developments and innovations taking place in other sectors, industries and countries. Indeed, many of the innovations introduced into hospitality businesses over the last twenty years or so have originated from other industries or countries. It would be dangerous in the extreme for tomorrow's hospitality manager to assume that the hotel, or any other kind of hospitality, business will remain basically as it is now in the future.

With the exception of Chapter 1, which has a slightly different purpose, all the chapters focus on a particular aspect of the hospitality industry and explore it in a comparative manner. The nature and focus of the comparative approach taken by each individual chapter does vary slightly in the light of the subject matter being dealt with. However, the purpose remains constant: to enrich your understanding of the structure and dynamics existing within the contemporary hospitality industry.

Chapter 1 is not concerned with a particular aspect of the industry. It is designed to provide you with an understanding of the principles underlying the nature and practice of the comparative approach to study. In this sense it is the chapter you should read first, as it will help to lay a conceptual foundation for you. This, in turn, should enable you to explore the other chapters with a more critical eye and gain more from reading them.

I hope you enjoy reading this book and find it stimulating. I am extremely grateful to all the contributing authors for agreeing to allocate some of their valuable time to the task of writing the chapters, and for translating my overall comparative perspective for the book into each chapter. Given their standing in the hospitality field it is not surprising that they have accomplished this with some aplomb, and responded to my badgering for the copy with typical good humour and professionalism. I just hope that I have not used up too many favours in the process!

I must also record my thanks to my wife, Penny, who once again has had to endure life for long periods of time with me tapping the proverbial keys. As ever she remains my rock and continues to hope that this might constitute the last writing project for a while. Of the former there is no doubt, the latter – well, we'll just have to wait and see! My thanks must also go to Sally North at Butterworth-Heinemann who was instrumental in helping me to get this project off the ground and has been extremely supportive throughout the time it took to write it. Her enthusiasm, patience and professionalism have been of immense help.

Finally, as is customary in ventures of this nature, I accept sole responsibility for any errors, omissions etc. in this text. Conversely, any value the text provides is solely due to its contents provided by my colleagues who wrote the bulk of the chapters. Without all their hard work this book would not exist.

Bob Brotherton

Abbreviations

AA	Automobile Association
ACAS	Advisory, Conciliation and Arbitration Service
ADS	alternative distribution systems
ADSL	asynchronous digital subscriber line
ARR	average room rate
ATM	asynchronous transfer mode
BACS	bank automated clearing service
BHA	British Hospitality Association
BTA	British Tourist Authority
CD	co-ordinating device
CD	compact disc
CPO	customer processing operation
CRS	central reservations system
DVD	digital video discs
EBMS	electronic bar management system
EDI	electronic data interchange
EFT	electronic funds transfer
EFTPOS	electronic funds transfer at point of sale
ELS	electronic locking system
EMS	energy management system
EPOS	electronic point of sale
EU	European Union
F&B	food and beverage
FTP	file-transfer protocol
GDS	global distribution system
GIS	geographical information systems
GM	general manager
GOP	gross operating profit
GP	gross profit
GPS	global positioning systems
HACCP	Hazard Analysis and Critical Control Points
HCIMA	Hotel and Catering International Management Association

HITIS	Hospitality Information Technology Interface Standards
HPA	Hotel Proprietors Act 1956
HRM	human resource management
HtF	Hospitality Training Foundation
ICT	information and communication technology
ID	interaction device
ILO	International Labour Organization
IRBS	in-room business system
IRES	in-room entertainment system
ISDN	integrated services digital networks
IT	information technology
JIT	just in time
LAN	local area network
LMS	leisure management system
MPO	materials processing operation
NIC	National Insurance Contribution
NMW	National Minimum Wage
NTO	national training organization
OS	operating system
P&L	profit and loss
PABX	private automatic branch exchange
PC	personal computer
PDA	personal digital assistant
PMS	property management system
POS	point of sale
RAC	Royal Automobile Club
RID	remote interaction device
RMS	restaurant management system
SIC	Standard Industrial Classification
SME	small to medium-sized enterprise
TCP/IP	transmission control protocol/Internet protocol
TMS	telephone management system
TRS	total rewards system
USAL	Uniform System of Accounts for Lodging
WAN	wide area network
WIRS	Workplace Industrial Relations Survey

The comparative approach

Bob Brotherton

Objectives

The general objectives of this chapter are to introduce you to the comparative approach to studying the hospitality industry, and provide you with an opportunity to explore some of the basic conceptual issues associated with this approach. Therefore, when you have read this chapter you should be able to:

1 Explain the difference between simply making comparisons and using the comparative approach.

2 Recognize the differences between comparative and other types of study.

3 Identify the features necessary to make valid comparisons.

4 Distinguish between different approaches to, and types of, comparative study.

5 Explain the difference between contextual and generic factors.

6 Explain what is required to establish an appropriate comparative base.

7 Distinguish between transferability and generalizability in comparative studies.

Introduction

As you will see in this chapter, and indeed the book as a whole, the comparative approach is potentially a very 'broad church' which can range from studies explicitly designed to compare two or more individuals to cross-national studies comparing an issue across at least two countries. In this sense it is an approach capable of embracing a wide range of possibilities in relation to the scope and specific focus of the study. For example, Nebel's (1991) study of the attributes associated with successful hotel general managers (see Case 1.1) was designed to make comparisons between individual general managers in order to establish those attributes common to all of them.

Case 1.1

What are the common characteristics of successful hotel general managers?

This was perhaps the key question this study sought to answer. To achieve this Nebel got ten very successful general managers (GMs) of American hotels to participate in his study. In selecting this group of ten he attempted to create a sample of GMs who were all highly experienced and successful, from both large and small hotels, national and international chains, and one independent hotel. By doing this he was hoping to be able to produce results which could be generalized to the wider community of hotel GMs. However, you may wish to question the extent to which this could be achieved, given the fact that the group chosen for the study was numerically small, based solely on American hotels, only contained one independent hotel GM and was comprised of males only.

The approach Nebel took to collecting his data was one that could be described as qualitative in nature, and the techniques he used would normally be described as non-participant observation and field interviewing. So what do these mean? Studies are generally grouped into two different types – quantitative and qualitative. Quantitative studies are designed to gather numerical or statistical data, whereas qualitative studies seek to obtain 'softer' data relating to perceptions, feelings, interactions between people

etc. Though Nebel did gather some quantitative data on the GMs' backgrounds, careers etc., what they did, and how frequently etc., his approach was predominantly qualitative in nature. The non-participant observation and field interviewing techniques Nebel used are best illustrated by his own words:

> I stayed as a guest at each hotel, joined the GM as he proceeded through his normal work day; observed and recorded his every activity. I attended the meetings he did, listened in on his phone conversations, watched him do paperwork, and lunched with him. I was, in effect, his shadow . . . I also conducted extensive interviews with each GM . . . I conducted additional interviews of about one hour each with the GMs' key division heads . . . The field research . . . resulted in over 700 pages of field notes.

One of the issues Nebel attempted to explore in this study was what the personal characteristics of an 'ideal GM' may be. As you might imagine this is a very difficult task because such a person is unlikely to exist! However, Nebel did recognize this problem and justified his decision to attempt this as follows:

No one manager will possess equal measures of each characteristic. But, characteristics that can be shown to be important to the effectiveness of hotel managers are important to know. So the process of trying to discern important, personal, success characteristics lends insight to what it takes to be successful in the hotel business.

In this sense Nebel was trying to recognize the influences arising from the personal characteristics of the GM's and reconcile this with those emanating from the nature of the job and hotel environment. In short, he was focusing attention on both content and context to identify the general and specific factors influencing the success, or otherwise, of the hotel GM.

By contrast, the study conducted by Kara, Kaynak, and Kucukemiroglu (1995) on consumer perceptions of fast food restaurants in three cities in the USA and Canada (see Case 1.2) was one concerned with more aggregate issues, used a questionnaire survey and was undertaken on a much larger scale.

Case 1.2

Marketing strategies for fast food restaurants

This study was interested in exploring consumers' perceptions and preferences for fast food outlets and how they differ across cultures/countries. The reason for this being that any similarities or differences could have implications for how the same type of fast food restaurants should be promoted and marketed in different countries. The overall aim of the study was 'to determine whether the same fast food restaurants are perceived similarly/differently across the two countries [the USA and Canada] and whether their positioning can be improved/changed through careful and selective promotion'.

To implement the study Kara, Kaynak and Kucukemiroglu first reviewed the relevant literature and identified nine fast food restaurant brands specializing in different types of fast food; including McDonald's, Burger King, Kentucky Fried Chicken and Pizza Hut, to compare across the two countries. In addition to this they also identified eleven attributes that could be used as a 'common' basis to ask the different sets of people how they perceived these restaurants. Together these two things helped to establish a common basis for comparison across the two

countries, as the same types of restaurant and questions were used in both countries. To extend this comparability further the cities/regions chosen to select the samples and the method used to implement the questionnaire were also 'matched' in the two countries. The combination of all these aspects acting to create a common and consistent basis to compare the responses of the US and Canadian consumers.

Perhaps not surprisingly, the results obtained from this study showed a number of significant differences between the perceptions and priorities of the American and Canadian consumers. It would not be appropriate to try and detail all of these here but the following examples will give you a flavour. While older (aged forty-six to fifty-five and above fifty-five) American consumers emphasized the importance of cleanliness, nutritional value and quality of taste, the same category of Canadian customers considered nutritional value and seating capacity to be the most important. On the other hand, the two sets of consumers did not differ in terms of the preferred time to consume fast food.

In practical terms the type of results obtained from a comparative study of this kind could be used to identify different segments of the fast food market and different consumer preferences and behaviours associated with these segments. This knowledge could help the company and/or the unit manager to develop more targeted and effective promotional messages. At an international level there would also be important issues raised over the extent to which a particular brand and product/service format could be exactly replicated, without any modifications, across a number of different countries. The key to making sensible decisions in any of these respects would be the identification of similarities and differences, and their implications.

Thus, at one extreme, the comparative approach may be used to explore an issue associated with particular types of individuals and, at the other, one associated with particular types of hospitality operations or activities across differing countries. In short, the scope for comparative study ranges from the individual to the international. In practice most comparative studies are conducted at a level between these two extremes. Studies that compare two or more companies in the same type of business are quite common, as are ones designed to compare one sector of an industry with another, and those concerned with comparing companies operating in different industries. These types of comparative study are often referred to as intra-sectoral, inter-sectoral, and inter-industry respectively. We shall return to these types later in the chapter and explore some examples of each.

The nature of the comparative approach

At a basic level the comparative approach is simply one of making comparisons, something we do constantly in our everyday lives. Indeed, as Swanson (1971: 145) succinctly pointed out many years ago: 'Thinking without comparison is unthinkable. And, in the absence of comparison, so is all . . . thought.' Thinking and learning by making comparisons is a very natural and intuitive process for us. We use comparisons extensively in our daily thinking and interactions with people and various objects. However, making comparisons is not necessarily easy or without its pitfalls. Any comparison may be appropriate and valid, or it may not. A comparison made between things that have some similarity to each other is more likely to be appropriate and valid than one trying to compare things that are totally different. Indeed, everyday expressions such as 'they are as different as apples and pears, or chalk and cheese' imply that it is very difficult to make useful comparisons between things that do not have any common features or characteristics. Therefore, this provides our first clue to what may be regarded as a useful and valid comparison, and what may not.

Conceptually we could view this situation as that shown in Figure 1.1. Here we have the two extremes of something being either identical or totally different. Any attempt to make comparisons between things lying at either of these extremes is likely to be a fairly pointless exercise. If two or more things are totally different, in every respect, then there is no basis to make a comparison. Similarly, if two or more things are identical this is all we can say about them. What is more interesting is the intermediate area between these two extremes, within which any things being subjected to comparison will not be either identical or totally different. In short, they will have some features or characteristics which are similar and others which are different.

Figure 1.1
Making comparisons

It is the exploration of these similarities and differences that makes the comparative approach so interesting. This now raises the issue of the extent to which the things are the same or different. For example, we might ask questions such as: is the process of producing food for a hotel restaurant the same as it is in school canteen or a burger restaurant? Are there any differences in the reservation systems used by hotels, airlines, or leisure centres? Do employment practices differ between contract catering and restaurant companies? In seeking to explore questions such as these we begin to adopt a comparative approach to study. However, we must be careful to do this in a meaningful and valid way.

To achieve this it is important that we do not fall into the trap of making surface or superficial comparisons. Things that may initially appear to be either very similar or different on the surface are often seen very differently when a more detailed, and in-depth, analysis is conducted. For example, at first sight a public house and a supermarket may appear to be totally different types of business operation with nothing at all in common. However, a more considered analysis of these two types of business may begin to indicate that they have more similarities than such a superficial analysis would suggest. Both have public and private areas, or a front and back of house, are involved in the retail sale of products to the customer, and regarded as 'service' businesses exhibiting direct service staff contact with the customer. In view of this you can see that it may be possible to undertake a valid comparative analysis of some aspects of public house and supermarket operations.

In addition, even where contexts have few, if any, similarities or common features they may still be used to conduct a comparative study where the issue to be studied becomes the 'constant' across these contexts. Perhaps one of the best known examples of this is the Peters and Watermans' (1982) *In Search of Excellence* study conducted in the USA. Case 1.3 contains a brief overview of this study and illustrates how such a comparative study may be designed and implemented in a valid manner.

Case 1.3

In search of excellence

The aim of this work was to study the most successful companies in America in order to discover why they were so successful and explore the possibilities for transferring their 'recipes for success' to other businesses. To study such a wide range of businesses from different sectors of the American economy clearly involved many varied contexts, and raised the question, how could such comparisons be made in a valid way? The first solution to this was to produce a definition of a 'successful company', regardless of the type of industry it was operating in. This definition was then used to select the sample for the study of sixty-three 'successful' companies from a wide range of industry sectors. In this way at least the study would be focused on companies who had a similar level of performance, and therefore were directly comparable.

However, this was not the end of the story. The next problem the study faced was how to ensure that there was some consistency in the data to be collected from each of the companies. To establish the reasons why these companies became excellent the study used a structured interview technique, supplemented by other published material on the companies. However, this gave rise to another issue. Even though the technique used for collecting the data from each of the companies was to be the same, the study could not allow the team of interviewers to simply go out and ask whatever questions they wanted to, or in any manner they felt appropriate. To be able to directly compare the responses given by the people to be interviewed it was necessary to create a common set of questions that each interviewer would ask in the same way to ensure that the technique would be implemented consistently in each company.

So far, so good, but of course all of this generated the further question, how do we decide what questions should be asked by each interviewer? To answer this Peters and Waterman turned to an existing theory for help. Previous research work had produced what is known as the McKinsey 7S model. This suggested that any attempt to study business organization and performance should examine the seven interrelated factors of – structure, strategy, staff, skills, style, systems and shared values. Hence, the 7S model was used as a framework to structure the interview questions and analyse the data collected from these interviews. At the end of this process the comparative study identified eight common or generic attributes associated with successful companies and ventured to suggest that if other companies adopted, or performed better, on these attributes they would be more likely to become successful or excellent. Therefore, because the design and implementation of the study was undertaken in this way it allowed its conclusions to be generalized to other companies.

As we have noted earlier, all thinking tends to exhibit varying degrees of comparison. However, not all study is explicitly designed to be comparative in nature. The occurrence of comparisons alone does not necessarily make a study comparative. For any study to be classified as comparative its overall aim or purpose should be explicitly comparative in nature and it should be designed with this specific outcome in mind. As Ragin (1996: 75) points out: 'there are important differences between the *orientations* of most comparativists and most non-comparativists and these differences have important ... consequences' (original emphasis). One such consequence is the particular importance given to 'contextual factors' by those who conduct comparative studies (Pearce, 1993).

As the comparative approach is essentially concerned with 'discovering similarities and differences among phenomena' (Warwick and Osherson, 1973: 7) the context(s) within which the phenomena exist are a vital part of the equation. For example, we could not undertake a valid comparative study of food service styles in fast food and fine dining restaurants without taking the influences of the two contexts into account. Neither could we satisfactorily compare the performance of companies in the bed and breakfast and upmarket hotel sectors of the industry without taking their different circumstances in account. Therefore, the explicit inclusion of 'contextual' factors is one feature that makes comparative studies different to non-comparative studies.

Intra and inter types of comparative study

Rokkan (1996) suggests that comparative studies may be divided into 'inter' (without) and 'intra' (within) types of comparative studies. The former is concerned with examining the questions or issues across the particular contexts selected for the study, i.e. companies, countries, cultures, etc., while the latter focuses on making comparisons between the relevant subunits included within the single context adopted for the study. The 'inter' type of study is essentially one involving horizontal comparisons across different contexts (see Figure 1.2).

Figure 1.2
Inter-comparisons

By contrast the 'intra' type of comparative study (see Figure 1.3) has a greater focus on making more detailed vertical comparisons within the boundaries of the single context used for the study (Janoski, 1991).

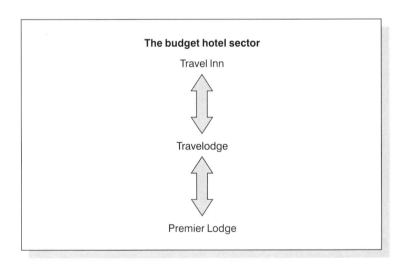

Figure 1.3
Intra-comparisons

This approach is not covered to any great extent beyond this point in this book. However, it is one you should be aware of because all the issues dealt with in Chapters 2 to 9 could equally be explored through this type of study. Instead of trying to compare, say, operating systems and products (Chapter 3) across the different sectors of the industry you might want to limit such a comparison to one sector and/or type of hospitality business. For example, you might wish to undertake a study designed to compare the purchasing systems used by different types of hotel company, or the nature of the accommodation product produced by different grades of hotel. Alternatively, you could be interested in exploring the extent to which management practices (Chapter 6) are similar in different fast food companies, or whether work patterns and employment practices (Chapter 5) differ between chain and independent hotels.

Positive and negative approaches to comparative study

Whatever the general purpose for the study Warwick and Osherson (1973: 52) contend that: 'Explanation or generalization through comparative [study] is usually sought via one of two paths: a *positive* approach in which similarities are identified in independent variables associated with a common outcome, or a *negative* one whereby independent variables associated with divergent outcomes are identified' (emphasis added). This may sound complicated, but it is really quite straightforward (see Figures 1.4 and 1.5).

The *positive* approach (see Figure 1.4) is suggesting that where a common outcome occurs within different contexts we would be interested in establishing the common reasons for this. In other words, the common, or generic, factors that create the same outcome.

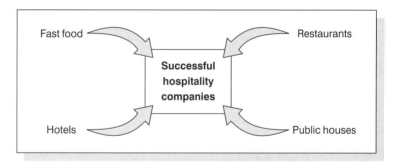

Figure 1.4
The positive approach

For example, we might be interested in discovering the reasons why certain hospitality companies are more successful than others, or why many different types of hospitality company face the problem of high staff turnover. Here the outcome – business success or high staff turnover – is the same regardless of the type and/or size of company. This suggests that there might be common or general reasons for this as it is highly unlikely that the same outcome will be created by entirely different factors operating in the different contexts. The task here would be to try and disentangle those factors common to all the contexts from those that are specific to a particular type(s) of hospitality business. If we can do this then we will be able to put forward a general explanation, or theory, to explain the reasons why the same outcomes can arise in very different contexts.

In the *negative* approach we are dealing with different, or divergent, outcomes but are still seeking to identify those factors which appear to be common to these outcomes (see Figure 1.5).

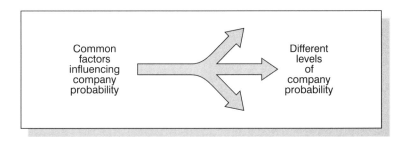

Figure 1.5
The negative approach

However, what we are more interested in here is not just identifying the common factors connected with different outcomes, but the level of 'performance' associated with these factors and the varying outcomes. For example, take a situation where the profitability of certain hospitality companies is far greater than that of others. Here we have a divergent outcome. If we examine the factors that could possibly affect the level of profitability in a company, we are likely to find that effective cost control is one factor that will influence this. Therefore, the different levels of profitability achieved by different hospitality companies may be explained, at least in part, by how well these companies design and implement their cost control measures. Some companies may do this poorly, and hence have low levels of profitability, others may do it well and have higher profitability. The same factor is connected to the different outcomes, but the reason for the latter is that the ability to control costs in some companies is better than it is in others.

How many comparisons?

Another issue common to all types of comparative study is the question of how many and what type of comparisons to include. In terms of our ability to make generalizations it may be trite, but perhaps true, to say that the more contexts used to make comparisons within the study the better. However, in reality there is frequently a trade-off between the number of contexts included in the study and the amount of data obtained. At its crudest this trade-off runs from one end of the continuum (few contexts/deep data) to the other (many contexts/surface data). The answer to the question 'how many comparisons?' is not simple or formulaic in nature.

Kohn (1996) advises that the choice of contexts, both in terms of their nature and number, should be informed by a type of risk analysis. As the selection of contexts for a comparative study is always something of a gamble, we need to carefully consider whether the potential payoff from increasing their number justifies the additional risk from doing so. This is really a matter of judgement. As we increase the number of contexts to be used for a study we potentially increase the likelihood of being able to transfer and/or generalize our findings to a wider range of other contexts not used in the study. On the other hand, increasing the number of contexts to be used in the study, particularly where they are very different, rapidly increases the scope, complexity and cost of conducting the study. In comparative studies, as with many other things, there is no such thing as a free lunch!

The selection of contexts for a comparative study should address what some authors (Ragin, 1994; Smelser, 1996) call the 'comparability problem'. Smelser (1996: 90) suggests that this problem raises questions such as: 'How can we be certain that the *events* and *situations* we wish to explain are comparable from one . . . context to another? How is it possible to compare very different . . . *units* (or . . . systems) with one another?' (original emphasis). These are significant issues facing the design of any comparative study and will be fully addressed in the discussion of *equivalence* contained later in this chapter.

Uses of the comparative approach

Antal, Dierkes and Weiler (1996: 10) suggest that the comparative approach can make a strong contribution to the development of appropriate policies: 'Structured comparison provides a framework for determining those aspects of a situation which are due to unique circumstances, and those which are more generally applicable – and therefore possibly appropriate to consider transferring to other contexts.' In this sense comparative research can inform policy determination by helping to identify those factors which are either generic or contextual in nature, and hence those which are amenable to general control or otherwise. Thus it can establish the 'transfer value' of the findings.

Antal, Dierkes and Weiler (1996) also propose that this type of research explicitly recognizes the generally greater degree of 'interdependence' characterizing the contemporary world. Sectors, systems, industries, national, and supranational entities are becoming increasingly interrelated and mutually dependent. Again, by studying the phenomenon in a range of contexts it becomes possible to disentangle its generic and contextual aspects. Despite differences in emphasis Antal, Dierkes and Weiler's (1996) purposes have a clear central theme, that of identifying similarities/differences, or convergence/divergence, to further an understanding of the phenomenon in question. Regardless of whether the comparisons are being made at the level of individuals, organizations, or between countries this central theme remains the same in any comparative study.

Establishing the comparative base

As has been noted earlier there are a number of specific issues associated with undertaking comparative studies. Though the nature of these issues does vary, there is no doubt that the most significant is that of *equivalence*. This lies at the heart of our ability to make valid comparisons, thereby addressing the 'comparability' problem referred to earlier. Any lack of equivalence creates problems of bias, which Van de Vijver and Leung (1997: 10) propose is 'a generic term for all nuisance factors threatening the validity of . . . comparisons . . . [and that] equivalence cannot be assumed but should be established and reported in each study'.

To establish a comparative base, or basis for comparison, we must be able to demonstrate that we are comparing 'like with like'. If we are not able to convince people that this is the case then we cannot expect them to view our study as being valid. The comparative base is the 'constant' in our study. It serves as the reference point, yardstick or spine to which all the data we collect can be related and compared. Depending on the nature of the study this can be very simple or more complex. For example, if we wanted to compare the food offer in different restaurants we could use the menu as the basis for comparison. Alternatively, any attempt to compare managerial careers in different international hotel companies would demand a far more extensive comparative base.

Conceptual or construct equivalence

The starting point for establishing equivalence, and hence the comparative base, is to focus attention on what some authors refer to as *conceptual equivalence* (Warwick and Osherson, 1973) and others as *construct equivalence* (Van de Vijver and Leung, 1997). This type of equivalence is concerned with establishing a commonality of meaning across the contexts to be used for the comparisons. Where the concept has a sufficiently similar, ideally identical, meaning across the contexts used for the study, there will clearly be significant degrees of construct overlap and hence this type of equivalence is likely to be high, and vice versa.

Though this problem is widely recognized by researchers to be particularly problematic in cross-national and cross-cultural studies (Anderson, 1996; Hantrais and Mangen, 1996) it often does not always receive the same degree of attention in comparative work that is not cross-national/cultural in nature. This frequently proves to be a significant mistake because even concepts and terms that appear to be unambiguous may not be so in reality. For example, the concept of 'gross profit' has a very different meaning in the hotel industry than it does in other industries. Similarly, concepts such as quality, productivity, empowerment, profitability, etc., may not be interpreted and used in the same way in different companies and industries. Hence, it is dangerous to make unwarranted assumptions about conceptual equivalence across the contexts in the study.

Contextual or functional equivalence

The issue of what Neuman (1994) refers to as *contextual equivalence*, and what other authors (Hantrais and Mangen, 1996; Janoski, 1991) tend to term *functional equivalence*, is also one which needs to be considered in establishing a sound comparative base. This type of equivalence focuses attention on the observation that either a concept may have different meanings in different contexts but essentially perform the same purpose, and/or that the same linguistic term may have different meanings and implications in different contexts.

In a similar, but slightly different, vein Hantrais and Mangen (1996) also raise the issue of the 'spatial equivalence' of units of analysis for cross-sectional studies. This is essentially a subset of *contextual equivalence* and refers to the variability that may exist between definitions of the unit(s) of analysis within the contexts in question. For example, studies designed to compare levels and volumes of hospitality activity on a 'regional' basis or across city or urban areas, particularly at a cross-national level, may be faced with the problem of non-standard statistical definitions of what a region or city is. If care is not taken to explore the specific nature of the definitions used to delimit these entities there are likely to be significant implications for comparability.

Transferability and generalizability

Equivalence per se is thus concerned with the threat of bias and, as comparative studies are designed to make valid comparisons, it is clearly a fundamental issue in establishing a valid basis for making such comparisons. In addition to the general issue of equivalence any comparative study will also need to consider the issue of *transferability* in relation to the comparative base. Transferability is closely associated, though not synonymous, with being able to generalize the study's findings to a wider context and is concerned with identifying and separating the contextual/situational and generic factors within the study.

Though establishing transferability will help to identify which relationships are contextually dependent (contingent) or independent (generic) this alone will not necessarily extend the ability of the study to generalize its findings on a wider basis. For example, where the study is limited to comparisons across two very similar entities or contexts, transferability may be high but the ability to generalize these results to very different contexts will be limited. In this sense the ability to transfer the findings of a comparative study is greater when the context(s) you wish to transfer the findings to are very similar to those used for the original study.

Conversely, the ability to generalize the findings of such a study depends on the extent to which they are applicable to a range of very different contexts to the original ones used. To illustrate this difference, consider the example of Nebel's (1991) study of the attributes of successful hotel general managers referred to earlier. The ability to transfer this study's findings to other hotel general managers is reasonably high. On the other hand, it would be difficult to justify any attempt to generalize these findings to general managers in other service or manufacturing businesses. As the contextual conditions and operating environments, and hence the demands placed on general managers, are different in these other types of businesses, it would be invalid to try and generalize the findings, at least in their entirety, to these other managerial situations.

Types of comparative studies

The two basic types of comparative studies are generally regarded as either *cross-sectional* or *longitudinal*. Essentially the difference between cross-sectional and longitudinal studies is the comparative reference point. In cross-sectional studies the comparisons are time constrained within a limited, predetermined and typically contemporary period. The primary focus of a cross-sectional study is to examine differences in the phenomenon across different contexts while time is effectively held constant. In longitudinal studies the reverse is true. Here identifying and explaining changes in the phenomenon over time is a central concern. As a consequence longitudinal studies invariably seek to limit the degree of contextual variation within the study. For example, the discussion of industry structure development models in Chapter 2 is limited to the hotel sector. Thus, in relation to the role of time, cross-sectional studies are often described as being synchronic in nature, while longitudinal studies may be described as diachronic.

All the chapters in this book, with the exception of Chapter 2, tend to take the cross-sectional approach to comparative study as their main focus. They are concerned with analysing their particular topic across the different sectors of the UK hospitality industry to explore similarities and differences across these sectors. This effectively means that each of the authors is holding time constant to focus on any inter-sectoral convergence or divergence. However, this does not mean that the time period used for this type of analysis is fixed at one exact point. It is reasonable for a cross-sectional study to adopt a given period of time, rather than one fixed point. Apart from the fact that it would be extremely difficult, if not impossible, to design and conduct such a cross-sectional study using one exact point in time, the use of a reasonable period of time allows the study to cope with different changes in each of the contexts over this period.

Cross-sectional studies

Cross-sectional comparative studies may be *case-* or *variable-oriented* in nature and conducted at a variety of levels, ranging from comparisons between individuals, groups, organizations, industry sectors, industries or countries, and may focus on phenomena relating to structures, products, processes, systems, cultures, etc. A detailed discussion of the issues associated with these options is beyond the scope of this book but if you need to explore this in more detail see Brotherton (1999) in the 'Further reading' section at the end of this chapter.

Case-oriented studies

A case-oriented cross-sectional study is one that seeks to compare two or more case studies. Case-oriented studies typically, though not necessarily, tend to be ones that are more limited in scope. Though it is possible to undertake case-oriented cross-sectional studies on a large scale, i.e. using countries as the cases, this is relatively rare because of the high levels of complexity and cost involved in such a venture. Because case studies usually deal with a limited context, and explore the issue(s) in depth within this context, the case-oriented approach to cross-sectional study tends to be used to compare individuals or companies rather than industries or countries. For example, see the studies by Figueiredo, Latas and Gomes (1995), Moncarz and Kron (1993), Royle (1995) and Boger (1995) in the 'Further reading' section.

Variable-oriented studies

The variable-oriented approach places less emphasis on the detail of the contexts used for the study and more on the generic nature of the issue(s) being investigated. Typically techniques such as questionnaire surveys, with large samples, are used in this approach in order to gather large amounts of data across fairly broad contexts. Hence, it is more common to find this approach used in larger-scale inter-industry and cross-national studies. The studies conducted by Hallam and Baum (1996), Pizam et al. (1997) and Van Hoof, Verbeeten and Combrink (1996) in the 'Further reading' section are all indicative of this approach.

Selecting cases and/or samples

In selecting the cases and/or samples for cross-sectional studies care should be taken to recognize and control for what Coolican (1994) refers to as the 'cohort effect'. Essentially this arises where there are significant differences in one or more of aspects of the samples' composition. For example, if one sample group is dominated by people in the age range forty-five to sixty and another by people who are in the twenty to thirty-five age range, any direct comparisons made between the two groups are likely to be extremely suspect because of the influence of inter-generational differences on the two sets of respondents. Similarly, where there are significant variations in other factors such as gender, socioeconomic group, occupation, ethnicity, etc., the cohort effect needs to be considered.

Clearly, the same issue arises in cross-sectional studies using organizations or countries as the basis for the cases or samples. These considerations also raise the issue of 'matched samples'. This is really the 'like with like' comparison issue again. I think you will agree that it would not be sensible to use two very different samples to make comparisons. If one sample comprised females and the other males, or very small and very large companies, we would not be comparing like with like. Similarly, if one sample contained 1000 respondents and the other fifty, we would be likely to question whether any comparisons based on such very different sample sizes could be valid. The technical considerations apart, this is really a common-sense issue. It is obvious that any comparison based on samples that have very similar compositions and characteristics is likely to be more appropriate and valid than one based on samples that are quite different.

Longitudinal studies

In longitudinal studies time and time intervals are of primary importance because the main goal of this type of comparative study is to analyse change and development in relation to some process which occurs over time (Adams and Schvaneveldt, 1991). This means that longitudinal studies are concerned with the direction (trend), speed (rate), nature (permanent or temporary) and degree (magnitude) of change taking place over time. Essentially, longitudinal studies attempt to map the patterns of such change and explain why they have occurred. To achieve this, attention must be focused on the sequence of events that collectively constitute the process the study is focused on. Of particular interest to longitudinal studies seeking to investigate a given process will be the order of occurrence, time gaps and nature of the transitions between the sequence of events constituting the process. Analysis of these will enable the study to establish and analyse the dynamic process relationships as they unfold over time.

While cross-sectional studies suffer from the 'comparability problem', as it is extremely difficult to be sure that the samples used in this type of study are sufficiently similar to allow valid comparisons to be made, longitudinal studies do not suffer from this problem to the same degree. By subjecting the same sample to repeated measures over time this problem is eliminated (Coolican, 1994). However, this does assume the absence of the 'sample attrition' problem. If this arises then the comparability problem will be evident in longitudinal work.

The sample attrition problem refers to the difficulty in maintaining the original sample over time. As time passes it is likely that some of the original sample will be lost, thus making comparisons over time more problematic. People leave jobs, move from country to country, companies go out of business or are taken over, new companies enter the sector/industry, etc. Changes such as these make it difficult to retain the original sample.

In addition, longitudinal studies should also recognize the potential impact of what Coolican (1994) terms the 'cross-generational problem'. This problem arises where a particular generation of people, organizations or countries is affected by significant events within a specific era while others are not. Thus, the pattern of change and development evident within this generation may not be applicable to other generations. For example, a longitudinal study investigating the views of human resource managers on industrial relations practices that began with a sample of such managers selected in the early 1970s is likely to encounter this problem. Particularly if the study attempts to generalize its findings to new, young managers who only entered their managerial positions in the late 1980s.

Conclusions

The issue is not *to compare or not to compare*, because, as we have seen, making comparisons is a natural thing for us to do. So, perhaps the issue is *how best to compare*. By now you will have realized that there is no single best way to make valid comparisons that can be applied to every type of comparative study. The different topics and contexts that can be explored through this approach, and the different purposes it can be used for, indicate that the way comparisons are made will inevitably vary. However, what should not vary are the underlying principles dealt with in this chapter. Whatever the specifics associated with any particular comparative study there is always a need to ensure that the comparisons being made are valid and reliable.

The hospitality manager can benefit greatly from the use of the comparative approach, as the other chapters in this book demonstrate. By comparing and contrasting the policies, processes and products that exist in the manager's company with those in others, it is possible to learn much. This is true even when comparisons are made between two hotel companies, but it is perhaps even more true when wider comparisons are made between one type of hospitality business and another, and truer still when the comparative scope is widened further to include comparisons with non-hospitality businesses. Similarly, much can be learned from comparing hospitality business practices in one country with those in another. So, the comparative message is do not be too parochial as a hospitality manager, take a wider view and use this to your advantage.

Summary

The key points to remember from this chapter may be summarized as follows:

1 The comparative approach to studying hospitality activities is one that can be applied to a very wide range of issues or questions, from individuals to international comparisons.

2 Comparative studies invariably try to identify and analyse those factors that are general in nature, and those that are specific to a particular context, of type of context.

3 Comparisons can be made on a 'within' (intra) or 'without' (inter) basis, i.e. between the same type of entity existing within the same sector, industry or country, or across different contexts.

4 The scope for a comparative study can range from individual people or positions, business units, companies, sectors and industries, to countries.

5 Comparisons can be made on the basis of a wide range of things, e.g. people, products, processes, systems, job types, etc.

6 Some comparative studies concentrate on situations where there are common outcomes (the positive approach) while others explore situations with divergent outcomes (the negative approach).

7 Establishing equivalence is vital to ensure that the comparative study will be valid.

8 Depending on the types of contexts used the results obtained from a comparative study can be transferred to other, similar, contexts or generalized to different contexts.

9 The two main types of comparative study are cross-sectional and longitudinal. The former being more concerned with investigating an issue at one point in time and the latter with investigating it over an extended period of time.

Review questions

1 What is the difference between making comparisons and using the comparative approach?

2 How do studies that are explicitly designed to be comparative in nature differ from studies that may include some elements of comparison but are not comparative in nature and/or focus?

3 What is the difference between intra and inter types of comparative study?

4 How do the positive and negative approaches to comparative study differ?

5 What is the significance of equivalence to comparative study?

6 What is the difference between transferability and generalizability?

7 For what types of comparative study would you use the cross-sectional and longitudinal approaches?

8 Under what circumstances would the case study-oriented approach be preferred to the variable-oriented approach when designing a cross-sectional study?

9 How would you need to take into consideration if you were designing a study to compare the management practices within McDonald's restaurants in the UK, Greece and Japan?

10 Why might it be difficult to compare the current financial performance of the major UK hotel chains with that of five, ten or twenty years ago?

Bibliography

Adams, G. R. and Schvaneveldt, J. D. (1991). *Understanding Research Methods*. 2nd edn. Longman.

Anderson, R. (1996). Part three: accessing information. In *Cross-National Research Methods in the Social Sciences* (L. Hantrais and S. Mangen, eds) pp. 105–108, Pinter.

Antal, A. B., Dierkes, M. and Weiler, H. N. (1996). Cross-national policy research: traditions, achievements, and challenges. In *Comparing Nations and Cultures: Readings in a Cross-Disciplinary Perspective* (A. Inkeles and M. Sasaki, eds) pp. 9–17, Prentice-Hall.

Coolican, H. (1994). *Research Methods and Statistics in Psychology.* 2nd edn. Hodder and Stoughton.

Hantrais, L. and Mangen, S. (1996) Method and management of cross-national social research. In *Cross-National Research Methods in the Social Sciences* (L. Hantrais and S. Mangen, eds) pp. 1–12, Pinter.

Janoski, T. (1991). Synthetic strategies in comparative research: methods and problems of internal and external analysis. In *Issues and Alternatives in Comparative Research* (C. C. Ragin, ed.) pp. 59–81, Brill.

Kara, A., Kaynak, E. and Kucukemiroglu, O. (1995). Marketing strategies for fast food restaurants: a customer view. *International Journal of Contemporary Hospitality Management,* **7** (4), 16–22.

Kohn M. L. (1996). Cross-national research as an analytic strategy: American Sociological Association, 1987 presidential address. In *Comparing Nations and Cultures: Readings in a Cross-Disciplinary Perspective* (A. Inkeles and M. Sasaki, eds) pp. 28–53, Prentice-Hall.

Nebel, E. C. (1991). *Managing Hotels Effectively: Lessons from Outstanding General Managers.* Van Nostrand Reinhold.

Neuman, W. L. (1994). *Social Research Methods: Quantitative and Qualitative Approaches.* 2nd edn. Allyn and Bacon.

Pearce, D. G. (1993). Comparative studies in tourism research. In *Tourism Research: Critiques and Challenges* (D. G. Pearce and R. W. Butler, eds) pp. 20–35, Routledge.

Peters, T. and Waterman, R. (1982). *In Search of Excellence.* Harper and Row.

Ragin, C. C. (1994). *Constructing Social Research.* Pine Forge Press.

Ragin, C. C. (1996). The distinctiveness of comparative social science. In *Comparing Nations and Cultures: Readings in a Cross-Disciplinary Perspective* (A. Inkeles and M. Sasaki, eds) pp. 74–89, Prentice-Hall.

Rokkan, S. (1996). Cross-cultural, cross-societal, and cross-national research. In *Comparing Nations and Cultures: Readings in a Cross-Disciplinary Perspective* (A. Inkeles and M. Sasaki, eds) pp. 18–27, Prentice-Hall.

Smelser, N. J. (1996). The methodology of comparative analysis of economic activity. In *Comparing Nations and Cultures: Readings in a Cross-Disciplinary Perspective* (A. Inkeles and M. Sasaki, eds) pp. 99–100, Prentice-Hall.

Swanson, G. (1971). Frameworks for comparative research: structural anthropology and the theory of action. In *Comparative Methods in Sociology: Essays on Trends and Applications* (I. Vallier, ed.) pp. 141–202, University of California Press.

Van de Vijver, F. and Leung, K. (1997). *Methods and Data Analysis for Cross-Cultural Research.* Sage.

Warwick, D. P. and Osherson, S. (1973). *Comparative Research Methods.* Prentice-Hall.

Further reading

For a more extensive and advanced treatment of the comparative approach/method, see:

Brotherton, B. (1999). Comparative research. In *The Handbook of Contemporary Hospitality Management Research* (B. Brotherton, ed.) pp. 143–172, John Wiley.

For examples of the comparative approach applied to a range of hospitality studies the following references may be useful:

Armstrong, R. W., Mok, C., Go, F. M. and Chan A. (1997). The importance of cross-cultural expectations in the measurement of service quality perceptions in the hotel industry. *International Journal of Hospitality Management*, **16** (2), 181–190.

Boger, C. A. (1995. A comparison between different delivery systems of quick service food facilities. *Hospitality Research Journal*, **18** (3)/**19** (1), 111–124.

Brotherton, B. and Burgess, J. (1997). A comparative study of academic research interests in US and UK hotel and restaurant companies. *Proceedings of the Sixth Annual CHME Hospitality Research Conference*, pp. 317–348, Oxford Brookes University.

Burrell, J., Manfredi, S., Rollin, H., Price, L. and Stead, L. (1997). Equal opportunities for women employees in the hospitality industry: a comparison between France, Italy, Spain and the UK. *International Journal of Hospitality Management*, **16** (2), 161–179.

English, W., Joslam, B., Upchurch, R. S. and Willems, J. (1996). Restaurant attrition: a longitudinal analysis of restaurant failures. *International Journal of Contemporary Hospitality Management*, **8** (2), 17–20.

Figueiredo, K., Latas, J. R. and Gomes, D. (1995). A strategic service vision in the hotel industry: some conclusions from case studies. In *Services Management: New Directions, New Perspectives* (R. Teare and C. Armistead, eds), Cassell.

Hallam, G. and Baum, T. (1996). Contracting out food and beverage operations in hotels: a comparative study of practice in North America and the United Kingdom. *International Journal of Hospitality Management*, **15** (1), 41–50.

Moncarz, E. S. and Kron, R. N. (1993). Operational analysis: a case study of two hotels in financial distress. *International Journal of Hospitality Management*, **12** (2), 175–196.

Morey, R. C. and Dittman, D. A. (1995). Evaluating a hotel GM's performance: a case study in benchmarking. *Cornell Hotel and Restaurant Quarterly*, **36** (5), 30–35.

Moutinho, L., McDonagh, P., Peris, S. M. and Bigne, E. (1995). The future development of the hotel sector: an international comparison. *International Journal of Contemporary Hospitality Management*, **7** (4), 10–15.

Papadopoulou, A., Ineson, E. M. and Wilkie, D. T. (1995). Convergence between sources of service job analysis data. *International Journal of Contemporary Hospitality Management*, **7** (2/3), 42–47.

Pizam, A., Pine, R., Mok, C. and Shin, J. Y. (1997). Nationality v industry cultures: which has a greater effect on managerial behaviour? *International Journal of Hospitality Management*, **16** (2), 127–145.

Royle, T. (1995). Corporate versus societal culture: a comparative study of McDonald's in Europe. *International Journal of Contemporary Hospitality Management*, **7**, (2/3), 52–56.

Sparrowe, R. T. and Poplielarz, P. A. (1995). Getting ahead in the hospitality industry: an event history analysis of promotions among hotel and restaurant employees. *Hospitality Research Journal*, **19** (3), 99–118.

Van Hoof, H. B., Verbeeten, M. J. and Combrink, T. E. (1996). Information technology revisited – international lodging-industry technology needs and perceptions: a comparative study. *Cornell Hotel and Restaurant Administration Quarterly*, **37**, (6), 86–91.

Industry structures and competitive environments

David Litteljohn

Objectives

The overall purpose of this chapter is to illustrate how an appreciation of concepts of industry analysis can help when understanding and investigating behaviours of organizations in the hospitality industry. After you have read this chapter you should be able to:

1 Define a number of key economic and industry terms and concepts.

2 Compare alternative models of hotel industry development.

3 Explain the supply-side view of the nature of competitive environments in the UK.

4 Describe the current structure of the hotel industry in the UK.

5 Suggest the possible future competitive contexts of the hotel industry in the UK.

6 Apply the economic and industrial structure concepts outlined in the chapter to other sectors of the hospitality industry.

Introduction

Before examining the factors influencing the development of industry structure it is important to define and illustrate a number of basic economic and industry structure terms. If you are to make comparisons across sectors, or indeed over time within a sector, then an understanding of the basic terms and concepts is necessary to ensure consistency.

Macroeconomic level analysis looks at very broad interactions that operate in an economy. Studies at this level deliberately simplify areas of activity in an economy in order to make visible the interaction of key variables in society. Variables at this level include such elements as levels of employment in the population and the amount of money businesses invest in their production. In this chapter macroanalysis will be used to discuss different stages of hospitality industry development. The variables investigated deal with a mix of social and economic factors at general, societal, levels. Of particular importance are the variables of demand and supply.

In economics demand means not only the amount that consumers buy of a particular good or service (e.g. trips to a cinema) but the way in which their purchase behaviour may change for different price levels. For example, would demand for cinema attendance double if prices were halved? At first glance this might appear to be logical but, naturally, many other factors are involved. Relevant aspects to examine could include levels of cinema-going already undertaken, prices of travel to and from cinemas, the availability and price of entertainment alternatives. Thus, research would be needed to establish relationships between prices and quantities purchased. Supply is the amount of a good or a service that sellers are willing to place on the market place at different price levels.

A market is the mechanism which equates demand to supply. It could be a defined place, as in the example of a farmers' weekly market. However, marketplaces are often national and international (and even virtual, as in the case of some e-commerce activities). In economies there are many different markets including financial markets (affecting, for example, the amount of capital for investing in hospitality enterprises) and eating away from home markets. Naturally the way in which macroeconomic factors interact with supply and demand will differ from market to market.

Market definition is important. Take the above example of eating away from home markets. Close examination indicates that the market can be subdivided into a number of different areas. For example, there is a particular market for 'eating out' for social reasons. Other distinct sectors of the market relate to eating at the workplace and to hospital patients (to give just two examples). In all cases the distinct sectors share a similarity in that they take place away from the households of consumers. Yet consumption and supply patterns will vary considerably in each. What is demanded, how and where it is demanded, and how it is provided might differ from market area to market area. In other words, the definition of markets requires careful consideration if they are to be investigated thoroughly.

A clear definition of what constitutes an industry is 'the set of all firms making the same product' (Begg, Fischer and Dornbush, 1987: 40). This simple statement belies a level of complexity that requires an analyst to consider the reason for their industry analysis. For example, consider discussion on an appropriate definition of the transport industry, particularly in the context of analysing environmental policy. If the term 'motor car industry' is considered, this will be narrow: motor cars form only one transport mode and run alongside air, rail and waterborne transport methods. Thus it would be useful, for this purpose, to consider a wide concept of the transport industry. Yet this outlook will not be necessarily be relevant if the analyst wishes to examine competition among motor car manufacturers. Here the narrow approach would seem more suitable. It is not that one definition is right and another is wrong – rather there will definitions that are more and less useful depending on your focus is.

In a modern developed economy characterized by affluence, appropriate market and industry, definitions, from a consumers standpoint, often are broad. For example, a meal out may be considered as an alternative to a cinema outing, nightclubbing, tenpin bowling and so on. An appropriate classification of 'industry' here could be *the leisure industry* rather than the *catering industry*.

This section has provided an introduction to some important terms and concepts that are used in investigating industry structure. It should also provide an indication that the precise meaning of terms needs to be judged in two particular ways – first, the purpose for which they are to be defined and, second, the way in which concepts change as society evolves.

The development of the hospitality industry: a macroanalysis

Different stages and models of hospitality industry development are proposed in this section. The analysis is a broad-brush one. As a consequence, the models do not bring out the full richness of change in hospitality environments and their effects on the industry. Furthermore, the analysis is deliberately non-specific about the precise periods for the different stages it proposes. This is because it concentrates on broad movements in societies, rather than providing watertight rules for industry stages. The emphasis is on appreciating the underlying dynamic of change. To simplify the analysis, the development of the hotel industry is discussed rather than broader hospitality sectors.

Thus the purpose of this part of the chapter is to illustrate the benefits of comparative investigation in hospitality, to encourage you to look behind industry 'snapshots' or time-bounded overviews in order to appreciate dynamic, evolving factors affecting industry composition and behaviour.

Model I

This model assumes that societies grow from scattered, low-density populations through stages of agrarian, commercial and industrial (manufacturing) activity to market-oriented economies where employment in services predominates. It is essentially a capitalist Western model, found in many Western Europe countries.

Stage 1

Society is characterized by feudal agrarian communities. Economies largely operate at near subsistence levels for the masses. Economic activities are primarily organized at local levels. Social activity similarly centres on local communities. Communication systems reflect local orientations – there are few national routes, and roads to regional centres are hardly much more numerous. Where concentrations of people, power and trade occur these are often at seaports or river and lake trade or communication hubs, as much communication is waterborne.

A feature of these economies is that there are high levels of barter: many products and services are not traded on a market. For example, there may be exchange of foodstuffs (vegetables traded for meat). Other interchanges are bound in social convention and power relationships. Feudal vassals are expected to offer their 'masters' certain goods and services as a right. For agricultural workers this would involve paying the 'Lord of the Manor' in agricultural produce and labour, in exchange for the use of land for smallholdings etc. In these type of communities hospitality is primarily carried out as a non-commercial activity and, like other non-trade goods and services, is bound by a complex pattern of social codes of exchange.

Travelling during this stage is inconvenient, uncomfortable and even hazardous. Most short-term travel is by the wealthy, those involved in affairs of the state and governing (e.g. law-keeping) and, of course, traders. Thus travel is a select activity among (relatively small) populations. The travel hospitality needs of the well-to-do people are catered for by other well-to-do people in their manors, hunting lodges, castles and palaces. They will wish to ensure protection and show their high social and economic standing. The needs of pilgrims and the less well-to-do people are often met by religious orders in monasteries and abbeys. Where commercial hospitality exists it is likely to be concentrated at population centres. Commercial lodgings grow around places where commercial meal and drink outlets have already been established to cater for local demand. These lodgings may not be predominantly used by short-term travellers. Undoubtedly travellers like traders, who stay for a few nights at a time, will use this type of accommodation. Some of the main users will also be those who stay away from home temporarily for longer periods, such as scholars.

Much hospitality is offered non-commercially and not traded in the marketplace. The manor house for gentry, the monastery for pilgrims, for example both played important roles in medieval Western societies and did not expect a commercial return for their hospitality. The traditions of hospitality prevalent during this stage provide an enduring legacy in symbols of safety, generosity, friendship, gift-giving and even kinship on expectations of hospitality in later periods. Indeed, no taverns offering regular overnight accommodation in England appear before 1300 (Quennel and Quennel, 1957).

Stage 2 · · ·

This stage spans the borders of pre-industrial society and early phases of early industrialization. It is characterized by increased economic sophistication as new commercial markets develop. Some countries acquire wealth through gaining possessions in different parts of the world, and there is a trend towards greater specialization in production. This is propelled by the increasing availability of labour, caused by migrations from rural locations to towns and cities, and the use of new forms of power and machinery together with the phenomenon of factory organization. These and other factors lead to changes in the nature of travel – for example for greater levels of transport of goods.

More raw materials are transported considerable distances, even sometimes from very distant counties. As a corollary, semi-finished and finished products need to be transported in greater numbers to new marketplaces. This all needs to be underpinned by the development of a communications infrastructure. At this stage, before the new mechanical technologies are applied substantially to the transport network, development is concentrated on improving land and water transport networks. Towards the end of this stage new inland canals are built, providing a significant impetus to economic growth.

Levels of wealth within the population rise and the spectrum of society travelling widens a little. However, most of the population still does not move far from home, with commercial trade and education needs remaining as important reasons for travel.

Taverns and inns offer commercial accommodation and deal with greater numbers as trade and economic activity grows. This specialization in provision is seen in the expansion of roadside commercial inns. Towards the end of the stage the commercial hotel is introduced. Originating in France (by former servants of aristocrats) during the mid- to late eighteenth century, hotels soon spread internationally. By 1780 Nero's Hotel in London is trading (Taylor and Bush, 1974). Hotels cater for well-off customers who, however, do not have the exceptionally high social standing or affluence to always expect traditional non-commercial type of hospitality. They also cater for rich customers who simply find it more convenient to use them.

Travel for pleasure for the affluent develops during this stage. In England, for example, a fashion to visit spas for health reasons becomes significant among the wealthy. Sometimes these travellers rely on non-commercial hospitality at the spas, or own or rent out houses (for themselves and their servants) at the new destinations. These substitute for inns, taverns or hotels at the destination, though travellers may have to use commercial lodgings on journeys to and from the location of their stay. However, some commercial lodgings now spring up at the more popular inland spas (e.g. Bath) and at the nascent seaside resorts (e.g. Brighton). Reflecting market demand these new institutions provide entertainment in the form of balls and dances as well as overnight accommodation.

Social aspects remain important in the provision of hospitality. While macroeconomic factors have increased national levels of prosperity wealth remains tightly controlled by an elite whose habits and customs are largely reproduced by those who join them, often through being successful in trade and foreign development. Even innovations like the hotel are modelled on traditional, aristocratic customs.

Stage 3

This stage is characterized by major industrialization. Production matures into a predominance of manufacturing modes. Wealth creation is facilitated by the development of new risk-takers in a growing industrial middle class. The application of new 'scientific methods' of production (extension of the factory system) as well as new science and technology increases to ensure goods are produced more efficiently and cheaply. The higher productive levels that are now being sustained lead to higher demand for labour. Wage rates move up somewhat from the quasi-subsistence levels of earlier stages. Societies enter a period of mass production and mass consumption. International trade, particularly trade to and from the colonies of the richer countries, is significant.

Much development is driven by the application of new technologies to transport. Though transport revolutions in their day, the canals of Stage 2 still used horses to pull barges. The steam trains and steamboats of Stage 3, introduced from 1830 onwards, ensure that passengers and cargo are transported further and faster with levels of reliability previously unknown. Centres of industry and commerce (e.g. London and Glasgow) see significant development in hotel type accommodation to meet commercial travel demand.

The growth in city populations is, to an extent, fuelled by a move from rural communities. This decline impacts on the demand for inns, taverns and hotels in parts of the country suffering depopulation. However, as overall levels of travel increase, new markets are created, so that the impact of declines in old markets is often softened by the arrival of new travel markets. The enlarging middle class, in particular, acquires new appetites for pleasure travel. Less well off sectors also acquire a liking for travel but, by comparison, this is often more locally based for they have greater constraints of leisure time and money.

As the internal combustion engine is developed and later air plane technology adds to the diversity of transport, new travel routes open. Decreases in the cost of transportation make it available to greater proportions of the population. Impacts of mass transportation methods cannot be understated. For example, in 1833 the UK's total inland passenger trips in England is estimated at 3.1 million. By 1863 the number rises to 204 million, and by 1881 the number of annual rail passengers alone is 623 million (Medlik and Airey, 1978). Later growth in airline passengers in the 1930s to 1960s is also exponential.

Legal frameworks adapt to the new conditions of trade and commerce. Changes in commercial law stimulate more innovation (or remove factors that inhibit innovation). For example, the introduction of limited liability (e.g. the Companies Act 1862 in the UK) facilitates greater risk-taking. This allows higher levels of investment in commercial accommodation. This is evidenced by the large number of hotels built in London from 1870 to the end of the century. Investment motives become more sophisticated. The coaching inns of Stage 2 were largely independently operated and met specific levels of demand. In Stage 3 a considerable injection of hotel investment is made by railway companies, often to secure a competitive advantage over rivals (Taylor and Bush, 1974). More than fifty years later, this approach is transferable to airline investment in hotels, as they expand networks after the Second World War.

Growth of leisure travel among the middle class can be judged as showing the beginnings of mass consumption for travel and hotel commercial accommodation. From an organizational perspective development here has strong parallels to that of industrial specialization. Early expansion is facilitated by new travel specialists – travel/tour operators who market travel itineraries within the UK and to Europe – such as the Englishman, Thomas Cook, who introduced the packaged tour to

England, Scotland and later to continental Europe. Hotels now deal with travel intermediaries as well as with travellers directly. They often have to gear up for large groups rather than individual or small-group travel. No longer is travel restricted to the upper echelons of society.

Other forms of commercial accommodation spring up to meet the needs of those who are less well off, but nevertheless economically independent enough to afford short stays at leisure locations not too far away from home. Boarding houses at seaside resorts, for example, meet this demand. These establishments have rules of what to do and when to do it (e.g. meal times and bathing) which are predicated on their desire to keep costs manageable. If not presenting a direct challenge to the hotels patronized by the affluent, they do introduce new precepts into the organization and provision of hospitality. However, not all travel requires commercial accommodation. For example, longer stays away from home can involve staying with relations. Better housing standards allow greater flexibility in offering accommodation to these visitors, no matter what the hosts' social standing.

Stage 4

Stage 4 again borders two economic phases – one which sees an acceleration of manufacturing activity as it continues to be the engine of the economy, and a later phase which sees its *relative* decline as societies rely less directly on manufacturing employment. This stage is one of post-industrialization. Productivity gains in manufacturing, the 'export' of many manufacturing processes to developing economies (to countries where employment is cheaper), the growth of more personal services in commercially traded forms ensure major changes in the ways in which economic production and work methods themselves are organized. Employment in service occupations of various types (professional services, administrative and management jobs, education, health, retailing and hospitality, for example) increase beyond 70 per cent of the working population. Changes in the structure of the workforce and in family life increase the power and impact of women on social institutions and markets.

At this stage travel for pleasure becomes a mass phenomenon. For example, by the 1970s 60 per cent of the UK population regularly travel away from home every year. A significant proportion of the less affluent can now pay for commercial accommodation for at least one stay away from home every year. Many of those who do not travel do so because of domestic and health reasons. Both leisure and business motivations feed hotel markets, and both these markets are affected by the enormous changes in travel habits engendered by high rates of car ownership and advent of cheap air transport.

Changing travel patterns of course impact on the location of hotel stock. Roadside accommodation and hotels at airports grow (while the stock of the previous transport revolution – railway hotels – often languishes or fights to find new markets). However, these relative changes mask the really large movements in the industry. One major change is the displacement of national holiday-taking, which grew in Stage 3 and the early phases of Stage 4, by high levels of international travel. While holidays abroad are limited to the higher income and a proportion of the middle classes during Stage 3, by the end of Stage 4 this has changed. Many in middle- and lower-income groups regularly take holiday trips out of the UK. While hotels are built at new resorts (e.g. Benidorm), guesthouses at traditional 'cold water' resorts such as Blackpool and Brighton go out of business as new international travel markets grow.

A more dispersed use of leisure time also means that many consumers regularly have more than one holiday. The market for mini-break holidays is an example of this. Thus hotels in cultural and business centres, as well as hotels at locations that have recreational and leisure attractions, can find weekend visitors, when otherwise they would be empty.

This stage is characterized by the commercialization of hotel markets to levels not previously seen. The new travel markets springing up mostly expect to have their accommodation needs met through commercial outlets. As hotels grow to meet these demands so do substitute forms of commercial accommodation. These include, for example, time-share developments and executive serviced short stay accommodation. Competition and rivalry means that operators increasingly try to differentiate themselves from rivals and may attempt to build customer loyalty through the use of branding.

Changes in business travel markets also impact on hotel demand. Previously travel demand came from two main areas: from the traders themselves (those organizing the purchasing, distribution and sales of goods) and from those who directly operated the transport systems. As societies become more affluent, information technologies become more advanced and firms grow in size and levels of internationalization, so service levels rise and an information society develops. In this context organizations wish to capitalize on their human resources as much as possible. This creates needs for communication, training and development. In order to achieve this, personal movement is necessary both in internal and external customer networks. Larger conference and exhibition markets also create needs for specialized facilities and access to major centres that can cater for 2000 or more delegates.

Government policy specific to hospitality operations becomes a more important factor at this stage. Potential government involvement in the industry becomes more widespread and pervasive. This can relate to the provision of infrastructure. Large hotel developments can impact on their environments (physical and social) in large and far-reaching ways. Thus, governments exert influence through planning controls. On the other hand, in countries that are changing their employment pattern from one that is manufacturing based, governments may wish to promote the growth or spread of tourism through financial incentives and regional development policies.

Governments may also want to enact developments to protect consumers either through law (e.g. fire precautions, food hygiene and hotel grading legislation) or through voluntary means (e.g. in the UK accommodation classification and grading schemes are voluntary rather than statutory). Finally, the growth in the size of operators may mean that governments wish to ensure that they do not have excessive market power.

At this stage hotel operations will face complex environments where customers are diverse, mobile (in spending as well by location) and have high expectations in standards. Responding to this market diversity, commercial accommodation develops distinct market areas or niches across the spectrum of travel motivation and budget range.

Investment criteria become more important. This is because commercial principles predominate as large operators who have stock market valuations provide greater levels of hotel stock. Also investment in hotels becomes more expensive as property values and building costs increase and need to be carefully justified.

Model II

This model assumes an economy that passes rapidly through agrarian and industrialization economy phases to a service economy phase. Model II is based on the experience of the USA since the influx of Europeans commenced in the sixteenth century. Among the main differences from Model I are a more sophisticated technological base at early periods of development and a population which is mobile and growing. The main similarity to Model I lies in its possession of a capitalist/free market system. The main difference from Model I lies in the fact that economic dynamism acts as a deterrent to social convention. Another difference lies in its large size relative to European countries. On the one hand, this means that it develops a relatively large and sustained travel market. On the other hand, its large size means that stages of economic development will differ at locations within its borders.

Stage 1

Early stages of economic and social development proceed quickly. Fed by trade, technology and labour 'imported' from other countries, the economy grows quickly. Progress at early established trade and commercial centres occurs in parallel with development at new locations as the activity expands to utilize new natural resources. High rate of economic change are maintained for a number of reasons including a growing population fuelled by large numbers of migrants with high levels of economic motivation, and the fast adoption of new forms of transport and communication.

Here hotels evolve as a prime social institution. They become cemented into the social fabric of growing communities from early in their development. Trade and demand from travelling migrants create needs for commercial accommodation at an early point in the evolution of communities. Boorstin (1965) states how USA hotels truly become palaces of the public. Among the first buildings to be built in towns, hotels become centres for social activities and day-to-day meetings between traders and business people. As many of their customers want to stay relatively long periods in a location (e.g. while they find a new home) many hotels cater for long-term resident markets as well as short-stay travellers. They develop many ancillary facilities for meals, drink and entertainment to cater for the local population as well as their resident customers. Thus while USA hotels share a common name with their European counterparts, their development pattern is distinctive.

In this type of context hotels are particularly responsive to market needs. Social conventions in the provision of hospitality are, of course, present. However, they are often mediated by more immediate commercial opportunism as many are developed where markets are non-existent and existing population bases are meagre.

Stage 2 • • •

Taking a national perspective it is difficult to develop a linear pattern to hotel development after Stage 1. This is partly a function of the comparatively large size of the country and the fact that economic development proceeds in a different way and at a different pace in different parts of the country.

Thus it more appropriate to appraise development at this stage by exploring the impact of the following factors in a particular location/area/state:

- the stage of economic development (see in particular Stage 4 in Model I)

- travel markets that might be attracted to the region (both for leisure and business purposes)

- travel/communications infrastructure

- local hospitality markets.

These factors, together with the fast development of economic infrastructure relative to Model I countries, result in a high focus on commercial hospitality. This does not mean that private, non-commercial aspects of hospitality are not important in the USA. However, the tradition of commercial orientation ensures that, as much as possible, these aspects are provided in the traded marketplace. To this desire is added the presence of chain hotel operations that develop national and state market positions and that earn scale economies to provide services to as wide a range of its market niche as possible.

Model III

Hotel development in this model is highly powered by incoming international markets. Here, the hospitality industry 'imports' segments of international demand (as described at Stages 3 and 4 in Model I). For the purposes of this chapter, Model III does not detail individual stages, but does discuss a post–1950 stage of development.

Holiday centres

The growth of the hotel industry is powered by importing leisure/pleasure travellers from abroad. The location of hotel capacity is predicated on the values of foreign tourists: e.g. a desire for sun, sand and sea holiday packages. The expansion of holiday resorts initially corresponds to the generation of demand from colder climate countries that are becoming increasingly affluent. Because much of this travel is organized by tour operators, who deal in mass/packaged tourism based on economies of scale, many hotels are large enough to deal with aeroplane loads of customers at one time. Invariably, their amenities are carefully designed to appeal to particular market segments, and they may appear bland and undifferentiated to more adventurous holidaymakers.

Holiday centres developed since the early 1960s are often subject to high levels of government policy. At early periods of centre development government policy may concentrate on financial incentives for increasing hotel capacity. Governments may also promote tourism to the new resorts by providing infrastructure (e.g. transport and sewage) to new locations. Later in the growth/maturity cycle governments may want to influence the nature of development (e.g. to stress quality of the location/holiday rather than quantity, or environmental conservation of natural resources). Examples of such holiday resort hotel development can be found in the Mediterranean (Portugal, Spain, Turkey) and the West Indies.

Business centres ▪ ▪ ▪

Business/production centres may also come into existence. These may be located because of natural resource availability – often where labour prices for all forms of production are competitively priced (usually through being lower) to those of the advanced service economies. This will mean that they can 'import' activities such as manufacturing which then export production globally rather than merely servicing local markets. This international marketplace, with the presence of firms from many countries will attract business travellers. Centres may also be strategically placed at communications hubs – reflecting a post–1950 emphasis, these will invariably relate to air transport and, for cargo, deep seaport facilities. One such business centre is Singapore in south-east Asia.

The classification of holiday and business centres is another simplification. For example, holiday resorts may deal with business travel (e.g. conference markets). Also, business stays and holiday tourism can develop at the same place, as is the case in Singapore, Hong Kong and Beijing.

However, it is a feature that hotels in either of these types of location are not, *in aggregate*, greatly affected in the short term by demands of local markets. Modern holiday resorts may be located at some distance from local centres of population. Market levels of provision and access factors are driven by the needs of international rather than local markets. This is not to say that local markets do not use hotels as holiday or business centres. They do, and may do so in increasing numbers as local economies evolve and rising affluence develops new markets. However, it must be noted that the concepts of commercial hospitality that have been developed may bear scant regard to the social and economic contexts of local populations. Thus, for example, hotels in devout Muslim countries may have special permission to offer alcohol to their primarily international customers.

The more a hotel industry is dependent on international markets the more its financial health is, naturally, related to events in the economies that create demand (e.g. how consumption patterns are changing). This is particularly the case for pleasure markets. For international business travel markets, levels of demand at any one time relate to the health of international economies and international levels of confidence in business growth, as well as those factors which attract industry to a particular location.

Critique of the model approach to hospitality development

The model approach has helped to underline that hospitality industry comparisons need to differentiate between stages of evolution and further to differentiate between contexts of evolution.

One major limitation of the analysis is its focus on hotel accommodation rather than a wider spectrum of hospitality. Other criticisms can be directed specifically at the use of a model approach. These include:

1 The lack of one comprehensive model of hotel development – in the above analysis three separate models are offered. This variety may create confusion when beginning to analyse a particular issue.

2 A lack of sufficient models of hotel development. For example, models used above may be criticized for being Euro- or Anglo-centric and concentrating on hotel development in capitalist societies. Naturally, present and future hotel development in China, likely to be the largest consumer market before the middle of the twenty-first century, will differ from the models advanced here. In China government control is exercised to a greater extent. Again, distinctive paths of hotel development occurred in European and USSR socialist states in the post–1950s. Here state organizations provided much hotel accommodation for local markets, giving the rise to social/government provided hospitality as opposed to private and commercially traded hospitality.

3 A lack of taking into account sufficient variables in the models.

4 A lack of clarity in the evolution of the stages within models which cannot be stated in precise, measurable terms.

It is accepted that the model approach developed here is not fully comprehensive. The models and stages rely more on economic factors than the social systems into which they fit. Expanding work on the social contexts of hospitality demand both at a cultural/ideological level, and plotting industry development within different forms of social organization might further our understanding of the comparative factors related to such development.

The model approach presented here is offered to counteract common-sense views which tend to assert that the more affluent societies become the larger and more sophisticated the hospitality/hotel industry becomes. This simplification assumes a national specificity and a homogeneity of industry structures, demand patterns and the behaviour of the industry suppliers. In fact, hospitality may frequently be distinguished by differences in paths of evolution. As levels of international travel and trade increase it is likely that understanding industry structures at any particular location will require the use of a number of different models/stages as a mix in order to develop new models of hotel evolution.

A supply view of nature of competitive environments in the UK

This section covers the basic conditions/characteristics of hotel supply, the structure of the UK hotel industry and the nature of competitive environments for UK hotels. Much industry structure literature proposes clear relationships between supply, demand and major economic variables to explain the nature and working of an industry. This section provides an indication of major aspects that should be understood when examining the structure of the industry at any single point in time.

Modern hotels are service providers. While they provide facilities, e.g. a bed and a room, it is the service element that gives the value added/quality level to customers. Services include the condition(s) in which the facilities are offered. As well as supplying *clean and comfortable* rooms and a *choice of well-prepared* meals a hotel may offer a range of other services. These include drinks from bars, conference and meeting rooms, shopping, entertainment and sporting amenities. Hotels also provide advance reservation services (complex when, for example, conferences are arranged), billing services and customer information services. Providing this mix effectively requires high levels of service capability. The range of provision, the different service levels and the nature of customization to individual patrons or events make service management complex as hotels become large and single-site management (an individual hotel) changes to multi-site management (a hotel chain).

Other authors in this book and elsewhere discuss particular characteristics of hospitality operations. For an initial understanding of industry structure, industry features may be characterized by seven main features. As in the previous section these are related to hotels in order to simplify the analysis. The seven factors are grouped under two main headings – investment supply specificity and service characteristics.

Investment supply specificity

1 Capacity specificity by location: at any one time industry capacity is fixed by location. This geographic distribution reflects past as well as present patterns of demand.

2 Investment specificity by use: at any time hotel capacity is fixed by purpose. In the short term, investment may allow flexibility in market levels, e.g. making a mid-market hotel into an up-market one. In the medium to long term, buildings (and thus industry capacity) may be subject to changes of purpose, e.g. a department store could be modified to a hotel. Alternatively, a small country house hotel might become a private residence or a nursing home. New hotels and change of use do require planning permissions, the availability of which may act as a brake or spur to development.

3 Capacity specificity by time: room nights are unstockable/ perishable. Capacity unsold one night remains a loss forever, in the same way seats at concert or a film which are unsold cannot be recycled for a following show.

Service characteristics

1 Sales flexibility: fixed capacity operations have high levels of flexibility in how they sell their capacity. Thus, for example, price levels may be designed to appeal to different market segments.

2 Service level and process flexibility: often being predominantly service operations, hotels may readily change (in principle) their operational methods. This may result in changing the elements of value added (service levels) or the systems used to achieve defined levels (operational processes).

3 Service intangibility: levels of value added are intangible and difficult to project to market decision-takers. In addition, as hotels provide high levels of individual/customized service, it may be difficult to convey their ability to cater for this diversity in a manner which does not dilute perceptions that they can adjust to individual requirements. Brand image is one way of projecting a strong image to a large market. Other strategies include developing customer loyalty and word-of-mouth recommendation and the sophisticated use of websites.

4 Service complementarity: hotel services fall within a spectrum of travel and leisure and/or business services consumed by travellers. For instance, to a package-holiday taker a hotel is one of a number of services that make a holiday experience (transport, shopping and tourist attractions – which may be natural and/or artificial).

The above analysis prompts two main deductions on the structure of the hotel industry. First, when demand is growing, there will be an emphasis on new investment. Location and investment specificity create a climate that encourages the specialized assets necessary. Second, at times of mature demand new investment is contained by the service flexibility shown by existing hotel operators. For example, operators may change service levels, price bands and their use of package operators to fill capacity in new ways and thus discourage potential entrants building new hotel capacity. This may make large-scale, long-term changes in hotel capacity within mature markets difficult to achieve. The risks that new operators run in establishing new capacity are perceived to be high. Because these factors operate at local levels this means that industry characteristics have to be understood in local contexts as well as in national terms. Thus, at any one time, no simple relationship exists between the underlying infrastructure and the markets that it serves in developed Western societies.

As well as understanding investment elements it is also necessary to understand the market factors affecting hotel demand. Hotel capacity may be marketed through three main approaches:

- using market niches (local, national and international) which allow specialized marketing effort

- using location as key and meeting the demands for accommodation effectively for that area

- the third strategy is a mix of the two above.

To be able to meet the requirement of the above strategies understanding demand is important. Whether pursuing niche or location strategies hotels are inevitably multi-market institutions. This springs partly from the fixed location they occupy and the need to maximize their sales at any one time. It also springs from the differentiated nature of demand. It is possible to simplify demand into four main market segments (see Table 2.1).

Demand behaviour differs by segment. For example, at a macrolevel, business travel demand and leisure use of hotels will respond to changes in the economic cycle in different ways. Differences in hotel market segment mix will also alter by location and facilities levels. It is not necessary for demand characteristics to be explored in depth here. It is important however, to note that the hotel industry structure in the UK will reflect these broad areas of demand and sales, and marketing strategies will match and react to changes in demand segments.

Table 2.1
Main hotel market segments (UK room nights sold 1998, million*)

		Leisure	Main purpose of travel Business
Visitor origin	National	Domestic leisure travel markets (10.70)	Domestic business travel markets (12.80)
	International	International leisure travel markets (8.80)	International business travel markets (5.75)

Note: * Figures for publicly quoted hotels in the UK.
Source: Slattery, Ellis and France, 1998.

Hotel industry structure

The two main supply groupings in the hotel industry are the corporate and the independent sector. The corporate sector comprises hotels that are financed by publicly limited companies and have a valuation on the stock market. The independent sector comprises those that do not have a stock market valuation but gain capital through private guarantees etc.

Hotel chains tend to be a corporate phenomenon but are not exclusively so. There can be private hotel chains and there are individually operated hotels in hotel chains. To understand hotel industry structure it is therefore necessary to identify different asset/affiliation patterns. The types of operation listed below provide an indication of these differences.

1 Ownership and operation: indicates that assets and operation are controlled by the same body. If hotels are corporately owned, i.e. operate as part of a chain, they are termed affiliated hotels.

2 Management contracting: asset ownership and operation are separated. The owner of the asset enters into an agreement with the hotel operator to run the hotel on their behalf in return for a management fee. Contracting is common in catering where food service operations at work, in retail, tourism attractions, leisure centres, etc. are often provided by a specialist company rather than the organization or employers responsible for the rest of the activities.

3 Franchising: asset ownership and operation are separated. The franchisor owns the business format, the trading name and all proprietary aspects of the property. The franchisee is given a licence to operate in the franchisor's name, in return for the payment of a royalty fee. A licence may be granted for one or several operations or it may be provided, on a corporate basis, for a region or a country. For the royalty fee, the franchisee will receive a standard operating format, with backup training manuals covering all aspects of operations, staff training assistance, advertising support and so on.

4 Consortium member: an arrangement where hotels co-operate to gain specific corporate benefits. These usually accrue through economies of scale from purchasing or marketing activities. A national consortium of independent budget hotels and a group of hotels in an area that join together to market bargain breaks under a particular name provide examples. By joining a consortium an independent may become an affiliated hotel.

The hotel industry in the UK has seen an increasing penetration of corporate activity. As Table 2.2 shows, in 1988, for example, the room stock owned by publicly owned companies was 107 851.

Organization type	Rooms, 1988	Rooms, 1998	% change
UK hotels plc	107 851	142 525	32.1
Unquoted hotel chains	36 770	43 270	17.7
Hotel consortia	26 035	54 135	107.9
Unaffiliated hotels	327 724	211 537*	−35.5
Total	498 380	451 467	−9.4

Note: * Includes 'quasi hotels'.
Sources: Slattery, 1992: 90–103; Slattery, Ellis and France, 1998: 27.

Table 2.2
Structure of the hotel industry, 1988–98

Ten years later this had climbed to 142 525 rooms, a rise of 32 per cent. This is all the more notable during a time when total capacity in the UK decreased by 9.4 per cent. The implication from Table 2.2 is clear – chain-type operations have grown, while (smaller) independent operators have decreased, both in total and as a share of the total industry capacity. In 1988 unaffiliated hotel rooms accounted for 66 per cent of capacity. By 1998 their share had fallen to 47 per cent.

Competitive strategies in the UK hotel industry

Branding has been widely employed as a competitive strategy across the hospitality industry as a whole. Hotel branding was pioneered in the USA by such established names as Holiday Inn and Sheraton. At its most advanced in the industry it currently involves standardizing aspects of design and service level through to, albeit a lesser extent, pricing. Until the early1980s UK corporate branding was largely a case of using (or adding) the company name to that of a hotel property. The reality was often that a disparate portfolio was promoted as a brand. Some years later in the UK, as spearheaded by US migrants and Forte, there emerged a trend towards stronger market focus. This encouraged a spate of branding activity, though this often replaced the previous *branding by name* to *branding by product type*. Branding is not a strategy solely adopted by the corporate sector. Independents join marketing consortiums partly to pool their resources and develop brand images that have high national or market niche recognition.

Larger and more consistent brands are mainly, though not exclusively, North American in origin. The growth of US brands has, conversely, occurred at a time of internationalization in their ownership. For example, UK companies now own Holiday Inn and Intercontinental (Bass), Hilton International (Ladbroke), Bildeberg (Queens Moat Houses), Meridien (Forte). Other international brands include Novotel (Accor, France) and Hyatt (USA).

Given the level of attrition of the non-affiliated sector shown in Table 2.2 the long-term survival of the sector may be raised. It unlikely that units in this sector will ever become extinct. Indeed, the wider availability of computerized technology and changes in distribution systems facilitated by the World Wide Web may increase their choices for survival rather than diminish them. Additionally, the local nature of many hotel markets may allow them to build competitive advantage over larger, international hotel companies.

Other competitive strategies include advance reservation systems (increasing market reach), yield management systems (capacity sales management) and budget hotel chains (creating market differentiation). In these respects larger companies may have advantages of scale. However, scale of operation has not provided immunity to failure. The health of the corporate sector stems from market success with customers and investors. Profitability, climbing property values and stock market rises in the 1980s made UK hotel companies attractive investments. The depression of the early 1990s saw demand and values tumbling. Stringent economy measures by the firms (including corporate-level redundancies) were outweighed by the effect of slack demand and vicious price competition. Development of package weekend holiday breaks helped counter the loss of business travel markets. Some corporate operations floundered or were taken off the stock market (e.g. Queens Moat Houses shares were temporarily suspended from trading). Forte, the UK's largest hotel operator, was taken over by Granada in 1996 in a hostile bid. However, as a sector, companies were able to show sufficient flexibility and innovation to avoid mass withdrawals of capital, although their reputation for following the boom–bust pattern of the economic cycle was reinforced.

In judging future trends in the structure of the hospitality and hotel industry it is important that demand and supply aspects are carefully investigated. It is also important, as shown in the earlier part of the chapter, that demand and supply are put within a macrocontext in order that changes in type of influence as well as more common-sense aspects are explored.

Conclusions

This chapter has explored the concept of industry structure. Initially it accomplished this by developing models. These stress comparisons by stage of industry evolution and by contexts of evolution. In later parts of the chapter the need to explain hotel supply in terms of investment specificity and service character-istics was explained. The conjunction of these two factors result in the need to take into account a number of special conditions when assessing the current hospitality industry structure and a need to assess locational aspects when studying structure and change to any depth.

This type of analysis allows general conclusions to be drawn on the nature and movements of hospitality operators. It cannot provide specific indications on the fortunes of individual enterprises – be they corporate or independent.

Future developments in examining elements of industry change where a deeper knowledge of industry structure could prove useful include:

- similarities/differences in industry structure at different locations
- product differentiation in hospitality operations
- advertising strategy of corporate and/or independent operators in hospitality
- empirical studies into the presence of economies of scale in hospitality sectors
- pricing strategies in hospitality
- profitability in the hospitality industry.

Summary

This chapter has illustrated the ability to use concepts from disciplines such as economics to analyse developments in hospitality. It has focused on hotel industry and organizations, but suggests that similar techniques can be used in other sectors of hospitality. This chapter has:

1 Used terms common in economics such as demand, supply, industry structure, cost structure and competition to explore the dynamics of the industry.

2 Developed models of the hotel industry that plot different stages of growth and different patterns of industry evolution.

3 Explained the nature of competitive environments in developed hotel industries which are subject to demand at national and international levels from leisure and business travellers.

4 Discussed the nature of competitive strategies from a supplier perspective.

There is no one recipe for analysing the hospitality industry which exhibits different characteristics in its different sectors. However, the approach adopted should allow considered scenarios to be developed for hotel industry futures as well as providing a foundation for analysis of other hospitality sectors such as eating out.

Review questions

1 To what extent could the models of the hotel sector's development outlined in this chapter be used to explore the development of other sectors of the hospitality industry?

2 How might knowledge of the structural characteristics of the sectors of the industry help you to compare them?

3 What data would you need to compare the nature of the markets faced by fast-food and hotel companies?

4 How could knowledge of the historical development of a sector of the industry help you to understand its present structure?

5 Why is a clear definition of the industry and/or a particular sector important for making comparisons?

6 To what extent could you apply the two groupings of industry features – investment supply specificity and service characteristics – outlined in the chapter to compare the hotel sector with others in the industry?

7 Ownership is a key feature of any industry structure. To what extent do the forms of ownership outlined in the chapter exist in other sectors of the industry?

8 Branding has become an important competitive strategy across the hospitality industry. Does this mean that it could be used to compare different types of hospitality operation in different sectors of the industry?

9 Would it be valid to compare the operations of a large chain hotel with those of a small owner-managed hotel?

10 What other criteria, beyond those outlined in the chapter, could you use to compare the structures/competitive environments of different sectors of the industry?

Bibliography

Begg, D., Fischer, S. and Dornbush, R. (1987). *Economics*. 2nd edn., McGraw-Hill.

Boorstin, D. J. (1965). *The Americans: The National Experience*. Penguin.

Medlik, S. and Airey, D. (1978). *Profile of the Hotel and Catering Industry*. Heinemann.

Quennel, M. and Quennel, C. (1957). *A History of Everyday Things in England*. Vol 1 (1066–1499), 4th edn. Batsford Putnam.

Slattery, P. (1992). Unaffiliated hotels in the UK. *Travel and Tourism Analyst*, no. 1, pp. 90–103. Economist Intelligence Unit.

Slattery, P., Ellis, S. and France, D. (1998). *European Quoted Hotel Companies, Rethinking Cyclicality.* Dresdner Kleinwort Benson Research.

Taylor, D. and Bush, D. (1974). *The Golden Age of British Hotels.* Northwood.

Further reading

Cabinet Office/Enterprise Unit (1985). *Pleasure, Leisure and Jobs: The Business of Tourism.* HMSO.

Foley, M., Lennon, J. and Maxwell, G. (eds) (1997). *Hospitality, Tourism and Leisure Management – Issues in Strategy and Culture.* Cassells.

Gratton, C. and Taylor, P. (1992). *Economics of Services Management.* Longman.

Hughes, H. (1990). *Economics for Hotel and Catering Students.* Stanley Thornes.

Taylor, D. and Bush, D. (1974). *The Golden Age of British Hotels.* Northwood Publications.

Tribe, C. (1995). *The Economics of Leisure and Tourism.* Butterworth-Heinemann.

Further reading on industry structures and contemporary trends in demand can be obtained from good quality industry market research firms such as *Keynote Publications* and *Mintel International* in the UK.

3

Operating systems and products

Peter Jones and Andrew Lockwood

The general objective for this chapter is to use the systems approach to compare and contrast the operational types found in the hospitality industry. At the end of this chapter you should be able to:

1 Recognize the nature of alternative approaches to classifying operations in the hospitality industry.

2 Identify how the industry may be classified on the basis of systems theory.

3 Identify the characteristics that make one type of operation different from another.

4 Explain how different types of operation require different approaches for their management.

5 Apply systems thinking and concepts to identify the basic structure, nature and purpose of alternative hospitality operations.

Introduction

It is clear that the hospitality industry is made up of a wide range of different types of outlet. In the accommodation sector, provision in the commercial sector includes five-star luxury properties, guesthouses and every type of hotel in between; while in the not-for-profit sector accommodation is provided in halls of residence, hospitals, prisons and hostels of all kinds. In the food service sector, food and drink is served in restaurants, pubs and clubs in diverse settings such as the high street, shopping malls, motorways, institutions (e.g. schools, hospitals and prisons), on railways, in aeroplanes and on board ships. From a systems perspective, the question is 'are these operations basically the same?' and if not, 'in what way are these operations different?'

In this chapter, we apply systems theory to a comparative analysis of the industry to identify similarities and differences between operations. Such analysis identifies key aspects of hospitality provision that explain how accommodation is different from food service, and how within these sectors there are also differences. The important point, however, is not that the hospitality industry can genuinely be divided into different types of operation, but the implications such differentiation has for the *management* of operations. In simple terms, if all hospitality operations were essentially the same, then a hospitality manager would need only one set of knowledge and skills to be able to manage any type of unit. If in some respects they are different, the manager may need a wider range of knowledge and skills from which to select the most appropriate set for the operation he or she is managing.

Classification of hospitality systems

The hospitality industry has been classified in many ways over the years. We shall consider here two main approaches – economic and market-based – before going on to look at a third approach – systems – which will form the basis for this chapter.

Economic classifications

The usual starting point for looking at alternative classifications is to start with the UK's official Standard Industrial Classification (SIC). An SIC was first introduced into the UK in 1948 for use in classifying business establishments and other statistical units by the type of economic activity in which they are engaged. The classification provides a framework for the collection, tabulation, presentation and analysis of data, and its use promotes uniformity. In addition, it can be used for administrative purposes and by non-government bodies as a convenient way of classifying industrial activities into a common structure. Since 1948 the classification has been revised in 1958, 1968, 1980 and 1992.

In this classification, the hotel and catering industry has been defined as 'establishments (whether or not licensed for the sale of intoxicating liquor) providing meals, light refreshments, drink or accommodation'. The hospitality industry is classified in Section 55: Hotels and restaurants and subsequently subdivided into five groups, as illustrated in Table 3.1.

The major problem with this classification is that although it is derived from data that is relatively easy to collect by government

55				**HOTELS AND RESTAURANTS**
	55.1			**Hotels**
		55.11		Hotels and motels, with restaurant
			55.11/1	Licensed hotels and motels
			55.11/2	Unlicensed hotels and motels
		55.12		Hotels and motels, without restaurant
	55.2			**Camping sites and other provision of short-stay accommodation**
		55.21		Youth hostels and mountain refuges
		55.22		Camping sites, including caravan sites
		55.23		Other provision of lodgings not elsewhere classified
			55.23/1	Holiday centres and holiday villages
			55.23/2	Other self-catering holiday accommodation
			55.23/9	Other tourist or short-stay accommodation
	55.3			**Restaurants**
		55.30		Restaurants
			55.30/1	Licensed restaurants
			55.30/2	Unlicensed restaurants and cafés
			55.30/3	Takeaway food shops
			55.30/4	Takeaway food mobile stands
	55.4			**Bars**
		55.40		Bars
			55.40/1	Licensed clubs
			55.40/2	Independent public houses and bars
			55.40/3	Tenanted public houses and bars
			55.40/4	Managed public houses and bars
	55.5			**Canteens and catering**
		55.51		Canteens
		55.52		Catering

Source: Office for National Statistics, 1999.

Table 3.1 The Standard Industrial Classification applied to hospitality

agencies, principally in the area of licensing the sale of alcoholic beverages, this does not adequately reflect the variety and complexity of hospitality businesses that comprise the contemporary hospitality industry. For instance, group 55.4 Bars derives from the data relating to the number of on licences issued by local magistrates. This can lead to a number of problems in finding an effective differentiation between restaurants and pubs, welfare feeding in hospitals and prisons, and transport food service, which is not identified at all.

A second source of data, and hence classification, from an 'official' source is the Hospitality Training Foundation (HtF) – which is the national training organization (NTO) for the UK hospitality industry. The HtF produces a statistical report on the industry (HtF, 1999), which identifies the size and scale of different sectors. This partially adopts the SIC classification, but also creates its own classification based on data from other sources, such as the British Tourist Authority (BTA).

Other organizations with an overview of the industry are trade associations, such as the British Hospitality Association, and professional associations, such as the Hotel Catering International Management Association. They routinely produce annual reports on the industry. For instance, *British Hospitality: Trends and Statistics 1999*, published by the BHA (1999), presents data on hotels, catering (divided into the profit and cost sectors), contract catering, motorway service areas and self-catering. Their data sources include government or quasi-government sources such as the BTA and tourist boards, market intelligence reports such as Mintel and Keynote, and consultancy reports.

In many respects, these economic classification systems derive from 'common sense', i.e. what most people regard as different sectors, and from pragmatic reality, i.e. what data is easily available. An alternative approach is to adopt a market-based approach. Such an approach classifies hospitality operations on the basis of the different customer groups or markets they serve.

Market-based classifications

A typical approach to hotel classification is to consider hotels ranging from one star to five stars, serving the so-called one star market and so on (see Case 3.1). It could be argued that this is not a market-based classification at all, since the organizations that classify hotels in this way, such as motoring organizations or government tourism bodies, usually do so on the basis of *product*, not market, criteria. This is a circular argument. Once a five-star hotel is built and operating, it is automatically used by customers from the five-star market segment. So a star rating is as much a market classification as it is a product classification.

Case 3.1

In 1999, the English Tourism Council, working in conjunction with the Automobile Association (AA) and the Royal Automobile Club (RAC), and in response to consumer demand, created a new rating scheme for hotels and guest accommodation in England, using stars to represent hotels and diamonds for guest accommodation (guesthouses, inns, farmhouses, bed and breakfasts). The scheme put greater emphasis on quality in hotels and guest accommodation, particularly in areas of cleanliness and guest care. To obtain a grading, the hotel or guest accommodation is visited overnight anonymously by qualified assessors.

The star ratings symbolize the level of service, range of facilities and quality of guest care that a customer can expect. Hotels are required to meet progressively higher standards as they move up the scale from one to five stars.

A *one-star* hotel must provide:

- Practical accommodation with a limited range of facilities and services, but a high standard of cleanliness throughout.
- Friendly and courteous staff to give the help and information the customer needs to enjoy a stay.
- Restaurant/eating area open to customers and their guests for breakfast and dinner.
- Alcoholic drinks served in a bar or lounge.
- 75 per cent of bedrooms have *en suite* or private facilities.

In addition a *two-star* hotel must provide:

- Good overnight accommodation with more comfortable bedrooms, better equipped – all with *en suite* or private facilities and colour television.
- A relatively straightforward range of services, including food and drink, and a personal style of service.

- A restaurant/dining room for breakfast and dinner.
- A lift is normally available.

In addition a *three-star* hotel must provide:

- Possibly larger establishments, but offering significantly greater quality and range of facilities and services, and usually more spacious public areas and bedrooms.
- A more formal style of service with a receptionist on duty and staff responding well to customer needs and requests.
- Room service of continental breakfast.
- Laundry service available.
- A wide selection of drinks, light lunch and snacks served in a bar or lounge.

In addition a *four-star* hotel must provide:

- Accommodation offering superior comfort and quality; all bedrooms with *en suite* bath, fitted overhead shower and a toilet.
- The hotel will have spacious and very well appointed public areas and will put a strong emphasis on food and drink.
- Staff will have very good technical and social skills, anticipating and responding to customer needs and requests.
- Room service for all meals and twenty-four hour drinks, refreshments and snacks.
- Dry cleaning service available.

In addition a *five-star* hotel must provide:

- A spacious, luxurious establishment offering the highest international quality of accommodation, facilities, services and cuisine. It will have striking accommodation throughout, with a range of extra facilities.

- Customers will feel very well cared for by professional, attentive staff providing flawless guest services.

- A hotel that fits the highest international standards for the industry, with an air of luxury, exceptional comfort and a sophisticated ambience.

Similar rating systems also exist in the food service sector, typically developed commercially as guides for consumers, such as the *Good Food Guide* or Egon Ronay guides. Tangible features such as price and service levels are used as criteria for this classification system, just as they are for hotels, but again the actual outcome is to differentiate operations based on different consumer market segments. Typologies explicitly developed to classify the sector adopt a similar approach. The American National Restaurant Association, in conjunction with CREST, has developed the idea of 'concept groups'. In this approach there are three main segments, each subdivided into concepts based on product or service style. The quick service segment is divided into concept groups such as chicken, donut, Mexican, pizza, etc. The mid-scale segment is divided into cafeteria, casual dining, family-style, hotel, steakhouse, speciality (seafood, ethnic) and varied menu. The upscale segment has concepts described as casual dining, high check (i.e. price), moderate check, hotel, speciality, and varied menu.

Systems classification

An alternative approach to classification is based on systems theory. In the hospitality industry, the terminology and jargon of systems is everywhere. Managers commonly talk about their management information system, property management system, central reservation system or food production system. These examples are all so-called 'hard' systems, based on technology. Just as important are other non-technological systems, sometimes called 'soft' systems, such as marketing planning, total quality management, budgeting or employee recruitment and selection policies and procedures.

The hospitality manager is well placed to understand systems thinking and systems concepts due to the inherent features of the industry. He or she has been trained to manage a system, e.g. use resources, oversee processes, measure outputs and act on feedback. Most management training (itself a system) follows the process of providing knowledge and skills in managing relatively simple systems, such as the bar, reservations or food service, through increasingly complex systems, such as rooms division or food and beverage, up to general management at unit level and then chain operations management.

Despite using the terminology and being trained to manage a variety of systems, most hospitality managers' understanding of systems principles is fairly rudimentary. A system may be defined as a set of components and the relations between them, usually configured to produce a desired set of outputs, operating in the context of its environment. There are three key aspects of systems theory, which enable classification to be made.

General systems view

Most managers will be familiar with the standard systems model of input–process–output–feedback. Inputs, or resources, are typically divided into materials, energy and information, while outputs are the same, although often described, especially in human-made systems, as product (inputs transformed in the desired way), waste (inputs transformed as a by-product) and residue (unused inputs). The conversion of inputs into outputs is achieved by some kind of transformation process that typically requires a physical infrastructure, order, structure, and capacity. Finally, this input–process–output activity is situated in a systems environment, i.e. all those things with which the system interacts.

Systems hierarchy

Most systems are related in some way to other systems. They are made up of subsystems and are themselves subsystems of a larger system. This concept of hierarchy is commonly applied in the hospitality industry to the way in which operations are organized. For example, a hotel chain (the principal system) usually comprises a head office, regional offices and individual hotels (the first-level subsystem). Each hotel is organized into departments such as food and beverage, front office and sales (second-level subsystem), which in turn are divided into sections or operating units such as bar, kitchen, coffee shop and so on (third-level subsystem).

Systems interaction

Implicit with the idea of hierarchy is the concept of system interaction. The outputs of one system form all or part of the inputs of another system.

A systems theoretical framework encourages the application of modelling to real-life situations to understand them as systems, identify hierarchies and analyse interactions. Such models are typical input–process–output models or so-called 'operations flow charts'. Jones (1996) has considered both accommodation and food service, developing systems models for them both.

Jones argues that for accommodation there is a *core* system comprising four subsystems of reservations, reception, overnight stay (housekeeping) and payment (or billing). This is illustrated in Figure 3.1. Besides these, depending on the type of market being served there are ancillary systems that may or may not be offered (also shown in Figure 3.1). These subsystems include laundry, restaurants, bars, business services and leisure services. He identifies that a hotel is largely a customer-processing operation, especially for the core system. He does not suggest how many different types of hotel arise from the potential combinations of the core system with ancillary systems, but *de facto* such a typology would resemble quite closely the typical approach to hotel classification.

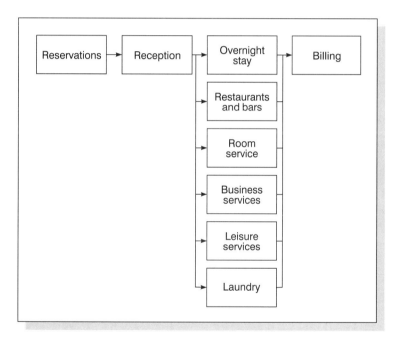

Figure 3.1
A systems model of hotel operations
Source: Jones, 1996

Even within a single type of hotel there can be some significant differences in the range of products or services offered to the customer (see Case 3.2). This example compares the product offered by three companies operating at the budget end of the hotel market, offering low prices but with a restricted offer. The three chains include Travel Inn, part of the Whitbread Hotel Company and operated exclusively in the UK, Granada Travelodge, part of the Granada group and operated under the brand name in the UK, and Fairfield Inns, part of the Marriott Hotel group and operated exclusively in the USA

Case 3.2

Travel Inn

For a single price per room per night, every Travel Inn offers:

- *En suite* bathroom with shower and bath.

- Double bed, with duvet.

- Family room that sleeps up to two adults and two children under sixteen.

- Remote control television and radio alarm.

- Tea- and coffee-making facilities.

- Spacious desk area.

- Licensed restaurant and bar (integral or next door).

Granada Travelodge

For a single price per room per night, every Travelodge offers:

- Spacious *en suite* rooms.

- Satellite television with a choice of cartoons, sports and films.

- Tea- and coffee-making facilities.

- Free newspaper.

- Free car parking.

- Friendly restaurants.

- Luxury 'Hypnos' beds.

- Easy check in and check out.

Fairfield Inns

For a single price per room per night, every Fairfield Inn offers:

- Free continental breakfast.

- Free twenty-four hour coffee and tea.

- Free local calls.

- Well-lit work desk.

- Fax and copy service.

- Fitness rooms at most locations.

- Swimming pool.

- Premium movies.

- Same-day laundry service.

Food service on the other hand is a materials-processing operation and customer-processing operation. Jones (1993; 1996) and Huelin and Jones (1990) have made a number of attempts to classify food service operations based on an analysis of their systems design, technology and configuration. They identify ten subsystems of food service, namely storage, preparation, cooking, holding, transport, regeneration, service, dining, clearing and dishwash. Jones (1996) goes on to suggest that these have been configured in a limited number of ways, within three broad categories, as illustrated in Table 3.2.

To provide an illustration of how this classification of food service operations can be used in practice see Figure 3.2 and Case 3.3. Figure 3.2 models a particular food delivery system, based on tray service, and Case 3.3 provides more of the contextual details lying behind this system operated by the in-flight catering company Alpha Catering Ltd.

System configuration	Operational types
Integrated food service systems	
Storage, preparation, cooking, service, dining clearing, dishwash	Conventional à la carte restaurant using fresh commodities
Storage, preparation, cooking, holding, service, dining, clearing, dishwash	Conventional table d'hôte restaurant
Storage, preparation, holding, service, dining, clearing, dishwash	Catering outlet serving only prepared foods, e.g. buffet or sandwich bar
Storage, cooking, holding, service, dining, clearing, dishwash	Conventional outlet using convenience products
Storage, preparation, cooking, holding, service, dining, clearing	Fast food
Storage, preparation, cooking, dining, clearing, dishwash	Japanese hibachi-style restaurant
Food manufacturing systems	
Storage, preparation, cooking, holding, transport	Cook-chill or sous-vide cooking from fresh raw materials
Storage, cooking, holding, transport	Cook-chill or sous-vide using convenience products
Storage, preparation, cooking, transport	Home delivery
Food delivery systems	
Transport, storage, regeneration, service, dining clearing, dishwash	Tray-serve systems, such as in-flight, hospital and so on
Storage, regeneration, service, dining, clearing, dishwash	Outlets serving fully prepared meals from supplier

Table 3.2 Food service systems and operational types

Case 3.3

Alpha Catering Ltd

With a production capacity of over 7500 flights per week, Alpha is responsible for the delivery of approximately 40 million meals per year. Besides the core activity of meal preparation for scheduled and charter airlines, the operations incorporate a complex exercise designed to ensure that food and equipment is ordered, packed and loaded on to aircraft within precise time frames. Typically, a scheduled Boeing 747 requires more than 40 000 items to be loaded, checked and packed into predetermined stowage on the aircraft. Allowing for choice, dietary and religious requirements, a long-haul flight can be supplied with over thirty different meal types.

Close attention to detail in all parts of the operation, including the food production process, precision delivery to aircraft and final handover to cabin crew, is paramount.

'Getting it right; first time; every time' is an operational credo that is especially pertinent to flight catering, since with a literally captive audience of up to 400 passengers at 30 000 feet, there is no second chance if something goes wrong. If no teapots are loaded, no tea will be served; if insufficient numbers of meals are loaded, some passengers may not get to eat. While a few additional meals are carried in order to provide some element of customer choice, with aircraft weight being the primary determinant in flight distance and number of passengers carried, there is simply no room to carry a large inventory of spares 'just in case', and so for the flight caterer there is only one chance to get it right.

For more than ten years, Alpha has used a form of purchasing that, though not always guaranteeing the lowest unit price, guarantees the freshest quality product at the best possible price, in direct relation to the level of service that their clients want them to provide. The just in time (JIT) process has its origins in manufacturing – in particular in the automobile industry – and is based around the belief that economies generated by volume purchases to achieve low unit costs, are outweighed by the diseconomies of the cost of carrying that inventory before usage. For Alpha, there is an additional diseconomy of loss of product quality in extended storage.

The key principle of JIT is the use of frequent deliveries of small amounts of product as close to an 'as needed' basis as possible, to minimize inventory levels. For Alpha, the commitment to this process over the last decade has led to an operating environment in which their manufacturing plants are built around the process rather than developing the production process around the constraints of the building structure. In the day-to-day operation of the plant, storage is avoided wherever possible – the raw product is delivered directly to the point of process. Similarly, the cooked products are also delivered directly to the point of process. For salad produce, there are up to three deliveries per day, again to the point of process.

The commitment to product freshness is obvious, but the gains to be made in terms of reduced inventory levels, reduced stock rotation requirements, and increased product control are also considerable. The Gatwick operation (see Figure 3.2) was the first purpose-built JIT plant in the company, and by introducing this process, inventory levels were reduced from over twenty days to less than five days – a greater than 75 per cent reduction which was directly attributable to the JIT process. The plan shows the simple factory-like layout with the flow of equipment and food moving round the operation to end up on the tray assembly line. It also shows the limited number of operations required for a food manufacturing system as described in Table 3.2.

Classifications compared

A summary of the different approaches to classification is provided in Table 3.3. We would argue that the most useful classification for understanding operations is that based on systems. Consistent with systems thinking is the notion of 'emergent properties'. That is to say, modelling a system and its subsystems identifies the specific characteristics of the system. Quite clearly, both accommodation and food service, have some systems that are relatively simple, such as the core accommodation system, buffet operations or fast food, and others that are complex, such as five-star hotels or cook-chill.

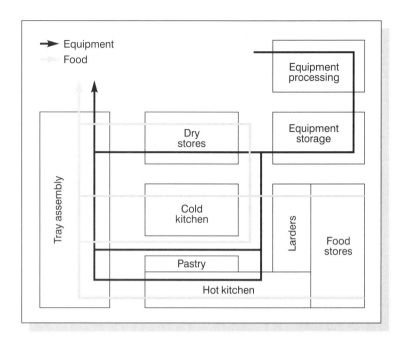

Figure 3.2
Alpha Catering Ltd flight catering kitchen, Gatwick

Before considering the implications of this, we need to consider whether modelling hospitality operations in this way helps to classify them in the context of operations as a whole, i.e. across all industry sectors.

Operations frameworks

The above analysis demonstrates that from a systems perspective there are differences in inputs, processes and outputs between different operations within the hospitality industry. How significant are these differences? To answer that question, hospitality operations need to be put into some kind of framework that differentiates between operational types.

It has been suggested by Schemenner (1986) that, in manufacturing, there has emerged a single framework of operational types, based on that originally developed by Hayes and Wheelwright (1979), that has gained wide acceptance. This framework has allowed the sharing of approaches and techniques across different manufacturing sectors and has allowed strategic decisions to be made about the implications of process choice. This framework identifies five process types that range from those that operate with a low output volume and high variety to those that operate at high volumes but with limited variety or high standardization. These types are project, job shop, batch production, mass production and continuous production, as shown in Figure 3.3.

In the top left-hand corner project activities are highly customized, one-off, highly complex and normally large-scale

S.I.C	Market based	Systems classification
Hotels		
Hotels and motels, with restaurant – licensed and unlicensed	5-star hotel	Full service hotel
Hotels and motels, without restaurant	4-star hotel	Mid-service hotel
Camping sites and other provision of short-stay accommodation	3-star hotel	Limited service hotel
Youth hostels and mountain refuges	2 -tar hotel	Hostels
Camping sites, including caravan sites	1-star hotel	Long-term residential accommodation
Other provision of lodgings not elsewhere classified	Hostel	
Holiday centres and holiday villages	Residential accommodation	
Other self-catering holiday accommodation		
Other tourist or short-stay accommodation		
Restaurants		
Licensed restaurants	Upscale restaurants	Conventional à la carte restaurant
Unlicensed restaurants and cafés	Mid-scale restaurants	Conventional table d'hôte restaurant
Takeaway food shops	Quick service restaurants	Buffet/sandwich bar
Takeaway food mobile stands		Call/short order
		Fast food
		Hibachi style
		Home delivery
	Transport catering	Tray serve
Bars		
Canteens and catering		
Canteens	Employee feeding	Assembly serve
Catering	Welfare catering	Sous-vide or cook-chill

Table 3.3 Comparison of alternative approaches to hospitality industry classification

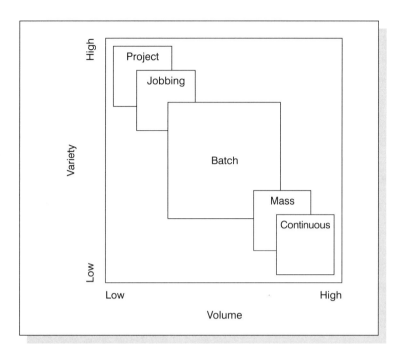

Figure 3.3
Manufacturing process types

activities such as the Channel Tunnel or a mission to Mars. At the other extreme, continuous production is exemplified by a chemical plant where there is a constant flow through a largely automated process with very limited flexibility. In between lie the jobbing, batch and line or mass-production process types. These types vary in their ability to produce a customized product and the volume of production. A job(bing) shop produces a wide range of products made to a customer order but shares resources between the different products. As bespoke products these will be at very low volume. The batch process generates a narrower range of products but produces small numbers of each at a time, so achieving higher volumes. Mass production, typified by the production line traditionally found in car plants, can produce large volumes of a single product but with only small variations being possible.

For many people, this framework works fine when applied to manufacturing but not when applied to service industries. In 1986, Roger Schemenner proposed a service framework that differentiated between different types of service operations, based on high or low labour intensity and the level of standardization versus customization. This resulted in four process types, which he called professional service, service shop, service factory and mass service. These have obvious similarities with the manufacturing process types but they do not use the same basic variables of variety and volume and it is therefore difficult to compare them directly.

Conversely, Silvestro et al. (1992) provide a way of classifying service processes that does, however, use the same variables. In this system, volume is measured in terms of the number of customers processed by an individual service unit per day and, indeed, many service operations can be described as customer processing operations (CPOs). The measure of variety used is based on six key dimensions ranked as either high, medium or low. These are equipment versus people focus, customer contact time, the degree of customization of the service, the degree of discretion allowed to customer contact staff, the emphasis on back of house versus front of house, and a distinction between a product – 'what the customer buys' – focus and a process-oriented – 'how the service is delivered' – approach. As the number of customers processed by a typical service operation increases, the general trends in terms of variety are a move from a people to an equipment focus, lower customer contact time, lower levels of customization and employee discretion, a move from a front to a back office focus and from a process to a product orientation. These elements are clearly evident in high-volume fast-food operations. This results in three generic service process types, which Silvestro et al. call professional services, service shop and mass services, as shown in Figure 3.4.

Hospitality is commonly seen as a service industry, so it would seem that the framework proposed by Silvestro et al (1992) would be the most relevant. As the discussion of food service operations identified, clearly there is also a degree of manufacturing

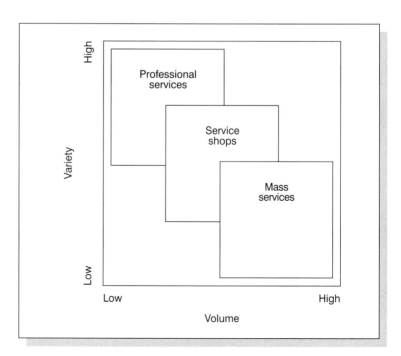

Figure 3.4
Service process types

involved in this area of hospitality, notably in the processing of foodstuffs into meals or what are often referred to as materials processing operations (MPOs). Indeed, as you have already seen, at least one sector of the industry, in-flight catering, in almost every aspect is quite clearly a manufacturing operation. The typical flight kitchen is located on an industrial estate, uses conveyor belts to transport equipment, uses assembly-line principles, and has large-scale output.

In fact, hospitality can be considered a hybrid operation, containing elements of both manufacturing and service. The former is typically carried out back-of-house, while the latter is front-of-house, naturally enough since this is the part of the operation used by the customer. So which framework – Hayes and Wheelwright's or Silvestro et al.'s– should be used to analyse the industry?

In Chapter 1, Bob Brotherton discusses the comparative approach and identifies that it is essential that 'we do not fall into the trap of making surface or superficial comparison'. He then goes on to discuss how to establish a comparative base, ensuring conceptual or construct and contextual equivalence. The hybrid nature of hospitality, however, makes it difficult to adopt a universally applicable conceptual framework that makes valid comparisons possible.

Hospitality operations comparison

We would suggest that an answer to this difficulty is not to try to compare services with manufacturing, i.e. CPOs with MPOs. Although the difference between processing people and things is often identified in the literature, rarely has it been *systematically* analysed to identify the implications of such differences. Clearly, customers are physiologically capable of action whereas materials are not. Such actions include the ability to move unaided, to apply the senses of sight, hearing, touch, taste and smell, and to communicate with the environment. As well as this physical interaction, customers also engage psychologically with their environment. This means that each customer's values and attitudes may be slightly different, they may perceive their experiences differently and hence they may respond to the service environment *heterogeneously.*

Two examples illustrate this difference between people and materials, and the gulf that therefore exists between CPOs and MPOs. When Disney opened its theme park in Paris, it applied years of experience to its planning and design. However, within a few weeks of opening, they found that Europeans, especially the French and southern Europeans, behaved very differently from the Americans and Japanese who predominantly visit their parks in California, Florida and Tokyo. The French do not like queuing, so they avoid it if they can. This meant that they would attempt to get on the major rides, for which long queues build up, by jumping the queue or accessing it by the exit. This was highly disruptive and led to the entrances to, and exits from, such rides having to be modified.

Likewise, people's perception of time while waiting has been shown to vary quite widely according to circumstances (Jones and Peppiatt, 1995). Time is perceived to pass more slowly if people have nothing to do, are anxious, queue on their own, wait in a 'preprocess' (as opposed to 'in-process') situation, do not know why they are waiting or how long the wait will be. Hence there are a number of probably apocryphal stories about how guest complaints about slow service have been eliminated by changing their perceptions, such as putting mirrors on each floor lobby to occupy guests' time whilst waiting for the lift to arrive.

We therefore propose that hospitality operations need to be modelled as either CPOs or MPOs. If an operation is a hybrid, i.e. it processes customers and materials, then it should be divided into its two constituent parts and each categorized accordingly. It should be noted that it is assumed that those operations where food items are mainly prepared from fresh ingredients are typically associated with table service, whereas those using convenience products are linked to cafeteria or counter-style operations. While this is generally true, the industry is con-siderably diverse in its practice. This classification, by its very nature, simplifies the complexity. Hence the operations identified in Table 3.4 are listed as either predominantly CPO or MPO or hybrid, then, hybrids are divided into their back-of-house and front-of-house systems.

Predominantly CPOs	Predominantly MPOs
Full service hotel	Cook-chill
Mid-service hotel	Tray serve
Limited service hotel	Home delivery
Hostels	
Long-term residential accommodation	

Hybrid operations	
Table service restaurant	A la carte kitchen; table d'hôte kitchen; call/short-order kitchen
Buffet/sandwich bar	Buffet/sandwich bar
Fast-food restaurant	Fast-food kitchen
Hibachi-style restaurant	Hibachi-style restaurant
Counter/cafeteria style	Assembly serve

Table 3.4
CPOs, MPOs and hybrids

To compare these we adopt the criteria of volume and variety as the key characteristics that differentiate between operations. This analysis is shown in Figures 3.5 and 3.6.

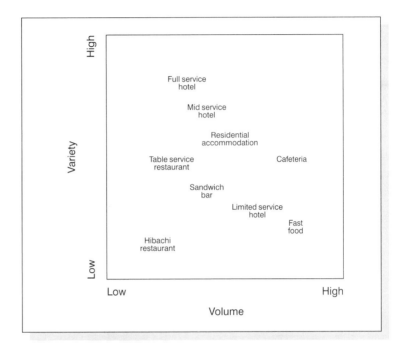

Figure 3.5
Classification of hospitality customer processing operations
Source: Jones and Lockwood, 1999

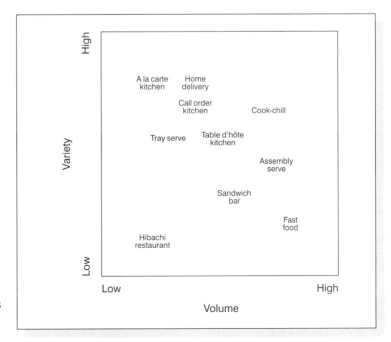

Figure 3.6
Classification of hospitality materials processing operations
Source: Jones and Lockwood, 1999

This comparative analysis of hospitality operations should immediately enable you to identify some key aspects of the hospitality industry:

1 Hotels are generally more complex than food service operations simply because, other than limited service hotels, they provide both lodging and food service.

2 Hybrid operations are more complex to manage than non-hybrid operations.

3 Hospitality materials processing operations are job shops (e.g. à la carte restaurant), batch production (e.g. cook-chill) or mass production (e.g. fast food).

4 Most hospitality customer processing operations are service shops (e.g. table service restaurant) or mass services (e.g. fast food).

5 There is generally a relationship between volume and variety, i.e. the greater the variety the less volume produced.

6 It follows therefore that hybrid operations that are batch production MPOs are typically associated with service shop CPOs, whilst mass production matches mass service.

Schemenner (1986) and Hayes and Wheelwright (1979) argue that it is logical for firms to 'move towards the diagonal', i.e. the line that represents a balance between volume and variety. Low variety enables the production of a high volume of standardized output. High volume is necessary as standardized products/ services tend to be viewed as commodities that attract relatively low profit margins. However, highly customized products and services can be sold at premium prices, thereby paying for the relatively inefficient high variety production.

Most of the hospitality operations we have analysed (in Figures 3.5 and 3.6) lie on this diagonal. One notable exception is the 'hibachi' restaurant, such as those found in the Benihana chain, which serves both a limited product and in relatively low volumes. The explanation can be found in the technology, i.e. the hibachi style of cooking. A hibachi table is a type of griddle on which items can be stir fried, around which customers sit, typically eight in number, waiting to be served food fresh from the griddle. This limits both the types of dishes that can be prepared and the numbers of people that can be served. This type of operation is therefore exceptional, which explains why it is not widespread.

As a key feature of this comparative analysis is to demonstrate in more detail how each operational type varies from the other we shall compare job/service shops with mass production/ service. A number of criteria can be used for identifying such differences, as illustrated in Table 3.5.

	Job/service shops	Mass production/service
Volume	Low	High
Mix of services	Diverse	Limited
Demand variation	Lumpy demand accommodated	Preferably stable demand
Pattern of process	Adaptable	Rigid
Process change	Easily accommodated	Costly
Role of equipment	Multi-use	Single use, often automated
Labour skills	Flexible, skilled workers	Generally lower skilled
Job content	Wide in scope	Narrow in scope
Work environment	Individual, craft based	Visible, paced performance
Economies of scale	Limited	Some
Bottlenecks	Movable and frequent	Identified and predictable
Additions to capacity	May be incremental	Difficult to adjust
Tolerance for excess capacity	Adapt activity of workforce	Adjust staffing levels

Source: adapted from Sasser, Olsen and Wyckoff (1978) and Schemenner (1986).

Table 3.5 Differences between job shops and mass production/service

The third major lesson that can be learnt from comparative analysis is how different types of operation demand different approaches to their effective management. It is clear from Table 3.5 that job or service shops present a number of challenges:

- extending demand to avoid peaks and bottlenecks and promote off peaks

- maintaining quality across a diverse and customized range of offers

- controlling costs with limited economies of scale

- encouraging flexibility and involvement in employees.

In response to these challenges, the industry adopts a number of strategies for managing its inputs, processes and outputs. These include:

- off-peak promotions such as two-for-ones, happy hours, and so on

- empowerment of employees – retention through involvement and intrinsic job satisfaction

- quality assurance

- emphasis on customer retention.

Mass service or production on the other hand has a set of different concerns:

- trying to ensure high levels of demand at all times
- matching levels of demand to staffing levels
- maintaining consistency of the products and services offered to support brand image
- maintain staff commitment in a low-skill highly repetitive task with limited customer contact
- reliance on the equipment and technology that drives the operation
- maintaining customer interest in a heavily standardized offer.

They respond to these challenges with:

- quality control
- forecasting
- high marketing and advertising expenditure
- training of employees, incentives, career progression from within – retention through extrinsic satisfaction.

Conclusions

One of the issues that can be identified from this comparative analysis is how change is acting on the industry. For example, is each of the different types growing at the same rate, or are some types expanding and others declining? Jones (1988) identified three key trends in hospitality operation design: production lining, decoupling and customer participation.

Production-lining refers to the concept of breaking down production activities into simple tasks so that they may be organized on a production-line basis, just as Henry Ford production-lined the motor manufacturing process in the 1920s. It has long been argued (Levitt, 1972) that services in general are moving towards more industrialized processes. Indeed, this has actually been termed the McDonaldization of society (Ritzer, 1993).

Decoupling refers to the idea of separating, both in place and time, back-of-house from front-of-house activity. Often the rationale for doing so is that one or the other (usually back-of-house) can be production-lined. For instance, a number of health authorities in the UK have created one large central production kitchen for a number of hospitals and introduced cook-chill, so that the kitchen may produce 5000 to 6000 meals for transportation the following day to five or more different hospitals.

Customer participation is otherwise known as self-service. Many hospitality operations now enable their customers to do things for themselves that were previously done for them. It is possible to check into a hotel by using a swipe card system, select salad items from a self-help salad bar and check out of a hotel using the in-room television set.

The introduction of these ideas into the industry has not only led to firms moving *towards* the diagonal, but also *along* it, away from high variety/low volume in the direction of lower variety and higher volumes. For instance, à la carte restaurants and full-service hotels have been around since the 1880s, whereas Kemmons Wilson only conceived the mid-service hotel, which he called Holiday Inn, in 1952. Fast food only really began when Ray Kroc took over the McDonald's chain when it had 200 outlets in 1961. Cook-chill and sous-vide are even more recent innovations.

As markets mature, there is also evidence of a fourth trend – the development of so-called micro units. These are food service outlets of a very small size aimed at serving often limited and/or captive markets. They include outlets in petrol filling stations, cinemas, sports stadia, the workplace, and so on. Their growth derives from the fact that more traditional sites are now unavailable and demands for eating out continues to grow, especially in the UK.

These trends reflect what has happened in many other industries. The final question is the extent to which the hospitality industry will follow other industries towards the notion of mass customization. In this context both high volume and variety are accommodated, using a range of different approaches to achieve this technically difficult task. This remains the biggest challenge for hospitality operators. How to serve large numbers of customers with high-quality food of their choice, at a low price, and at sufficient speed.

Summary

1 There are three basic ways in which the hospitality industry may be classified – economic, market and systems.

2 The accommodation sector has been classified as a core system to which other subsystems may be attached (Jones, 1996).

3 The food service sector has been classified into ten distinct systems (Jones, 1996).

4 Accommodation provision is largely a CPO, while food service includes some MPOs.

5 When classified in the context of manufacturing and service as a whole, two main distinct types of operation emerge – the job shop and the mass production/service operation.

6 These two types of operation have quite distinct characteristics and set different challenges, to which management responds in quite distinct ways.

7 The overall trend has been for hospitality operations to seek a balance between volume and variety of output, and from job shop towards mass production/service.

Review questions

1 Brainstorm a list of hospitality operations to give as wide a coverage as possible. Think of all the situations in which food, drink and accommodation are provided for people outside their homes. Now classify all the operations using the SIC framework. Which operations were difficult to place? Which operations did you find it impossible to classify? What are the advantages and disadvantages of the SIC?

2 Identify two food service outlets in your local area, one being a typical job shop and the other a mass production/service operation. What evidence is there that they exhibit the characteristics identified in this chapter?

3 If hotels are primarily CPOs, what other types of service businesses could also be classified as CPOs, and why?

4 To what extent would you regard a takeaway-only fast food business to be the same as a supermarket?

5 What other market-based criteria could be used as a basis to classify and compare hospitality operations?

6 What particular problems do the hybrid operations shown in Table 3.4 give rise to for anyone wanting to compare them?

7 To what extent does the use of the systems approach mean that the normally problematic issue of culture can be ignored when comparing hospitality operations in different countries?

8 If mass customization can solve the variety–volume trade-off referred to in this chapter does this mean that the classifications shown in Figures 3.5 and 3.6 will become redundant?

9 If hotels, cruise ships and aircraft all provide forms of accommodation, food and drink for their customers are they all the same type of operation?

10 What implications for the CPO and MPO approach to classifying and comparing hospitality operations do you think the application of information technology will have in the future?

Bibliography

British Hospitality Association (BHA) (1999). *British Hospitality: Trends and Statistics 1999*. BHA.

Hayes, R. and Wheelwright, S. (1979). Linking manufacturing process and product life cycles. *Harvard Business Review*, **57** (1), 133–140.

Hospitality Training Foundation (HtF) (1999). *Key Facts and Figures*. HtF.

Huelin, A. and Jones, P. (1990). Thinking about catering systems. *International Journal of Operations and Production Management*, **10** (8), 42–52.

Jones, P. (1988). The impact of trends in service operations on food service delivery systems. *International Journal of Operations and Production Management*, **8** (7), 23–30.

Jones, P. (1993). A taxonomy of foodservice operations. 2nd CHME Research Conference, Manchester.

Jones, P. (1996). *Introduction to Hospitality Operations*. Cassell.

Jones, P. and Lockwood, A. (1999). *Hospitality Operating Systems*. Distance Learning Unit, University of Surrey.

Jones, P. and Peppiatt, E. (1999). Managing perceptions of waiting times in service queues. *International Journal of Service Industry Management*, **7** (5), 47–61.

Levitt, T. (1972). Production line approach to service. *Harvard Business Review*, **50** (5), 20–31.

Office for National Statistics (1999). http://www.ons.gov.uk/data/cu/intro.htm

Ritzer, G. (1993). *The McDonaldization of Society*. Pine Forge.

Sasser, W. E., Olsen, M. and Wyckoff, D. D. (1978). *The Management of Service Operations*. Allyn and Bacon.

Schemenner, R. W. (1986). How can service businesses survive and prosper. *Sloan Management Review*, Spring, 21–32.

Silvestro, R., Fitzgerald, L., Johnston, R. and Voss, C. (1992). Towards a classification of service processes. *International Journal of Service Industry Management*, **3** (3), 62–75.

Further reading

Medlik, R. and Ingram, H. (2000). *The Business of Hotels*. Butterworth-Heinemann.

Lane, H. E. and Dupré, D. (1997). *Hospitality World: An Introduction*. Van Nostrand Reinhold.

CHAPTER ● ● ● ●

4

The physical environment

Hadyn Ingram and Josef Ransley

This chapter aims to explain the nature and importance of the physical environment in the UK hospitality industry. By the end of this chapter you should be able to:

1 Define the physical environment.

2 Appreciate the importance of the physical environment for hospitality operations.

3 Explain the generic process of developing properties.

4 Recognize the nature of physical environments in different contexts, especially internationally.

5 Discuss the likely effects of trends on the development of physical environments for hospitality operations.

Introduction

In these early years of a new millennium, service industries seem set to provide a future of industry expansion, excitement and advancement for the aspiring manager. Compared to the traditional manufacturing industries that are declining, service industries are expanding. In particular the UK, and indeed global, hospitality industry is growing in size and becoming a more professional but complex activity that demands a greater level of managerial competence. The unit hospitality manager of the future will need to be competent in both operations and strategy because, while operations can affect short-term performance, it is strategy that shapes the future of the unit. Unit managers have overall responsibility for making sure that customers are satisfied with the physical environment of the property so that they will enjoy their visit and return. Properties need to be maintained, developed and improved if they are to contribute towards making the unit a good place to work and visit. This chapter considers the nature, importance and development of the physical environment in three sections. The first establishes the nature of the physical environment and considers a model of property development. The second uses the five components of the model as comparative bases for the physical environment:

- concept

- planning

- building

- operations

- maintenance.

The final section suggests how current trends might affect hospitality properties in the future.

The nature of the physical environment

Although many practitioners and academics in a range of applied business disciplines might agree that the physical environment is important to their particular activity of interest, there has been little research on its nature, particularly in the hospitality industry. Paradoxically, it is often property maintenance and development issues that can take the time of a busy unit manager and cause the greatest frustration, yet have the greatest effect on the business. In this section of the chapter the physical environment is defined and its importance explained, particularly in relation to the hospitality industry.

Definitions

The environment is defined as 'physical surroundings, circumstances etc.' in which people live and work (Oxford University

Press, 1996). In a commercial environment this means the surroundings, property, plant, machinery, offices, and so on, where work is done. For the purposes of this chapter, we define the physical environment as, the physical property that forms the locus (place) where business for profit is conducted and where manufacturing and/or service processes take place.

Such activities can take place in a range of different commercial contexts: factories, retail parks, farms, banks, shops, consultancies, hospitals, breweries, accounting practices, pubs, solicitors offices or hotels.

Importance of the physical environment

Most commercial activities need physical premises where those operating the business can work together to produce goods and services for sale to customers. In some types of business, notably manufacturing industries, the premises are important in that they enable goods to be produced with the assistance of plant and machinery. Here, the physical environment serves the functional purpose of manufacturing goods that are distributed, perhaps through a wholesaler, to a retail outlet where they are sold to the consumer. In service industries, the physical environment forms part of the product/service because the consumer usually visits the premises to consume that product/service. Physical premises in service industries, therefore, serve not only a functional purpose, but also a cosmetic one because the consumer will judge the quality of the product/service partly on the characteristics of the physical environment. Many of us might think of examples where we have not enjoyed a hotel, restaurant or pub because it was uncomfortable, dirty or unpleasant.

In the hospitality industry, the physical environment is important for a number of reasons as it:

- is a locus or place for the delivery of the product/service
- forms an integral part of the product or experience
- defines the form, scale and nature of the property, which also influences the character, and nature of its locality
- provides a visual image that defines identity or 'look' of the premises and its facilities, increasingly as part of a brand identity
- constitutes a physical presence that can attract customers who might be passing or recognize a favoured brand identity
- influences consumer choice that is, at least partly, based on the 'look' of the premises and its facilities, which are often published and classified in guidebooks. The harmonized English Tourism Council guidelines for accommodation classification are an example of giving consumers a wider choice by describing facilities and services

- adds value, or otherwise, to the experience by enhancing atmosphere, ambience and enjoyment to, for example a visit to a restaurant or club

- enables the physical flows of people, systems and information to take place efficiently

- serves to protect those within the environment from safety, fire and security hazards

- can make profit possible for owners and provide a return on their investment.

Location

The decision to site a business at a particular location is an important one, which will affect its future competitiveness and success. In the past, the location of manufacturing premises was often determined by the location/availability of raw materials. For example, the carpet factory at Wilton (Wiltshire) was built close to the wool market and the River Nadder (for transport and for the manufacturing process), and several beer breweries at Burton close to supplies of suitable water on the River Trent. Today, such is the importance of site selection that a number of location theories have been spawned that can be reduced to an algorithm and evaluated using computer technology. Hekman (1982) suggests that the five most important locational factors are:

- local industrial climate

- labour productivity

- transport

- land availability and room for expansion

- cost of land and construction.

Other researchers point out factors such as the social and cultural environment (Hack, 1984), building and energy costs and population density (Schemenner, Huber and Cook 1987); and proximity to markets (Schemenner, 1982). Karakaya and Canel (1998) also argue that there are many variables other than cost, some of which are qualitative and intangible in nature, and that such variables are often industry-specific.

Location and the hospitality industry

In the hospitality industry, as in many others, site decisions are often made on the basis of availability rather than choice. When acquiring a hotel, for example, it can be easier to buy an existing hotel than to convert a large building or build from scratch. As businesses in the UK hospitality industry are predominantly owner operated, the desire of the owner to live in a particular area can be a key locational decision (Galbraith, 1985). Ghosh and Craig (1986) maintain that a good location strategy should give a firm a competitive advantage that is difficult to copy. As hospitality properties primarily aim to provide accommodation with or without ancillary services for those travelling away from home, the location is a key factor in consumer choice. Nevertheless, as Bull (1994) remarks, location is the only attribute of the hotel product that is fixed; service design and décor styles can be changed, but the geographical location cannot. Therefore, hospitality units should be located with a view to access (transport, road, rail, ports), convenient for the purpose of the visit (business, sightseeing, special events) and suitable for the target customer market (facilities, quality and price), all of which influence the nature of its physical environment.

Katsigris and Thomas (1999) pursue this issue of the importance of location further and suggest that business survival can depend upon prudent site selection criteria including:

- access by customers, parking and access to utilities (such as gas and main drainage)

- previous ownership

- traffic generators that bring people into the area, such as local attractions

- proximity to the workforce that is needed to run the business

- ownership: short leases, for example of five years or less prohibit hospitality businesses from realizing their full potential

- elevation affects gravity that, in turn affects water pressure and drainage efficiency

- local restrictions: e.g., on the sale of alcohol.

In the UK, for example, proposed sites for the construction of new Post House Hotels in the 1980s (now a Granada Plc Hotel brand) were required to meet the following locational criteria:

- major cities with a population in excess of 150 000 inhabitants

- airport locations that dealt with at least 4 million passengers per year

- major employers in the locality, not in traditional heavy industries but more in sectors that generated demand for hotel accommodation

- local attractions within a maximum of a 25-mile radius that could be promoted to attract weekend stays at the hotel
- other weekend demand generators such as universities or public schools were seen as a potential bonus, as were major sporting venues
- passing trade from the motorway/trunk road should be composed of a large proportion of distance traffic as opposed to local commuting traffic
- no other group hotel in the city, that might compete with the new development.

The continued success of these roadside motor hotels is, perhaps, a testament to the extent to which these locational considerations were specified in advance.

Developing the physical environment

We have suggested that it is important for hospitality properties to be continually improved and modernized, but how should this be done? Because property development can involve heavy capital investment and risk, care must be taken in planning to amend or extend existing premises/facilities, or perhaps to add new buildings. Whether existing or new, the diagram in Figure 4.1 shows the process that can be adopted in developing hospitality properties.

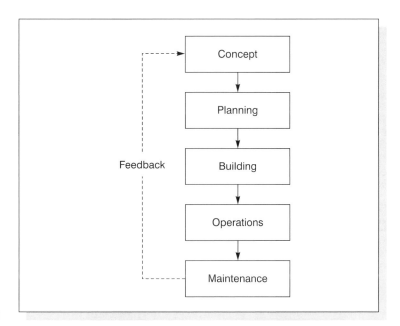

Figure 4.1
The hospitality properties development process
Source: Ransley and Ingram, 2000

Processes like these can be mapped so that those involved are clear about the order and sequence of plans. Figure 4.1 shows that the process of developing the physical environment can be divided into five stages:

1 *Concept*: the first task in the development process is to decide, in broad conceptual terms, how the finished product might look and what market it might serve. This usually entails communication between the developer and a designer to draw up plans and concept drawings. For larger organizations, this might be part of an overall strategy to develop brands or concepts, so that the firm's assets are maximized.

2 *Planning*: the concept or idea must be planned and costed so that it can be completed within a suitable budget and to an agreed standard. This usually includes a feasibility study that shows the possible costs and returns of the project.

3 *Building*: the building stage is when the property is actually constructed or adapted in a physical way. This process may involve the services of experts, such as architects, quantity surveyors and building contractors.

4 *Operations*: after construction has been carried out, the building must be commissioned and handed over to the operations team. The construction contractors need to complete on time and to a specified quality, while the operations team has to prepare itself for a new facility.

5 *Maintenance*: the final stage in the process is the ongoing maintenance and repairs that are necessary to comply with legal requirements and to keep the property in good working order. This function may be outsourced to specialist facilities management organizations.

This, however, is not the end of the process because every commercial property needs to be periodically reviewed to ensure that it meets the purpose for which it is intended. Factories need retooling, shops need refurbishment and hospitality properties need modernizing. So the property improvement cycle begins again.

Comparative bases

Having established the nature of the physical environment and introduced a model for property development, this second section uses the five components of the model as a comparative base to explore the UK hospitality industry, especially how it compares internationally:

- concept

- planning

- building

- operations

- maintenance.

Concepts

Since the early 1970s, there has been a move to market service industry offerings as brands or concepts. From the consumer's point of view this means that much is usually known about the nature of the concept or brand before it is consumed or provided. Many concepts have originated in the USA, and this is particularly true of hospitality and catering products. For example famous fast-food, motel, budget hotel and soft drinks brands have migrated from west to east. This does not necessarily mean that Americans are more skilled in the quality delivery of hospitality services, rather that they were more empowered to internationalize the industry at the time. At the same time, methods of financing and ownership in their different forms, such as franchising, management contracts, joint ventures and other variants related to investment requirements were evolved. These methods and standards have subsequently been adopted by other non-American based businesses in their international hospitality expansion strategies.

Some examples of these hotel products are original US brand names, like Ritz Carlton, Hyatt, Hilton, Sheraton, and Holiday Inn Inc. (now owned by Bass Hotels & Resorts). At that time, towards the end of the twentieth century, European companies such as the Ritz Group, Trust House Forte, Grand Metropolitan, Steigenburger and Wagon Lits were effectively still national, rather than international chains.

The 1980s saw the development of new hospitality concepts in the form of low-service hotels, for example, Holiday Inn Garden Court and HI Express. Other examples are Travelodge in the UK and the French ACCOR group's equivalent, Formula 2. These were closely followed by Apart hotels, Conference hotels, Town house and Club hotels, and a range of niche products such as the Paramount in New York, No. 1, The Aldwych, London and the Bleibtrau Hotel, Berlin. The latter examples are traditional full-service hotel products that have established a specific product image through interior design styling. Their contribution to the industry has been to demonstrate that style solutions (except the standard mid-Atlantic hybrid or classical reproductions) provide an alternative to market segmentation or price. The main attribute of such variants, importantly, is to remind the hotel industry that their product is in part, competing in the same marketplace as other consumable products. The industry must understand that the customer, in allocating disposable income, may be choosing between a new dress, golf club or night away from home. This imperative reinforces the importance of ensuring that the product appeals to the customer, to remind the industry of the diversity of its competition. If product appeal is relegated to secondary importance, and assumptions are made that customers are happy with the existing product, the result can be an out-of-date, new hotel, opening two years later!

In the case of restaurants, Katsigris and Thomas (1999) have suggested that concept development is essentially a process involving the identification, definition and collection of ideas that constitute what the guest will see as the restaurant's image. For Lundberg and Walker (1993) restaurant development begins with ideas about the concept, with a number of important considerations following on from this. These involve more specific questions about location, style and positioning of the restaurant. From a comparative perspective Lundberg and Walkers' model (see Figure 4.2) is useful as it identifies a number of criteria that could be used to compare different restaurant concepts and operations. Indeed, there is no obvious reason why a similar model could not be developed to compare different hotel or public house concepts. You may find this a useful approach if you want to compare these, or other, types of hospitality operation.

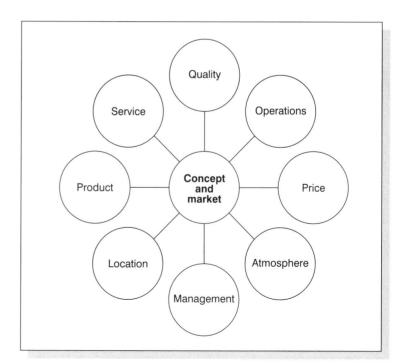

Figure 4.2
The restaurant development process
Source: Lundberg and Walker, 1993

Design

Design is both functional and sensory. It has visual appeal and emotion through, for example, lighting, richness of colour, texture of furnishings. Mirrors, lighting and sound can transmit excitement and atmosphere in hospitality properties. It is necessary to design a room size and its proportion in relation to the purpose and the number of people who may use it. Public areas, for example, should give sensory clues as to the quality and prices of the services on offer and present a warm and inviting ambience. Warmth or coolness can be created using materials, textures and colours, and variations of light and shade can give the illusion of space and form. The extent and importance of these as design features will depend upon the market that is being targeted. Customers in the luxury market will expect greater aesthetics, and may be more appreciative (and perhaps critical) of items such as antiques and paintings placed to create an atmosphere of sophisticated elegance.

The atmosphere that can be created by design, including feelings such as calmness, sociability and intimacy augments customers' satisfaction with hospitality products and services. Mood can affect the way that an individual responds to an experience and mood can be affected by social and environmental conditions. Hospitality products are often consumed in social conditions, so that an individual might be more aware of others in a half-empty restaurant or bar, than in one which is crowded with people. Paradoxically, some hospitality units are all the more desirable for being crowded, and it is the job of the designer to help to create a balance between size and atmosphere. It is often style that distinguishes a property from those of competitors by branding or product differentiation. In design, there is a trend towards cleaner, simpler, less fussy lines, which reflect the contemporary lifestyle and are easier to maintain.

Planning

There are many factors that influence the planning and design of hospitality properties. Internationally, these include:

- local regulations on fire, safety, building standards, health and safety and hygiene
- location, development and infrastructure
- staff costs and operational methods
- climate and environment
- building techniques, methods, costs and resources
- accessibility and lifestyle
- type of facility.

The most important factor, however, is communication. The most common communication errors are based in the tacit assumptions made between the internal and external members of the development team. It is all too often assumed, when dealing with another nationality, that usage of a common language automatically guarantees understanding. This situation is normally compounded by a natural desire to avoid embarrassment or cause offence, either by appearing to be patronizing or misinformed. The golden rule should therefore always be to ask the same questions or describe a requirement in a number of different ways. It is far better (and usually less expensive) to be considered slow-witted but to achieve the objective.

The basic principles of construction are universal and transitional, and it is in the detail that the variance is meaningful. For example, if a local engineer in a developing country were to be asked if the electrical supply is reliable, he is most likely to answer in the affirmative. There is no point in feeling aggrieved to discover that the electrical supply fails once a week, after all, locally this may mean a good standard of reliability. Local standards, therefore, may be regarded as satisfactory within the local context but at the same time unacceptable to international operators.

This analogy will generally also apply to local regulations for fire safety, building standards, health and hygiene, and other regulatory requirements. For international hospitality groups, this is of particular importance, as the international customer will expect to enjoy the same level of safety precautions in the hotel irrespective of the country it is located in. Consumer protection law in some Western countries is such that, when booked before departure, the customer is legally entitled to such expectations. Therefore, the sensible international operators will define their own minimum requirements and ensure that these are implemented, even if they are of a higher standard than local requirements.

Equally, space standards will vary subject to location. The most common factors that impact on space standards are:

1 *Financial*: cost of land or construction.

2 *Storage*: are deliveries made daily, weekly or even monthly?

3 *Site constraints*: high or low rise, singular or multiple accommodation blocks.

4 *Climate*: including internal and external circulation, leisure facilities, balconies, water storage, capacity.

5 *Culture and lifestyle*: such as dining contexts (al fresco), personal hygiene and consumer preferences.

The effect of these factors will vary according to location. For example, land availability in Hong Kong is not compatible with the Midwest of the USA. The availability and storage requirements for food and beverage provisions in Banjul, Gambia, are very different to Paris. Similarly, there would be no reason to provide an in-house laundry in Frankfurt or consider external corridors and courtyards in Helsinki, which, like restaurants and bars, are a standard option in St Lucia. Many Japanese visitors will shower before soaking in a full bathtub, while no one in Nairobi would sleep without a mosquito net. These examples illustrate the need to review local conditions prior to formalizing the briefing requirements and planning of an international hotel. In developing countries, where staff costs are low and it is politically desirable for the international hospitality company to create jobs, high-tech equipment to reduce staffing levels may not be as necessary or as economic as it would be in a developed country.

These, as well as other factors need to be considered at the early stages of planning and design for an international project. Irrespective of how fixed corporate standards may be; they will require adjustment to suit local conditions.

Building

Building the property requires skill, materials and personnel, all of which can vary according to the project and country. Undoubtedly, common sense in considering the use of historical building methods (whether for construction or services) will gain prominence, or at least, influence new technology. As Case 4.1 illustrates, utilizing the latest green technology that works with systems such as air displacement and other methods can help to solve problems that the application of 'imported' solutions may help to create in the first place.

Case 4.1

Electricity in Zanzibar

Zanzibar Town gets frequent cuts in the electrical supply. To overcome this, most of the hotels have generators, but some of the small ones don't, which means no lights or fans. If the lights go out, kerosene lamps may be provided but it's best to have a torch or candles handy just in case. When the fans stop working there's not much you can do, and inside rooms can get unbearable, during Zanzibar's hot season. Bear this in mind when choosing a place to stay. Hotels that have been built recently rely on a constant electrical supply to work the fans or air conditioning. Older hotels have been built to withstand the hot weather using designs that date from before the invention of electricity. If you can't find a genuine old hotel, look for one built in traditional style – with large windows, thick walls, high ceilings, courtyards, wide verandas and even a double roof, not just a pseudo-oriental façade. If all the new hotels were built using genuine traditional designs, fans and air conditioning would be unnecessary, Zanzibar would not need to burn so much imported oil, and tourists would be more comfortable during the power cuts.

Source: Else, 1998.

Equally important in the method of local construction is the availability of utilities and materials as well as their maintenance. Hotels located in humid areas, especially with low season occupancy, do not lend themselves to the use of wool carpeting which tends to rot in such conditions. Similarly, Cuba for instance, is severely restricted in what it can import, so it is not unusual to find electrical wiring with more different colour coding than a painters palette, which is somewhat disconcerting when trying to differentiate live from neutral electrical terminals!

Operations

Operating hotels internationally is not only different than operating nationally, but it can also be demanding for senior and local management. The one area that both levels of management might see as very different is that international operations are more time-consuming, predominantly in staff and employment issues. This can mean more time is devoted to managing the operation and less time is available to develop the business both locally and strategically.

Table 4.1 shows comparisons between employee statistics in hotels in London and Hong Kong. Interestingly, in 1992 (at the time the survey was compiled), staff costs for a 4-star hotel in London were double (HB) and treble (LB) those of Hong Kong. At the same time the Hong Kong hotels employed 59 per cent (HB) and 86 per cent (LB) more staff. However, the overall earnings per employee in London compared to Hong Kong was not very different, as shown in Table 4.2. These figures show that, while the financial efficiency of using more staff in Hong Kong

	London		Hong Kong	
Employees per available room:	*HB	LB	*HB	LB
5-star hotel	1.36	1.22	1.43	1.27
4-star hotel	0.83	0.70	1.32	1.31
Sales per employee/US $:				
5-star hotel	88 058	91 551	51 505	46 155
4-star hotel	90 713	92 712	45 985	47 024
Costs per employee/US $:				
5-star hotel	29 059	27 477	16 612	12 253
4-star hotel	26 241	30 097	13 894	11 981

Notes: *HB means high profile corporate branded hotel (international); LB means lower profile hotel operator (national).
Source: Howarth Consulting, 1993.

Table 4.1 Comparative employee statistics in hotels in London and Hong Kong (employee statistics)

4-star hotel	*HB	LB
London	28.90	33.22
Hong Kong	30.21	25.44
Variance	+1.31	−7.78

Note: *HB means high profile corporate branded hotel (international); LB means lower profile hotel operator (national).
Source: Howarth Consulting, 1993.

Table 4.2
Costs per employee in hotels in London and Hong Kong (percentage cost per employee to sales per employee)

compared to London was not very different, the management time required to manage nearly double the number of staff in a (LB) Hong Kong hotel must be much greater.

While social costs in other European Union (EU) countries are generally higher, labour in these countries is more unionized and personal taxation higher. This can result in higher-paid but less flexible staff. This can affect management's ability to maximize efficiency in an environment of complex employment legislation and union dominance. Conversely, in the economically emerging countries, management time may not be as demanding in terms of legislation or dealing with unions. However, in these countries, the effort and time expended on training and politics is normally much greater.

Other aspects that are different operationally include:

- minimal availability of support services

- high rates of inflation requiring regular salary reviews

- two-tier room rate structures – government-fixed local rates and floating international rates

- isolation from head office – little support for local sales and marketing

- difference in investment criteria – conflict between prestige and rates of return

- international brand loyalty – high with international travellers, but national customers loyal to their own national brands

- language skills

- distance learning and training

- work permit problems for skilled expatriate management staff.

In developing countries, local management often find that in addition to the above, the hotel's status usually means it is the epicentre of society in the community. The hotel general manager's role is a much higher social profile, with frequent exposure to national politicians. This means the time and attention paid to national politics is much greater and, in some cases, it is an everyday task. This can be even more demanding as it is quite normal in these countries for politicians and/or governments to be part owners in the hotel property.

Certainly, in such locations forward planning is essential, and hotel mangers have to become familiar with importing supplies and goods direct. They have to be able to deal with import duties, letters of credit etc., as it can take up to three or four months to deal with large currency transfers. At the same time, regular business with airlines and tour operators, for instance, tends to be negotiated locally, as are the conditions of contract. All these factors, including working in a different culture where living standards are much lower than the operational environment, place a high demand on managerial time. Obviously, the upside for managerial staff locally, usually is the weather, status and lifestyle when the time is available to enjoy it. For senior management profitability and property value growth, especially, can be rewarding.

Maintenance

In most developed countries, the issue of maintenance is similar to the UK or the USA, however, generally utility costs will be higher and this certainly will be the case in such areas as the West Indies and Africa. Electricity costs in the Caribbean, where every room is air conditioned for instance, can be 15 per cent of total sales compared to 3–4 per cent in the UK. Most hotels will have their own water desalination plant and sewage treatment units. In some ways, therefore, the hotel or resort property functions are similar to those of a small town in the UK. The big difference, of course, being that in the UK and other developed countries there is easy access to skilled tradespeople and spares – replacing spares in underdeveloped countries means either directly importing them or, sometimes even worse, through local agents.

As in operations, it is imperative to plan well ahead and these issues ought to have been considered at the development stage when equipment and systems that rely on imports can be minimized. For example, the logistics of importing 200 air conditioning filters at the development stage, may not have been a complex issue. However, for maintenance purposes, one or twenty replacements, in practice, can take four months to obtain. Developers should consider the maintenance strategy at the outset, including stock levels and costs, as well as the storage and security of spares. Equally, tasks that may be simple for a trained engineer in the UK can be more complex in a country where such engineers are not available. Multiply this single element by the hundreds or thousands of components needed in a fully serviced hotel, with limited skilled staff available, and maintenance can take on a different perspective.

Equally, different climates and habitats provide some interesting maintenance and safety requirements. A common procedure in West Africa is to train security staff in the use of long poles to catch the occasional snake that may choose to sunbathe with guests by the poolside. Equally, the prevalence of Aids in many African countries casts the provision and maintenance of medical and first-aid services in a different light. Security and guest relation staff need to be sensitive to dealing with local cultural issues that can range from dealing with local population sensitivities to being photographed, to appeasing the local witch doctor. Similarly, hospitality staff in many Caribbean countries need overcoats to wear when using the freezer stores. On the other hand, in Sweden and Finland, keeping the service yard or access drive clear, requires overcoats to deal with a different climatic problem.

Examples of the differences abound, however, most can be addressed with a little common sense, at least for those who enjoy a different challenge. Nevertheless it is imperative that issues of health and safety, for guests and employees alike, together with regular and long-term maintenance issues are considered at the outset.

As the industry continues to grow globally, more people involved in the sector will inevitably work in foreign places. It can be expected that there will be an emerging need for those developing hospitality services to give more consideration to local people, culture and custom in the future. As the world continues to become a smaller place, the hospitality industry's economic future will depend on preserving these resources, while at the same time providing the customer with the opportunity to enjoy and take pleasure in cultural diversity.

Trends and developments

The hospitality industry has evolved slowly over the centuries, spurred by developments in transport technology, such as railways in the nineteenth century and motor cars in the twentieth century. For example, the availability of the motor vehicle for all has been the single most important factor in the emergence of motor hotels in the USA lodging industry. Similarly, the growth in air transport has driven the internationalization of the hotel and tourist industry in the latter part of the twentieth century.

New techniques of evaluating and managing assets developed in other industry sectors have been adopted by the hospitality industry. Airlines, for example, have led the way with technology to manage reservations and yield; and retailers have focused upon techniques to evaluate financial performance and space planning.

The structure of the hospitality industry has changed from ownership in wholly autonomous units to the emergence of powerful groups of operators that can derive competitive advantage using economies of scale, bulk purchasing and marketing muscle. Such groups are increasingly becoming service providers and management operators rather than property owners. Similarly senior management is reallocating many traditional responsibilities from operational managers to corporate managers as the focus continues to switch from the provision of hospitality per se to the generation of profits, the latter also being driven by greater institutional investment in the sector and the emergence of asset management and yield technology

Juxtaposed on this is the observation that branding has become the success story of the age. Multi-unit hotel, restaurant and pub companies invariably arrange their units into categories and aim them at specific market segments. Examples include limited service (HI Express, Travelodge, etc.) mid-service (Holiday Inn, Marriott, Forte, etc.) and premier service brands (Intercontinental, Ritz Carlton, etc.), that are being further augmented by living style products that focus on image rather than service levels (Malmaison, One Aldwych, etc.). Similarly, many properties deliver a specific product that is dependent upon their location, such as conference hotels at airport or motorway junctions, luxury hotels in capital cities, etc.

Social trends, such as the increase in consumerism, greater propensities to travel, higher levels of discretionary spending and greater consumer awareness have given rise to a more discerning customer. Similarly, levels of income and leisure time continue to rise in developed countries enhancing demand in both developed and emerging markets. These factors, as well as improved levels of education and communication, have influenced the nature of the service provider and customer alike. The customer has become more discerning and the service provider more sophisticated.

Greater professionalism and continued improvement in performance will be demanded of hospitality practitioners in the future, and the physical environment is often the starting point for this activity. Operations may well still be the central activity of hospitality managers, but product and service offerings will need to be adapted more frequently if units are to retain or improve market share. As information becomes more widely available, and technology breaks new boundaries there will be greater choice for all. Technology can help with planning the physical environment as well as in using better materials for the comfort of guests and enhanced operational efficiency.

Consolidation within the industry, with the resultant benefits for brand globalization and corporate profits, will continue to be driven by international groups and institutional investors.

Similarly, the growing confidence of the discerning customer will create more opportunities for the niche operator. This may well cause planning to become more centralized and building to become more modular. For example, budget hotel bathrooms can be prepared off site and plumbed into the bedroom.

An increasing customer focus on image and entertainment together with increased pressure on land use and value, may see further evolution in the form of the 'limited life cycle building product' as well as more 'multi-use hospitality and entertainment properties'. A 'limited life cycle building product' could be defined as a building designed to provide a single function, presented in a given form and style for a specified time period. For example, if a limited service hospitality unit is expected to have a product life of twenty-five years, is there any benefit in designing the building fabric and services to last more than thirty years? If not, can the building be realized for a lower capital cost, thereby enhancing profitability?

It could justifiably be argued that many buildings that are totally refurbished with increased building services such as air conditioning etc., would be cheaper to realize by demolishing the existing building fabric and developing a new unit. Even if this process meant a marginal increase in capital costs the efficiency gains in operation and reduced running and maintenance costs would offset the same. Equally, the ability to control the product image, content and style rather than adapt these to suit the existing building structure would be beneficial. While not advocating the demolition of buildings of historical merit, consideration of the value of a building in the context of site or land value and operational profitability rather than bricks and mortar is likely to influence future refurbishment or rebuilding.

Historically location and consequential trading has been the main driver in hospitality property values. Essentially one could argue the land area and its location has an inherent value, whereas the building, if we consider it a 'product', has a value relative to its financial performance only. For example, the Angel Inn in Guildford High Street, an old coaching inn refurbished on numerous occasions, was eventually sold as a low-performing hospitality asset. Converted to a mixed-use building, with a basement restaurant, ground floor retailing and two upper floors of exclusive accommodation, its financial performance for each product type (retail/catering/room letting) increased dramatically. The change in 'value' was occasioned by the social and environmental changes that transpired over a twenty- to thirty-year period in the town and its development. While one cannot easily predict the nature of any future change on this location, or any other, one can be confident change will be of similar import over the next fifteen to twenty years.

Conclusions

This chapter has considered the nature of the physical environment as the place in which goods are produced and services offered. The physical environment is important for any business, but for hospitality operations it is essential because customers must travel to consume their products/service. As a result, the location of a hospitality unit will have the greatest effect on its success or failure.

Another important success factor is the extent to which service firms develop their facilities to retain and attract customers. As hospitality outlets are so visible, they need to ensure that their facilities and services are in tune with the needs of customers and of competitors, and this requires careful forward planning. Figure 4.1 proposes a generic property development model in five stages, from planning to maintenance, recognizing that there is a feedback loop that recommences the process. Building new properties or refurbishing existing ones is always a multifaceted activity in any industry, but for hospitality companies it may be even more complex. There is greater complexity when the facility is to be refurbished and business must continue, with the need to separate noisy and dirty building work from people who are eating, drinking or sleeping.

We maintain that successful development is a team-based activity that should be controlled by the client, who should have a clear idea of the final outcome of the project. The key issues in successful hospitality developments are:

1 *Research*: it is important that developers have as clear an idea as possible of their market and its needs. Projects must create a product, building or refurbishment at an agreed cost that customers like, or risk failure.

2 *Awareness*: developers need to be aware of the planning process and its critical points. Similarly, there needs to be an awareness of the specialist advice that is necessary for the project and where to go to find it. There are so many specialists and consultants, both good and bad, that personal recommendation by industry peers and colleague often leads to successful working relationships. As with other professional services, cheap advice can be expensive in the long term.

3 *Planning*: major projects need to be carefully considered by owners and developers because, if they are unclear or have not thought through their strategy, the project is unlikely to meet their needs and provide the required financial returns.

4 *Communication:* the need to co-ordinate activities and to advise the necessary parties of the relevant information at the appropriate time and in the correct manner starting with a clear and concise project brief.

The overall conclusion to be drawn from this chapter is that hospitality products and services need to be regularly reviewed as an issue of quality management. As the physical environment is such an integral part of the hospitality experience, in the future it will become more important than ever to ensure that the interior and exterior of the property remains interesting to the customer, and operationally efficient.

Summary

1 The physical environment is a much underresearched area of the hospitality industry, but one that is a crucial and integral part of the hospitality product.

2 The location of hospitality premises can be absolutely vital for the success of the unit as this is the one aspect of the physical environment that cannot be changed.

3 Therefore, site selection is a very important aspect of the physical environment.

4 In seeking to compare the physical environment occupied by different hospitality operations the model outlined in this chapter provides a set of common criteria that can be used as a basis for making valid comparisons.

5 Local, contextual factors act to modify the application of these common criteria and must be taken into account when comparing such physical environments, especially when international comparisons are being made.

6 The increasing importance of branding in the hospitality industry has had a major impact on the design and life spans of its physical environments.

7 Technology and new business combinations are likely to have significant implications for the design and use of hospitality premises in the future, in particular mixed or multi-use sites are likely to create additional problems for making direct comparisons between very different physical environments.

Review questions

1 Compare the characteristics, importance and location of the physical environment for a five-star hotel, a garage and an insurance call centre.

2 Why is it necessary for properties to be periodically developed? What circumstances might cause this process to start or be delayed?

3 Outline some factors that affect the development and operation of properties internationally and suggest how current trends might affect these processes.

4 How might the design of the physical environment for a restaurant brand need to be modified in different countries?

5 Could this be done without losing the desired degree of consistency in the brand?

6 In seeking to compare hospitality properties, why might it be important to examine the both the context and the content of the physical environments?

7 Is the function, and therefore the design of the physical environment, the same for a hotel bar and for a public house?

8 What criteria could you use to group or categorize the different types of locations where hotels are found, and how might this help you to understand some of the similarities and differences in the physical environments displayed by these hotels?

9 What is the relationship between quality indicators, i.e. hotel star rating, Michelin restaurant stars and the design of hospitality environments?

10 All hospitality operations provide accommodation for their customers, not just bedroom accommodation, and food or drink. How does the purpose and the design of accommodation vary between different types of hospitality environment, and why?

Bibliography

Bull, A. O. (1994). Pricing a motel's location. *International Journal of Contemporary Hospitality Management*, **6** (6).

Else, D. (1998). *Guide to Zanzibar*. Bradt.

Galbraith, C. S. (1985). High technology location and development: the case of Orange County. *California Management Review*, Fall, 98–109.

Ghosh, A. and Craig, C. S. (1986). An approach to determining optimal locations for new services. *Journal of Marketing Research*, **23**, November, 354–62.

Hack, G. D. (1984). The plant location decision making process. *Industrial Development*, **153**, September–October, 31–33.

Hekman, J. S. (1982). Survey of location decisions in the south. *Economic Review*, June, 6–19.

Howath Consulting (1993). *The Case for Management Contracts*. Howarth Consulting.

Karakaya, F. and Canel, C. (1998). Underlying dimensions of business location decisions. *Industrial Management and Data Systems*, **98** (7), 321–329.

Katsigris, C. and Thomas, C. (1999). *Design and Equipment for Restaurants and Foodservice*. John Wiley.

Lundberg, D. E. and Walker, J. R. (1993). *The Restaurant from Concept to Operation*. 2nd edn., John Wiley.

Oxford University Press (1996). *Concise Oxford Dictionary*. D. Thompson, ed., 9th edn. BCA.

Ransley, J. and Ingram, H. (2000). *Developing Hospitality Properties and Facilities*. Butterworth-Heinemann.

Schemenner, R. W, Huber, J. and Cook, R. (1987). Geographic differences and the location of new manufacturing facilities. *Journal of Urban Economics*, **21**, January, 83–104.

Schemenner, R. W. (1982). *Making Business Location Decisions*. Prentice Hall. World Tourism Organization (1996). *Towards Environmentally Sustainable Development*. Agenda 21. UNCED WTO.

Further reading

Baud-Bovy, M. and Lawson, F. (1998). *Tourism and Recreation: Handbook of Planning and Design*. Butterworth-Heinemann.

Borsenik, F. D. and Stutts, A. T. (1992). *Management of Maintenance and Engineering Systems in the Hospitality Industry*. John Wiley.

Cecil, R. (1993). *Client's Guide to Building*. Legal Studies Publishing.

Construction Industry Research and Information Association (CIRIA) (1995). *CDM Regulations*. CIRIA Report R145.

Construction Industry Research and Information Association (CIRIA) (1995). *Planning to Build? A Practical Introduction to the Construction Process*. Special Publication 113. CIRIA.

Construction Industry Research and Information Association (CIRIA) (1996). *Value Management in Construction: A Client's Guide*. Special Publication 129. CIRIA.

Dyson, J. (1997). *Accounting for Non Accounting Students*. Pitman Publishing.

Institution of Civil Engineers, and the Faculty and Institute of Actuaries (1998). *RAMP: Risk Analysis and Management for Projects*. Thomas Telford.

Janssens, D. (1990). *Design and Build Explained*. Macmillan.

Jones, C. and Jowett, V. (1998). *Managing Facilities*. Butterworth-Heinemann.

Lawson, F. (1994). *Restaurants, Clubs and Bars: Planning, Design and Investment for Food Service*. Butterworth-Heinemann.

Lawson, F. (1995). *Hotels and Resorts: Planning, Design and Refurbishment*. Butterworth-Heinemann.

Lawson, F. (1999). *Conference, Convention and Exhibition Centres*. Butterworth-Heinemann.

Royal Institution of Chartered Surveyors (RICS) (1996). *The Procurement Guide*. RICS Business Services.

Rutes, W. and Penner, R. (1985). *Hotel Planning and Design*. Watson-Guptill.

The Building Round Table (1995) *Thinking of Building?* The Building Round Table Ltd.

CHAPTER 5

Work patterns and employment practices

Rosemary E. Lucas and
Roy C. Wood

Objectives

The overall objective of this chapter is to alert and sensitize you to the types of work patterns and employment practices that exist in the hospitality industry, and the influences which have created, and tend to maintain, these patterns and practices. More specifically, by the end of this chapter, you should be able to:

1 Explain the meaning of the terms 'work patterns' and 'employment practices' and apply them to the hospitality industry.

2 Explain the related concept of the labour market and its operation within the hospitality sector.

3 Identify the various sub-elements that constitute work patterns, employment practices and the labour market, and explain the interrelationships among these.

4 Identify the significance of key internal and external influences on work patterns and employment practices in different areas of the hospitality industry.

Introduction

In this short introduction we wish to spell out how we intend to interpret the comparative approach outlined in Chapter 1. We will also introduce and define the two terms that are at the heart of this chapter, namely 'work patterns' and 'employment practices'.

In terms of the comparative approach, for both work patterns and employment practices we will compare cross-sectoral and, briefly, selected cross-national data. By cross-sectoral we mean data relating to different sectors of the hospitality industry. Here, the focus of the examples employed will be the UK. By cross-national, we mean comparing certain aspects of the British sectoral data to similar information from other countries. In the case of the latter, we emphasize the selective nature of what appears in this chapter. For quantitative data (i.e. statistics) it is sometimes possible to compare certain trends across countries, even when these countries have different ways of collecting and presenting data. Sometimes there are data from supernational organizations relating to many countries (for example, as is the case with the International Labour Organization, ILO).

For qualitative data, the source of cross-national information is likely to be individual studies undertaken by academic researchers and published in books or academic journals. Taken together, these studies do not represent a comprehensive or systematic body of work, because the research has been undertaken in different countries, different sectors of the hospitality industry and at different times. It is our job to make sense of this disparate data and here we do so in a somewhat sketchy and abbreviated form. To see how the task has been achieved on a larger scale you may wish to follow up certain issues raised in this chapter by reading our books (Lucas, 1995; Wood, 1997).

We now turn to the terms that define the content of this chapter. By 'work patterns' we mean the group of factors that define *how* people work in the hospitality industry. This embraces the composition of the workforce according to basic, largely unchangeable factors rooted in our biology, for example, gender (male/female), ethnicity and race, and age. However, the term 'work patterns' also relates to ways in which the workforce is structured as a result of some human choice or choices. This means we can include modes or methods of working (e.g. whether full- or part-time, seasonal or casual) and the various subsets of these (for example, zero hours contracts) as well as patterns of reward. Also included is the location of work or, put another way, the distribution of employment (i.e. who works in what sector of the hospitality industry, e.g. in hotels, restaurants, pubs). Work patterns are influenced by human choices but these choices are not necessarily in any sense natural or democratic (indeed, they rarely are). Employers determine most employment practices and hence work patterns, but they in turn are influenced by the legal constraints placed upon them by governments as well as constraints that arise in their own organizations.

Turning now to employment practices we wish to emphasize that while these to a degree arise from the work patterns that prevail in a given organization, sector or industry, these practices often 'feed back' to qualify and change such patterns. Employment practices are defined as methods of people management most commonly found in organizations in a sector or industry. These practices may be formal (e.g., arising from employers' or managers' legal *obligations* or organizational *policy*) or informal (e.g., arising from managerial or employee *behaviour*).

Work patterns

Because organizations do not function in isolation from their external environments, a complex mix of external factors influences work patterns. While these influences shape the context within which organizations function, they do not necessarily determine organizational choice. Thus, within the organization there are also internal influences affecting work patterns. For example, while the legally enforceable UK National Minimum Wage (NMW) is set (in 1999) at £3.60 an hour for workers aged twenty-two and above, organizations may choose to pay a higher minimum rate of pay. We now explore some of the main external and internal influences affecting work patterns.

External influences

External influences on work patterns in hospitality organizations operate on different levels and may be international, transnational, national, regional or local. There are numerous external influences, including cultural differences and the political climate that are, in total, too numerous to be considered in this chapter. The specific influences considered here are:

- measures that have legal authority;

- collective agreements and social partnership;

- demographic, social and economic factors;

- the way in which labour markets function; and

- particular labour market policy initiatives.

Each of these will now be considered separately, although it is important to bear in mind that they are not discrete but are interrelated influences and that various combinations can have many different effects across a diverse range of contexts.

Measures that have legal authority are designed to ensure that minimum standards are enforceable at law. At an international level, the ILO aims to promote social justice throughout the world by establishing humane conditions of labour. This aim is pursued by the adoption of international standards in the form of Conventions and Recommendations. Transnationally, the European Union, through a wide-ranging programme of Social Directives and other measures, has been a major influence on member states' work practices since the 1970s. Directives have required the UK to introduce national employment protection legislation and regulations covering areas such as sex discrimination, equal pay, maternity and parental leave, working time and giving part-time workers equal treatment with full-time workers by entitlement to *pro rata* pay and conditions. As you will see, these aspects of legal regulation have particular relevance to hospitality organizations because of the high proportion of female, ethnic minority, and part-time labour employed in such organizations (Lucas, 1995).

Collective agreements made between representative groups of employers' and workers' representatives, usually trade unions, are often a preferred method of setting pay and conditions. They have had very little effect in the UK hospitality industry where trade union membership is marginal (consistently below 5 per cent during the present decade – see Cully et al., 1999; Lucas, 1995) as employers prefer to adopt a non-interventionist stance at industry level. However, these arrangements are much more influential in Europe, where national practice is to reach an agreement rather than pass legislation to implement Directives on matters such as working time and part-time workers. Also, a new form of collective agreement known as social partnership is emerging, often involving non-trade union representation, and this is likely to become more influential in the UK.

A combination of demography (size, structure and distribution of the population), social trends and norms (increased participation in paid employment by females) and economic conditions (recession or buoyancy) influence work patterns. While the UK population is relatively constant, there has been a trend to a greater concentration of the population in the south of England, where a large part of the hospitality industry is also geographically concentrated. There have been some significant shifts in the age structure and ethnic mix of the UK's labour force. The average age of the labour force has been increasing, while among the reduced proportion of young people in the labour force there is a proportionately higher concentration of young people from ethnic minority groups. Such groups tend to be geographically concentrated in particular regions, cities and towns.

Social attitudes to women taking paid employment have altered. Around half the working population is female, many of whom work on a part-time basis, often to undertake jobs for which there is no full-time requirement, although part-time working may suit some women's needs as well. When the economy is doing well, labour demand rises, but skill shortages may occur where there are insufficient workers to fill specific vacancies. When the economy is doing badly, unemployment rises as organizations make adjustments to their work patterns by downsizing their workforce. Less drastic measures might include a reduction in the hours of existing employees, or a switch to the employment of a more part-time or casual workforce.

Although globalization has increased the importance of international labour markets, it is at regional and local levels in particular where the labour market exerts most influence on hospitality organizations' work patterns (Riley, 1996). The labour market is where employers seek new employees (labour demand) and people seek employment or try to change jobs (labour supply). At a local level, the state of the labour market is influenced both by demand and the type of organizations (e.g. large and small firms) that are located there and the nature of the labour supply (including gender, ethnicity, race and age). It is now increasingly recognized that labour markets operate in imperfect conditions, because not all participants have access to relevant information that would enable a fair wage bargain to be struck. The presence of a few large firms and a plentiful supply of labour that is desperate to work gives these firms the upper hand in dictating terms and keeping pay and conditions to the bare minimum. This can be exploitative, as would be the use of underage labour or paying workers below the NMW.

By way of contrast, where there are too many firms seeking staff with a scarce skill (e.g. chefs), such workers are in a strong position to demand exceptionally good working terms and conditions. At a more practical level an imbalance between labour demand and supply can often be corrected by the introduction of new working patterns which are not necessarily exploitative. Thus an organization may find that the only way to fill a full-time vacancy is to recruit part-time labour instead – females or young students who do not wish, or are unable, to work on a full-time basis (Lucas, 1995).

As part of economic management, governments make policy initiatives affecting the labour market. These in turn influence work patterns. The government sets a threshold below which National Insurance Contributions (NICs) and income tax do not have to be paid. This means that workers take home more pay and employers' wage costs are less, generally where weekly hours are twenty or fewer. While this may encourage part-time working, the downside for employees is that they may not be able to claim any entitlements that are based on NICs, such as statutory sick pay. Measures to increase participation in education of young people have reduced the supply of young workers able to work on a full-time basis. Changes to retirement age and pensions have affected the supply of older workers in the labour market. Thus many people in these age groups work part-time.

Measures designed to 'upskill' the labour force include National Traineeships and Modern Apprenticeships while the 'New Deal', aimed at the unemployed, also extends to older unemployed people. Employers are paid a subsidy by way of an incentive to engage workers under these schemes, so they do not need be paid normal wages like employees. The opportunities to use these alternative labour sources may be relatively limited, particularly in small hospitality firms.

Internal influences

Organizations are able to exercise choice over their work patterns. These we call internal influences because they arise, for the most part, from decisions made by people working within organizations, although, of course, the decisions reached are not immune from the external influences identified above. The extent to which different organizations' choices are affected by the external environment will vary, depending on the level at which they operate. Thus a large international organization's choices are conditioned at a variety of levels by international, national and local influences, whereas the overriding influence on the choices made by the proprietor of a small firm operating in rural Wales is most likely to be the local labour market.

There are many formal and informal internal influences affecting organizations' work patterns. While we focus on the formal in this part of the chapter, later we also show how employment practices are very much a function of informal influences. The specific influences considered here in relation to hospitality organizations are:

- company operating standards;

- organization size and management style; and

- skill requirements and the application of technology.

Organizations can choose their opening hours, and what products and services are available at particular times of the day, week, month or year. Pubs can choose to open all day or stick to conventional lunchtime and evening opening hours. They may serve food only at lunchtime, or in the evening as well, offering different menus at particular times of the day. They may not serve any food at all. All these choices affect their work patterns.

Organizations also choose to operate to a particular standard within their given market. Here the nature of the product market is important because it determines whether the business operates at the quality or budget end of the market, although many businesses fall somewhere between. Hotels with a five-star rating operate high standards of personal service and are people intensive. They may operate stable full-time work patterns for most jobs, with the exception of banqueting functions, where casual staff are engaged as required. Hotels in the budget sector will operate on lower guest:staff ratios, because they are offering a more basic standard of service, and may use higher levels of part-time employment.

The level of demand for products and services also affects the number and type of staff employed, methods of working (full-time, part-time) and patterns of reward. Similarly, operating standards and worker availability will also affect these work patterns. The need for workers to be reliable, in the sense that they actually turn up for work, may lead a hotel to target older part-time female labour for early morning hours on the breakfast shift. Why? Simply as they happen to be available at this time whereas students would be otherwise occupied at school or college. Yet the same hotel might prefer students for food and beverage service in the evenings and at weekends, partly because of their availability and, perhaps, owing to a perception that they can be used more cheaply and flexibly.

The issue of image is also important because theme restaurants and pubs might wish to project their brand through the type of staff they employ. Thus a trendy, fast-moving and colourful image might be achieved by employing young workers, while an ethnic restaurant might prefer to employ staff of requisite ethnicity to convey authenticity. This may be problematic, demonstrated by the fact that many organizations continue to report skill shortages. This suggests they may be ruling out potentially suitable recruits from others parts of the labour force, particularly older workers (Hospitality Training Foundation, 1999) and could even be engaging in unlawful discrimination.

Although many hospitality organizations are large, employing thousands of workers, and are managed by professionally qualified managers and functional specialists (including human resource, marketing and finance managers), most are small owner-managed outlets employing fewer than ten staff. Labour costs are an important consideration to all organizations, but the sheer size of the wage bill in large organizations may lead managers to make a conscious decision to change work patterns in order to reduce and control labour costs. One choice might be to pursue more flexible labour policies, including the employment of cheaper young labour. The use of zero hours contracts enables the employer to call on the worker as required but only to pay them for hours worked, provided this complies with the working time and minimum wage regulations.

In small firms, managerial choice may be constrained by different organizational circumstances (we shall learn more about management style later). Thus in a very small hotel with a restaurant open only in the evening, the manager and partner might be the only full-time workers. While one may be a qualified chef, neither may have any management qualifications, yet they would be acting as overall managers, chef, front of house and restaurant managers. Their only staff could be three part-timers – a room assistant/cleaner during the day, and a restaurant assistant and a kitchen assistant in the evening. The business could not operate without them, although some minor variations to their working hours might be possible. Thus work patterns in small firms like this are less open to managerial manipulation.

Work patterns are also a function of the organization's skill requirements. Although the industry is regarded as being low skilled, skills can be a subjective concept. It is still clearly the case, even though misplaced and discriminatory, that women are perceived as being most suitable for hospitality work such as making beds and cleaning because these are unskilled 'women's tasks' and so they do not need training. Similarly, the perception that hospitality work is physically demanding might lead an employer to prefer a younger worker to an older worker, as in fast food. But technology also plays a part. Food production and service in fast-food establishments are based on high-tech systems necessitating only unskilled labour, a requirement that young workers also fulfil. Changes in the skills base of organizations may coincide with the adoption of new work patterns. Here the deskilling of work enables work patterns to be based on the use of more part-time labour, typically older women and young students, rather than on the more traditional full-time job model (Lucas, 1995).

What do contemporary hospitality work patterns look like?

Having identified some specific external and internal influences, let us now examine the reality of work patterns in the hospitality industry. As we have more data about the UK, we can explore work patterns in the industry's constituent sectors – hotels, restaurants, pubs, clubs, bars and contract catering in the context of the UK as a whole. A more detailed analysis from 1993 statistics and earlier can be found in Lucas (1995: 49–79). The figures used here are based on more recent labour market data, mainly from 1996 and 1998 (Hospitality Training Foundation, 1999; Office for National Statistics, 1998a; 1998b), and can be used to update this earlier analysis. Examples of non-UK data are taken from international statistical sources and other reports. These data are useful indicators of cross-sectoral and cross-national similarities and differences, but as the sources of information are not identical, making comparisons is not easy and extreme care needs to be taken in such a venture!

Table 5.1 shows that the hospitality industry has a total labour force of 1.263 million, including the self-employed who are typically owners-managers. This figure rises to 1.88 million (8 per cent of the workforce in Great Britain) if hospitality services (including the medical and educational sectors) are counted. The two biggest sectors – pubs, clubs and bars, and restaurants, together employ 64 per cent of the total labour force, while hotels employ 23 per cent. The largest occupational groups (200 000 or more) are cleaners and domestics, chefs/cooks, catering assistants, and waiting staff. The smallest occupational groups are housekeepers (21 300) and hotel porters (11 200).

Table 5.1
Number of employees by sector

Hospitality businesses	Number
Hotels	259 000
Restaurants	332 000
Pubs, clubs and bars	399 000
Contract catering	150 000
Self-employed	123 000
Sub-total	1 263 000
Hospitality services	617 000
Total	1 880 000

Source: Annual Employment Survey, 1996, and Labour Force Survey 1998, adapted from Hospitality Training Foundation, 1999: 15, table 2.1.

The industry continues to be dominated by small establishments (85 per cent employ between one and ten employees). The hotel sector has the highest proportion of large establishments (10 per cent with over twenty-five employees) while the restaurant sector has most very small establishments (nearly 90 per cent with one to ten employees). Between 1991 and 1998 the percentage of businesses with over twenty-five employees increased from 3 per cent to 4 per cent of all establishments. There is now more employment in larger workplaces with 41 per cent of employment in establishments employing twenty-five or more employees (from 36 per cent in 1991), while 59 per cent of employment is in establishments with fewer than twenty-five employees (from 64 per cent in 1991). Over the decade all sectors in the hospitality industry continued to grow, with the exception of hotels.

Six out of ten employees work part-time, which is markedly different from the patterns of part-time working in the UK as a whole (Table 5.2). Within hospitality, the patterns of part-time working vary by sector, with pubs, clubs and bars having the highest proportion of part-time workers. Considerably more females work part-time than do males. The occupational groups with the highest proportion of part-time workers are cleaners and domestics (78 per cent), waiting staff (77 per cent), bar staff (73 per cent) and kitchen porters (68 per cent). Only 5 per cent of hotel and accommodation managers and 10 per cent of restaurant managers work part-time. Although these figures do not detail seasonal, temporary and casual working, these are significant minority practices. When these are added to part-time employment, this feature of 'atypical' employment constitutes a core not peripheral component of the hospitality workforce.

Sector	Full time	Part time
Hotels	53	47
Restaurants	40	60
Pubs, clubs and bars	29	71
Contract catering	54	46
All hospitality	41	59
All industries and services	75	25

Notes: Part-time is defined as weekly hours of thirty or less in the Annual Employment Survey, while the Labour Force Survey allows respondents to classify themselves.

Sources: Annual Employment Survey, 1996, and Labour Force Survey, 1998, adapted from Hospitality Training Foundation, 1999: 19, Table 2.4; Office for National Statistics, 1998b: 18, Table 8.

Table 5.2
Distribution of employment by sector (percentage)

When we look more closely at actual working hours, average male and female full-time and part-time hours in the hospitality industry are lower than average working hours in the UK as a whole (Table 5.3). However, although average figures give a useful overall indication of differences a more reliable measure is often to be found in the distribution of hours. Given the importance of part-time working, a more detailed sectoral analysis for females (detailed data for males are not available) is

	Full-time, male	Part-time, male	Full-time, female	Part-time, female
Hotels*	41.8	-	40.1	18.2
Restaurants*	42.5	-	38.9	17.5
Bars	42.1	14.8	38.8	15.0
Canteens	44.3	-	40.3	20.4
Hotels and restaurants*	42.5	16.6	39.4	16.8
All industries and services	45.0	20.7	40.2	19.0

Notes: *Hotels and restaurants refer to the SIC 1992 used by the government to classify the hospitality industry for official statistical purposes.

Source: Office for National Statistics, 1998a, Part C, Tables C1 and C2, and Part F, Tables F31 and F32.

Table 5.3 Average weekly hours of manual workers by sector (including overtime)

shown in Table 5.4. This merits further comment. First, more hospitality workers than workers generally have no specified hours and may be employed on highly flexible hours contracts, including zero hours contracts. Second, while nearly three-quarters of male and female part-time workers in hospitality work twenty-one hours a week or less, there are marked sectoral differences. Bars have the highest concentration of short part-time hours or, put another way, the most flexible workforce.

These patterns of flexibility are unlikely to be replicated in other countries where there is stricter regulation of employment contracts. In the Netherlands all hospitality workers are covered by a national collective agreement. While 38 per cent of workers are employed on 'on-call' contracts, after six months they are entitled to three hours' pay per call-up, even if fewer hours are worked (IDS, 1998a). In France most workers are employed on permanent or fixed-term contracts, although there have been moves to greater flexibility. In 1995 one-third of restaurant waiting staff and hotel administrators were working part-time, of whom over 60 per cent were women (Burrell et al., 1997a).

In Italy there is detailed legislation to protect and safeguard employees' rights. Four new collective agreements have been signed for the hospitality and tourism sectors that specify a minimum working week of fifteen hours. Any hours worked above contracted time must be paid at a premium of 30 per cent (IDS, 1999). In Spain where the hospitality industry is highly seasonal, temporary and seasonal contracts are permitted, over

	No specified hours (% in sample)	Below 8 hours	8–16 hours	16–21 hours	21–30 hours	Average weekly hours
Male:						
Hotels and restaurants*	22.3	17.8	17.8	35.6	28.7	16.6
All industries and services	15.5	12.7	27.7	18.9	40.7	20.7
Female:						
Hotels	21.6	13.6	31.3	22.4	32.6	18.2
Restaurants	8.8	17.1	30.0	17.1	36.0	17.5
Bars	15.3	20.2	41.2	18.7	19.9	15.0
Canteens	11.6	12.6	28.7	18.6	40.2	20.4
Hotels and restaurants*	14.5	17.1	35.4	18.9	28.5	16.8
All industries and services	9.5	11.3	31.8	23.6	33.2	19.0

Notes: *Hotels and restaurants refer to the SIC 1992 used by the government to classify the hospitality industry for official statistical purposes. Row percentages do not sum to 100 due to rounding.

Source: Office for National Statistics, 1998a, Part F, Tables F41 and F42.

Table 5.4 Distribution of weekly hours of part-time manual workers by sector (percentage)

200 000 agency temporary workers are employed (IDS, 1998b). Additionally within the EU the UK has the lowest level of labour taxes (percentage of pay) standing at 27 per cent, which serves to encourage labour flexibility. With the exception of Luxembourg and the Irish Republic, employers in other member states must pay between 36 per cent and 56 per cent.

More females work in hospitality than in the UK economy as a whole (Table 5.5). Hotels have the largest proportion of male employees, although this is still a sizeable minority. The gender balance in some managerial occupations is relatively even – hotel and accommodation managers (47 per cent male, 53 per cent female), restaurant and catering managers (55 per cent male, 45 per cent female). On the other hand, there is sharp gender divide within many other occupations. Females dominate these groups: housekeepers (98 per cent), catering assistants (82 per cent), cleaners and domestics (81 per cent), waiting staff (75 per cent). Conversely, at the other end of the scale, only 4 per cent of hotel porters are female.

Table 5.5
Employment by gender (percentage)

Sector	Male	Female
Hotels	39	61
Restaurants	33	67
Pubs, clubs and bars	32	68
Contract catering	29	71
All hospitality	34	66
All industries and services	53	47

Sources: Annual Employment Survey, 1996, and Labour Force Survey, 1998, adapted from Hospitality Training Foundation, 1999: 23, Table 2.8; Office for National Statistics, 1998b: 18, Table 8.

The UK pattern of female working in hospitality is not replicated elsewhere. For example, the gender split in France and the Netherlands is 50:50, while more men work in hospitality than women in Italy (54 per cent) and Spain (59 per cent). These differences may be attributable to the fact that a greater proportion of employment comprises self-employment, employers and family workers in these countries (Burrell et al., 1997a). Comparable figures on men and women by occupation are difficult to obtain. In France, Spain and Italy, apart from housekeeping, reception (except Italy) and the restaurant (except France and Italy), men are more likely to work in management, supervision, kitchens, and the bar than women (Burrell et al., 1997b).

Half the UK hospitality industry's workforce is aged between sixteen and thirty compared with a quarter in the economy as a

	16–30	30–50
All hospitality	50	35
Great Britain	26	50+

Source: Labour Force Survey, 1998, adapted from Hospitality Training Foundation, 1999: 4, Fig. 4.

Table 5.6
Employment by age
(percentage)

whole (Table 5.6). In comparison with the national average nearly six times as many sixteen- to nineteen-year-olds and twice as many twenty to twenty-four year olds work in restaurants. Pubs, clubs and bars, and hotels follow a similar pattern, but not to the same extent. Conversely, older workers are less likely to work in hospitality than in other sectors of the economy.

The hospitality industry workforce in the Netherlands comprises one-third under the age of twenty-three and nearly half are aged twenty to twenty-nine years (IDS, 1998a). In New Zealand 57 per cent of employees are under twenty years of age, and are most commonly found in fast food outlets (Ryan, 1997).

The hospitality industry also employs a higher proportion of ethnic minority workers than the economy as a whole (Table 5.7). This is thought to be so because of the large number of ethnic restaurants. Occupations with the highest concentrations of non-white workers are restaurant and catering managers (15.9 per cent) and chefs/cooks (12.5 per cent).

	White	Non-white
All hospitality	89.2	10.8
Great Britain	95.1	4.9

Source: Labour Force Survey, 1998, adapted from Hospitality Training Foundation, 1999: 21, Table 2.6.

Table 5.7
Employment by ethnicity
(percentage)

Finally, hospitality pay is lower than pay in general in the UK, making it among one of the lowest paid industries in the UK (Table 5.8). Males earn more than females, and full-time workers earn more than part-time workers. As a consequence the NMW introduced in April 1999 is expected to benefit proportionately more hospitality workers (an estimated 30 per cent of the total workforce) than those in any other industry.

In keeping with the UK, in countries like France, Spain and Italy low pay tends to correlate with the degree of feminization in

	Full-time, male (£)	Part-time, male (£)	Full-time, female (£)	Part-time, female (£)
Hotels	5.57	–	4.59	3.93
Restaurants	5.00	–	4.20	3.82
Bars	4.87	3.72	3.96	3.61
Canteens	6.21	–	4.57	3.98
Hotels and restaurants*	5.29	3.84	4.27	3.80
All industries and services	7.10	5.53	5.14	4.67

Note: *Hotels and restaurants refer to the SIC 1992 used by the government to classify the hospitality industry for official statistical purposes.

Source: Office for National Statistics, 1998a, Part C, Tables C1 and C2, and Part F, Tables F31 and F32.

Table 5.8 Average gross hourly earnings of manual workers by sector (excluding overtime)

the job (Burrell et al., 1997). Equal pay has not been achieved because occupational and sectoral segregation are found in all four countries, but lower pay for part-time work is mainly a UK phenomenon (Price and Stead, 1996).

Employment practices

In the Introduction to this chapter, we argued that employment practices are methods of managing people most commonly found in organizations in a sector or industry. We said that these practices may be formal (e.g. arising from managers' legal obligations or organizational policy) or informal (e.g. arising from managerial or employee behaviour). In this section, we discuss the major employment practices common to most sectors of the UK hospitality industry. The majority of these are highly informal in nature. They relate to:

- the style of people management which is often unsupported by extensive formal personnel and human resource management policies and procedures;
- a reliance by management on low-paid, 'marginal' members of the workforce;
- a tendency to use labour in a highly flexible manner; and
- the discouragement by management of collective action among employees, especially in the form of trade unions.

We will now consider each of these in turn.

Style of people management

The hospitality industry is characterized by a predominance of small owner-managed businesses. Often the proprietors and

managers of these businesses have little, if any, formal management training, let alone training in people management, and their
employment practices are frequently arbitrary and inexpert.
While there are many large hospitality chain organizations,
whose business goals and broad procedures are specified by
senior company executives, the managers of individual units
within these chains possess a great deal of personal autonomy
and have considerable latitude to select the methods by which
these goals are achieved and the policies observed. In many
cases, as far as people management is concerned, employment
practices parallel those found in small independent businesses.

This absence or marginalization of the personnel and human
resource function in hospitality organizations reflects the degree
of informality of employment practices. In the late 1970s Johnson
(1978) noted that few units had dedicated personnel managers,
with responsibility for personnel matters often resting with unit
managers who, in turn, frequently devolved this important
function to others in the unit. This is still a feature of employment
practices in hospitality organizations today, with few, if any, of
those with responsibility for personnel at unit level possessing
formal qualifications or experience in the field.

More recently Kelliher and Johnson (1987) undertook two
parallel studies of hotel personnel practice in Ealing, London,
and in Leeds. In the Ealing study, only 42 per cent of
establishments surveyed employed a full-time personnel manager. The likelihood of finding a member of the hotel management team with primary responsibility for personnel was closely
related to the size of the unit. Some 96 per cent of hotels with
more than 200 bedrooms employed a personnel manager, often
with a backup team of specialists. In many smaller establishments the personnel function was delegated to a wide variety of
people. These included the managing director, the head receptionist and, in one instance, the general manager's secretary.
Many medium-sized hotels delegated responsibility for personnel matters to assistant managers who, however, had other
important duties.

In the Leeds study, Kelliher and Johnson (1987) discovered that
half of all personnel managers had never held a personnel
position before their current post, nor did they have formal
training in personnel management. The researchers found that
across both studies, the role of those with personnel management
responsibilities was narrowly defined in terms of recruitment and
training, and to some degree, welfare matters. In an extension to
this work, Kelliher and Johnson (1997) revisited the earlier study
to track developments since the first research project. Again it
was found that only large hotels tended to have personnel
specialists. A change had occurred in the main duties and
activities of personnel and related managers, however. Recruitment and training remained important, but counselling and

welfare roles had increased in significance, as had dealing with grievance and disciplinary procedures.

In a further study, Croney (1988) examined pay systems, recruitment, selection and employee participation in four hotel groups. He found a considerable difference between statements of corporate philosophy and practice on personnel matters and the views and practices of unit managers. The latter often employed informal recruitment and training methods even where formal practices were recommended by 'head office'. Personnel managers, where employed, effectively were confined to implementing the decisions of departmental heads.

One of the most important recent studies of personnel practice in the British *hotel* sector is that by Price (1993; 1994) (see also Hoque, 1999, for a different, if eccentric, view and, for a thorough comparative review of personnel practice and the state of people management in the wider UK hospitality industry based on data from the 1990 Workplace Industrial Relations Survey (WIRS), Lucas, 1995). By way of summarizing the current state of play Price (1994: 44) notes that:

> no amount of image-massaging is likely to be effective unless the poor employment conditions and personnel practices prevalent in the industry are fundamentally improved. Employers' attempts to sell the industry seem hollow when placed against a range of studies which paint a picture of low status work carried out by exploited employees.

Price (1994: 49) also confirms the findings of much earlier research while uncovering new information about the informality of employment practices. These include the following.

1 There was a strong correlation between unit size and the extent to which establishments had introduced personnel policies and procedures that satisfied legal requirements. This was in the main attributable to the presence of unit-level personnel specialists or ease of access to a central personnel department.

2 Only 39 per cent of respondents referred to all the legally required terms and conditions in the written particulars for their contracts of employment.

3 Only 24 per cent of respondents followed completely the recommendations of the Advisory, Conciliation and Arbitration Service (ACAS) code of practice in their disciplinary procedures.

4 Twenty-eight per cent of respondents never used job descriptions; 37 per cent never used person specifications, making it difficult to ascertain freedom from bias in their employee selection procedures.

5 In many cases, 'word of mouth' was the preferred means of recruiting low-skill and casual staff.

6 Attitudes to training, especially in personnel matters, were inconsistent. Many respondents paid lip service to the principle of good training but few were prepared to pay for it. Only 19 per cent of respondents were willing to pay more than £100 per day per person for training, 37 per cent more than £80 per day, and 40 per cent only between £51 and £100 per day.

Reliance on low-paid, 'marginal' workers

In the preceding discussion, we noted how many low-skill and casual workers are recruited informally, by 'word of mouth'. In point of fact, many operative employees in all sectors of the hospitality industry are remunerated by means of hourly rates. In the earlier section on 'work patterns' it was also stated that many employees in the industry are young, female, work part-time and are generally low paid. These marginal workers are drawn from groups in society who have little bargaining power and whose choice in employment is severely curtailed by factors such as lack of qualifications and experience; multiple-commitments (e.g. domestic management, child-rearing) which make them available for work only on a part-time or casual basis, and/or wider discriminatory factors within society (as is often the case with members of ethnic minorities). The use of the term 'marginal' in this context is not pejorative but rather an indication of the extent to which employees with these characteristics are perceived in terms of their labour value.

The link between marginality and pay lies in the fact that workers who possess the characteristics described above are not in a position to demand high wages. Sometimes, employees accept work in the hospitality industry not through principled choice, but because there are no alternatives (Wood, 1997). Relatively speaking, the supply of such workers from an employer's point of view is plentiful. In economic terms, therefore, a plentiful supply of labour to some extent drives down their remunerative value (see also Lucas, 1995).

The employment of many low-paid marginal workers has two important consequences for employment practice: the prevalence of informal rewards, and high levels of labour instability.

Informal rewards

The hospitality industry has always had a reputation for poor pay and conditions of employment. Indeed, government-inspired wages regulation has existed in the sector for much of the twentieth century, latterly in the form of wages councils. However, these were abolished by the Conservative government in 1993. In 1999, the Labour government introduced a generic National Minimum Wage (as noted earlier) but it is too early to tell how successful this will be in assisting the poorest paid.

Hospitality industry employers were among the keenest proponents of abolition of the old wages councils, arguing that they imposed unnecessary costs on businesses and discouraged job creation. Similar arguments were marshalled in lobbying against the introduction of a minimum wage, employers arguing that such a wage would destroy jobs. There is little evidence that in either case these forewarnings of doom have been realized. We should not be surprised at this. There are sound economic reasons for arguing that a business which cannot pay its employees a decent wage is one which is either inefficient (and thus of questionable value to the wider economy) and/or more concerned with maximizing profits for owners or shareholders.

A more important argument advanced by employers against the statutory regulation of wages is that formal remuneration (i.e. the wages paid by the employer) of employees in the hospitality industry is supplemented by numerous benefits, notably tips. Academics have coined the term 'total rewards system' to describe the hospitality industry's employee remuneration package (Mars, Bryant and Mitchell, 1979; Johnson, 1983; Wood, 1997). The total rewards system (TRS) comprises formal rewards which are basic pay + subsidized lodging (where the employee 'lives in') + subsidized food (meals on duty and the like) + other benefits supplied by the employer (e.g. uniforms and free cleaning thereof, bonuses, productivity payments, free transport to and from work) together with informal rewards which include tips and so-called 'fiddles' and 'knock-offs'. Many workers receive some or all of these elements as part of their job rewards but, equally, many do not. Furthermore, the quality of these benefits, where received, varies considerably in their intrinsic quality and utility.

For example, free or subsidized meals often comprise low-grade foods that have to be eaten quickly in short, prescribed, periods. The utility of these meals may represent a genuine supplement to the income of the single worker but for those with partners and/or families, the value of meals on duty is substantially reduced as others still have to be fed at a cost. Similarly, the quality of live-in accommodation has been found to be highly variable (see Wood, 1997, for a review of the evidence). Live-in workers are also more prone to be 'on-call' because of their proximity to the workplace and enjoy very little privacy.

The biggest debate over total rewards, however, concerns tips. The first thing to note here is that not all workers are in a position to receive tips, which are most routinely given to workers in those occupations with direct customer service contact. Dronfield and Soto (1980) estimate that 50 per cent of the workforce in hotels have no direct contact with customers and thus no direct access to tips. More important is the point that except in rare circumstances, tips are unlikely to compensate sufficiently for low basic wages. Indeed, in many cases, employers use tips to subsidize wages. In the age of credit card payment where the slip the customer signs has a space for a gratuity to be added, it is worth reflecting that any amount inserted is by no means guaranteed to go to the employee.

Employers can (and do) use income from tips to contribute towards the monies available for paying wages. Employers also set wage rates to reflect tipping opportunities, Lyons (1994) reports the case of a hotelier who engaged in the fairly common practice of adjusting basic wage rates to allow for the monies that should be earned from tips. Not only does this make an assumption about tipping potential that may never materialize, but also it can negate any supplementary effect of tips. It is important to note that since the introduction of the NMW, only tips, gratuities and service charges that are paid through the payroll count towards NMW pay. Any tips or gratuities paid directly to the worker by the customer and kept by the worker do not count.

Finally here, we can consider 'fiddles 'and 'knock-offs'. The term 'fiddles' refers to petty monetary theft and a 'knock-off' is a particular type of fiddle entailing the taking by employees of small items, normally but by no means exclusively, food. Fiddles are either at the expense of the employer or customer. Knock-offs are invariably at the expense of the employer. Research indicates management's collusion in these activities in most hospitality organizations. That is, management tolerates a degree of fiddling and knocking-off on the tacit understanding that such activities lead to employee benefits that are a legitimate part of the reward package. The degree of such tolerance is ambiguous, however, and it is easy for such tolerance to be temporarily withdrawn with workers disciplined or dismissed for stealing. As with tips, the scope for fiddling and knocking off is often restricted to certain kinds of workers who benefit from a context that facilitates such activity. There is also a suggestion that modern systems of electronic control make it more difficult for fiddling and knocking off to take place. This view is untested and should be treated with caution as the scope for these activities remains considerable in most hospitality organizations.

Labour instability

Low wages and poor conditions of employment in the hospitality industry can lead to high levels of labour instability. Historically, labour turnover in the hospitality industry is high when compared with other industries (see Wood, 1997, for a review). Rates of 70 per cent annual staff turnover are typical but incidences of 400 per cent are on record. Despite this, the demand by the industry for labour seems insatiable. There are many reasons for this high turnover.

First, managers rely heavily on the external labour market for recruitment and do not engage extensively in those activities such as training and development that might improve staff retention. Second, low pay contributes to low morale and workers are more readily prepared to change jobs than would be the case in other industries in order to gain even minor incremental improvements to their wage. Third, management in the industry is traditionally heavy-handed, with employees often dismissed for quite trivial reasons. Finally, pressure at work can drive people to seek alternative employment that they believe (whether rightly or wrongly) will be less stressful.

Some academic commentators have argued that labour turnover is detrimental to the industry, not simply because the replacement process can be costly but because instability contributes to unpleasant and uncertain working environments. Others have suggested that since employers recruit mainly from external labour markets and require for the most part employees with limited skills, labour turnover is a normal even healthy phenomenon that allows workers to develop their skills by moving from job to job in search of skill and pay betterment. Both arguments are flawed. Replacement costs are generally low precisely because employers rely on local labour markets and recruit principally through informal means. The argument from skill development is flawed for the same reason: in most local labour markets there are a finite number of hospitality working environments (units) and thus a finite scope for skill self-improvement. The debate over the significance of labour turnover is an interesting one, however, and repays close study. There are clear sectoral and intra-sectoral differences, which means that generalizations about the advantages and disadvantages of turnover must be treated cautiously.

Labour flexibility

We have already noted how the hospitality industry depends to a very large degree on part-time workers. There is also a reliance on casual labour, particularly in areas such as banqueting. In crude terms, this is an example of the use of flexible labour. It is often argued that the use of part-time and casual workers in the hospitality industry is necessary because of the uneven nature of demand for the hospitality product. This is a misleading position. Business levels do vary but in the main can be planned for fairly easily. Flexible working in the hospitality sector is a preferred practice, one reason for this being that by varying labour inputs to the organization according to need, the cost of labour can be more readily controlled (and usually kept low). However, another reason for the persistence of these forms of flexibility is a reluctance or inability to see a more efficient way of working – an industry 'blind spot'.

Following the model developed by Atkinson (1984) it is conventional to identify four types of labour flexibility. These are as follows.

1 *Numerical flexibility* involves varying the number of workers or hours worked in response to demand by the utilization of temporary, part-time or casual workers, increased overtime and changes in shift patterns. This pattern of flexibility is most suited (and most frequently found) in organizations with generally low skill requirements where little or no training is required.

2 Functional flexibility involves attempts to gain greater flexibility in skills utilization and competencies that allows employees to perform a variety of jobs at similar or different levels in the organization (termed horizontal and vertical flexibility respectively). This form of flexibility is often referred to, only partly accurately, as multiskilling.

3 Pay flexibility occurs when the form and delivery of rewards is adjusted to encourage functional flexibility and includes such things as bonus schemes, merit rewards, productivity payments and other forms of performance-related pay.

4 Distancing strategies are where employers contract out certain types of work and functions in order to redistribute risk and uncertainty within the organization. In the hospitality industry this can presently be seen in the contracting out by hotels of room cleaning, laundry services and, in some cases, the food and beverage function (hotel restaurants).

Academic interest in organizations' flexibility practices has increased dramatically in the late 1980s and 1990s. Ironically, numerical flexibility has existed in the hospitality industry for many years before such expressions of interest. This being a view at least partially confirmed by the National Economic Development Council (1986) who found that flexible working strategies were not a priority for service sector firms in general because they already existed by tradition. Indeed, functional flexibility is the most common form of flexibility in the hospitality industry, as would be expected from the variety of features of the industry we have discussed in this chapter. In contrast, researchers have found little evidence for the existence of extensive numerical flexibility, despite various attempts at multiskilling by many hotel corporations over the years (see Hales, 1987; Wood, 1997).

Having said this, a note of caution must be sounded. By their very nature, many small and medium-sized enterprises by definition tend towards the functionally flexible with a small group of people performing many different tasks. This is rarely if ever planned, however, and should be seen as part of the culture of small businesses and distinct from our understanding of functional flexibility in larger organizations. With regard to the extent of pay flexibility in the hospitality industry we know little. Senior managers in larger organizations are certainly subject to such elements as performance-related pay but it is unusual to find pay flexibility on any scale applied to employees further down the hierarchy. Finally, as we noted earlier, distancing strategies have perhaps grown in significance in some hospitality organizations but overall, probably remain only a small part of the industry's flexibility strategies.

Discouragement of collective action

The relatively small size of hospitality units compared with other industrial organizations means that the management of employees is often direct and 'hands on', with many operative employees experiencing regular contact with their line and senior unit managers. Such direct relationships are thus characterized by more individualistic relationships between management and other employees. Managers are able to exert more influence and control over their employees in these circumstances. Systematic research into the nature of these relationships has shown that hospitality managers value such individualized control for operational and social – often paternalistic – reasons, and discourage collective relationships and collective action among employees (Lucas, 1995).

The relative absence of trade unions in the UK hospitality industry (which we noted earlier has been less than 5 per cent over the course of the decade according to data from the Workplace Industrial Relations Survey, 1990, and the Workplace Employee Relations Survey, 1998 – see Lucas, 1995; Cully et al., 1999) arises partly because of the active discouragement of unionism by employers, but also because hospitality managers in general possess an almost supernatural belief in the power of their own management style (Lucas, 1995). Collective representation of employee interests is seen as necessary only when individual managers' style fails (see Wood, 1997; for a detailed study of particular instances of this kind of belief see Aslan and Wood, 1993). Naturally, such beliefs are self-serving but they are held sincerely by many managers who genuinely believe that is their duty and responsibility to 'look after' their employees properly, a responsibility most believe they discharge reasonably well.

International aspects of employment practices

Everyday conversation would frequently have us believe that employment in hospitality services in the UK is atypical and that in other countries (France and the USA are popularly cited examples) there is a positive culture of performing service jobs. Furthermore, that these jobs are in some way qualitatively better and more highly paid. There is some truth in this, but such an assertion should be treated with caution. Employment in the hospitality industry is not as stigmatized in some countries as it is in the UK – this is true. In many developing countries hospitality service work is much sought after and, relative to other local economic and employment conditions, can be well paid with good terms and conditions of employment (Baum, 1995). The keyword here is 'relative'. If you have a steady job in a hotel as opposed to being permanently unemployed or engaged in some form of subsistence labour, in agriculture or extractive industries for example, then of course you might think yourself lucky. The important issue to bear in mind in this context is that the proper comparator when considering the value of occupational remuneration is the relative value of other jobs in the same economic system, not the same jobs in other countries or regions.

When considering hospitality jobs in other developed economies, the problems are even greater. One feels it is intuitively true, for example, that in many other EU countries, hospitality industry workers are better paid than in the UK. There is, though, limited evidence to support this view. In several such countries, a good many jobs are better paid than in the UK but this ignores factors like the operation of a national minimum wage (wage regulation is more sophisticated in much of the EU) and differences in taxation and the culture of employment. It is one thing to be paid twice the average hourly UK rate in France or Germany and quite another to have to pay twice as much in direct taxation.

We do not have sufficient space in this chapter to detail all the available evidence on employment conditions and remuneration in hospitality services around the world (see Baum, 1983; 1995; Wood, 1997 for extensive reviews). Save to say, there is much diversity of practice but a discernible trend of which the UK is a part. In other words, the grass is not always, if ever, greener elsewhere. Reference to the sources cited above leaves a distinct impression that despite local variations, employment in hospitality services across the world shares many more characteristics, including most of those discussed in this chapter, than there are differences. This is perhaps unsurprising given the nature of the hospitality business and the increasing tendency toward the globalization of employment practices.

Conclusions

Any attempt to analyse the present, never mind to predict the future, is always a hazardous occupation. This is particularly the case in activities that involve a myriad of human interactions. As you will have gathered by now, the variety and complexity evident in the hospitality industry makes such an endeavour problematic with regard to work patterns and employment practices. However, notwithstanding these difficulties, it is possible to identify elements of commonality across different hospitality contexts. On the other hand, this is an activity best conducted with considerable caution.

The hospitality industry is a global industry but one in which small indigenous businesses will continue to play a significant role. While it is possible to establish sources of similarity and difference across the globe in work patterns and employment practices, there remains considerable diversity in legal regulation, employer attitudes and, of course, the perception and status of hospitality work. In this chapter we have sought to capture some of the flavour of these similarities and differences. It seems likely that such patterns of employment and employment practices will continue for some time to come, ensuring that the hospitality industry remains a fascinating focus for the study of work in the age of globalization.

Summary

The key themes and issues to arise from the discussion in this chapter can be summarized as follows.

1 Work patterns describe *how* people work (e.g. modes of working, patterns of reward, and distribution of employment) whereas employment practices describe the methods of people management found in work organizations.

2 The UK hospitality industry labour force numbers around 1.263 million. Some 60 per cent of employees work part-time. More women and members of ethnic minority workers work in the hospitality industry than in the UK economy as a whole. Half of the workforce is in the age range sixteen to thirty. The largest sectors by numbers of employees are pubs, clubs and bars, and restaurants (accounting for 64 per cent of employment). Hotels account for 23 per cent of employment in the industry. Small firms continue to dominate the industry, some 85 per cent of all firms employing between one and ten persons.

3 European Union comparisons suggest that the UK hospitality sector has many distinctive characteristics. Two are especially notable. First, contractual arrangements, especially as regulated by law, mean that hospitality industry workers elsewhere in the EU are not expected to work as flexibly as their UK

counterparts who tend to have more open arrangements and are less likely to have precisely specified times of working. Second, the gender split in the workforce encountered in the UK is not as marked as in other EU countries where male workers are found in greater numbers.

4 Pay is lower in the UK hospitality industry than elsewhere in the EU. Part-time work in particular is lower paid than in these countries.

5 Employment practices in the UK hospitality industry are marked by informality of management practices, especially with regard to personnel and human resource management (HRM). Few hospitality organizations have effective personnel and human resource policies and training is limited. Management can be heavy handed and inexpert. The industry is characterized by high rates of labour instability and an emphasis on informal rewards.

6 Employment practices elsewhere tend to be strongly correlated to the degree of legal regulation of employment that exists. There is a perception that in many countries, the hospitality sector offers comparatively good and well-paid jobs. Such claims must be viewed in the light of appropriate comparisons relative to the local contexts in which the hospitality industry functions.

Review questions

1 Explain why the pattern of part-time hours varies in different sectors of the hospitality industry.

2 Is the hospitality industry's high reliance on female workers justifiable and sustainable?

3 Assess the benefits and disadvantages of using young labour in different types of hospitality organizations.

4 Explain how and why work practices in different countries might vary.

5 Assess the benefits and disadvantages of relying on a low-paid workforce.

6 How could labour turnover in hospitality organizations be reduced?

7 Is tipping a sound and moral practice? Does it benefit workers in the hospitality industry?

8 To what extent are conditions of employment in the UK hospitality industry being globalized?

9 What problems are likely to be encountered in trying to compare hospitality employment statistics from different countries?

10 If the external influences are basically the same for all organizations operating in a given sector of the hospitality industry to what extent would it be true to say that any differences in employment patterns and/or work practices between these organizations are due solely to differences in the internal influences within each individual organization?

Bibliography

Aslan, A. and Wood R. C. (1993). Trade unions in the hotel and catering industry: the views of hotel managers. *Employee Relations*, **15** (2), 61–69.

Atkinson, J. (1984). Manpower strategies for flexible organizations. *Personnel Management*, August, 28–31.

Baum, T. (ed.) (1983). *Human Resource Issues in International Tourism*. Butterworth-Heinemann.

Baum, T. (1995). *Managing Human Resources in the European Tourism and Hospitality Industry: A Strategic Approach*. Chapman and Hall.

Burrell, J., Manfredi, S., Rollin, H. and Price, L. and Stead, L. (1997a). Equal opportunities for women employees in the hospitality industry: a comparison between France, Italy, Spain and the UK. *International Journal of Hospitality Management*, **16** (2), 161–179.

Burrell, J., Manfredi, S., Rollin, H. and Price, L. (1997b). Women's employment in France, Italy, Spain and the UK. *Council for Hospitality Management Education (CHME) Sixth Annual Research Conference Proceedings*. Oxford Brookes University.

Croney, P. (1988). An investigation into the management of labour in the hotel industry. Unpublished MA thesis, University of Warwick.

Cully, M., Woodland, S., O'Reilly, A. and Dix, G. (1999). *Britain at Work: As Depicted by the 1998 Workplace Employee Relations Survey*. Routledge.

Dronfield, L. and Soto, P. (1980). *Hardship Hotel*. Counter Information Services.

Hales, C. (1987.) Quality of working life: job redesign and participation in a service industry: a rose by any other name? *Service Industries Journal*, **7** (3), 253–273.

Hoque, K. (1999). New approaches to HRM in the UK hotel industry. *Human Resource Management Journal*, **9** (2), 64–76.

Hospitality Training Foundation (1999). *Key Facts and Figures for the Hospitality Industry*. Hospitality Training Foundation.

Incomes Data Services (IDS) (1998a). 'Atypical' jobs sustain growth in Dutch hotels. *IDS Employment Europe 442*, October, 18–20.

Incomes Data Services (IDS) (1998b). Pay and conditions in Spanish hospitality sector. *IDS Employment Europe 443*, November, 18–19.

Incomes Data Services (IDS) (1999). New agreements set minima in Italy's hospitality sector. *IDS Employment Europe 449*, May, 20–21.

Johnson, K. (1978). Personnel matters: an overview or an oversight? *Hotel, Catering and Institutional Management Journal*, January, 21–23.

Johnson, K. (1983). Payment in hotels: the role of fringe benefits. *Service Industries Journal*, **3** (2), 191–213.

Kelliher, C. and Johnson, K. (1987). Personnel management in hotels: some empirical observations. *International Journal of Hospitality Management*, **6** (2), 103–108.

Kelliher, C. and Johnson, K. (1997). Personnel management in hotels – an update: a move to Human Resource Management? *Progress in Tourism and Hospitality Research*, **3** (4), 321–331.

Lucas, R. (1995). *Managing Employee Relations in the Hotel and Catering Industry*. Cassell.

Lyons, V. (1994). Tips sliding away. *Caterer and Hotelkeeper*, 12 May. 32–36.

Mars, G., Bryant, D. and Mitchell, P. (1979). *Manpower Problems in the Hotel and Catering Industry*. Gower.

National Economic Development Council (1986). *Changing Working Patterns*. Report by the Institute of Manpower Studies. National Economic Development Office.

Office for National Statistics (1998a). *New Earnings Survey Parts A-F*. The Stationery Office.

Office for National Statistics (1998b). *Labour Force Survey Quarterly Supplement No 3*. November. The Stationery Office.

Price, L. (1993). The limitations of the law in influencing employment practices in UK hotels and restaurants. *Employee Relations*, **15** (2), 16–24.

Price, L. (1994). Poor personnel practice in the hotel and catering industry: does it matter? *Human Resource Management Journal*, **4** (4), 44–62.

Price, L. and Stead, L. (1996). Pay inequality in four European countries. *Council for Hospitality Management Education (CHME) Fifth Annual Research Conference Proceedings*. Nottingham Trent University.

Riley, M. (1996). *Human Resource Management in the Hospitality and Tourism Industry*. Butterworth-Heinemann.

Ryan, R. (1997). *Employment Relations in Hotels, Cafes and Restaurants: Summary of Survey Results*. Industrial Relations Centre, Victoria University of Wellington.

Wood, R. C. (1997). *Working in Hotels and Catering*. International Thomson Business Press.

Further reading

Baum, T. (1995). *Managing Human Resources in the European Tourism and Hospitality Industry: A Strategic Approach*. Chapman and Hall.

Gabriel, Y. (1988). *Working Lives in Catering*. Routledge and Kegan Paul.

Goldsmith, A., Nickson, D., Sloan, D. and Wood, R. C. (1997). *Human Resource Management for Hospitality Services*. International Thomson Business Press.

Guerrier, Y. (1999). *Organizational Behaviour in Hotels and Restaurants: An International Perspective*. John Wiley.

Lashley, C. (1997). *Empowering Service Excellence: Beyond the Quick Fix*. Cassell.

Lucas, R. (1995). *Managing Employee Relations in the Hotel and Catering Industry*. Cassell.

Mars, G., Bryant, D. and Mitchell, P. (1979). *Manpower Problems in the Hotel and Catering Industry*. Gower.

Riley, M. (1996). *Human Resource Management in the Hospitality and Tourism Industry*. Butterworth-Heinemann.

Wood, R. C. (1994). *Organizational Behaviour for Hospitality Management*. Butterworth-Heinemann.

Wood, R. C. (1997). *Working in Hotels and Catering*. International Thomson Business Press.

Management practices

Clare Kelliher and Keith Johnson

Objectives

There are a host of interrelated factors that can influence how management is conducted within hospitality organizations. The general objective of this chapter is to introduce you to a range of these factors and to illustrate how they might influence the practice of management in specific sets of circumstances. Using the comparative approach as a basis, you should be able to make some sense of the complexity, variety and richness of hospitality management practices and activities. In particular, having read this chapter you should be able to:

1 Recognize a variety of definitions and observations covering the practice of management.

2 Identify some common elements of the practice of hospitality management.

3 Identify differences in management practice.

4 Recognize hospitality management as a heterogeneous activity composed of both generic and idiosyncratic elements.

5 Explore some of the variables which cause the balance between generic and idiosyncratic elements to change in particular circumstances.

6 Compare and contrast management activity in a variety of hospitality settings.

Introduction

To address the comparative agenda constituting the theme of this book we start to examine management practice in the hospitality industry from the standpoint of first principles. In this sense we begin by exploring the nature of management itself as there would appear to be little point in trying to investigate how management practice may differ or not without identifying what management is in the first place. This is not an easy task, as the voluminous body of research literature on management readily illustrates. However, even though there are a number of theories concerning management and its practice, many of which differ in their construction and predictions, there are some generally agreed fundamentals of management that can be used as a starting point. An examination of these will enable us to identify some aspects of potential commonality in management practice across different contexts, and at different levels.

Using this as a foundation the chapter then proceeds to add in the complications arising from contextual variations. Here you will begin to appreciate the individual, organizational, and environmental influences on management practice that tend to lead to its different manifestation in different organizations and industry sectors. As you might imagine this could be a very complex endeavour as there are literally thousands of potential influences, and many more combinations of these, that serve to affect how management is practised in any given situation. To explore this systematically, let alone in its entirety, is clearly beyond the scope of this chapter. Therefore, our exploration of these influences is a partial one designed to sensitize you to some of the key influences. Having read this part of the chapter we are sure you will be able to start identifying other potentially significant influences for yourself.

The nature and context of management

Management is all around us. Everybody can see the consequences of managerial actions. Some organizations appear to be well managed, others less so. The question is, what is it that makes this difference? Management is a definable activity. Put simply, it is the process of administering and co-ordinating resources in an effective and efficient manner in an effort to achieve the goals of an organization. Despite the fact that it is an activity conducted in a variety of organizations, each operating within its own specific context and environment, a number of characteristic elements enable the activity to be recognized and defined.

While there are numerous definitions of management (see Table 6.1 for some examples of these) which reflect the diversity of its occurrence, it is also true to say that a consensus exists concerning the essential features of the activity. Drucker (1974) suggests that managers give direction to their organizations, provide leadership and decide how to use organizational resources to accomplish organizational goals. Daft (1995) suggests that management is the attainment of organizational goals in an effective and efficient manner through planning, organizing, leading and controlling organizational resources.

- 'A multipurpose organ that manages a business and manages managers and manages workers and work' (Drucker, 1954: 19).
- 'arranging things and getting things done' (Brech, 1975: 12).
- 'The process of achieving desired results through efficient utilisation of human and material resources' (Bedeian, 1986: 4).
- 'all those activities involving responsibility for the work of others' (Deverell, 1985: 12).
- 'The process of planning, organising, leading and controlling the work of organisation members and of using all available organisational resources to reach stated goals' (Stoner, Freeman and Gilbert, 1995: 10).
- 'simply a matter of running an organisation so that the variety of people who want something out of it will go on supporting it in such a way that it is able to continue its existence into the future' (Watson, 1994: 10).
- 'One way in which management differs from many other types of work is that managers are not paid for the hours they put in. Instead, they are paid to get results (Morris, 1988: 11).
- 'All managerial activity is directed at either Breakthrough or Control. Managers are busy doing both of these things, and nothing else . . . Breakthrough is the creation of good changes, whereas Control is the prevention of bad changes' (Juran, 1964: 4).
- 'The functions that seem to distinguish management positions from others in the organisation are those related to keeping the organisation together (the 'glue' function), giving purpose and direction, co-ordinating the various subparts, ensuring that it meets its objectives effectively, acquiring resources from the external environment, keeping that environment as nourishing and predictable as possible, and creating buffers as needed to protect the organisation against threats form the outside' (Martin, 1983: 31).
- 'Any definition of management must be right because almost any definition must fit something so amorphous and shifting. Achieving results through other people is one of the more popular definitions. It applies to the president of General Motors, but also fits the madam of a brothel. And she is an executive facing real problems of personnel selection, marketing and accountancy, not to mention her tax and legal arrangements' (Heller, 1990: 2).

Table 6.1
Definitions and observations of management

Planning, organizing, leading and controlling are widely recognized as the cornerstones of management practice. Fayol (1916) and others identified these basic activities at the beginning of the twentieth century. The long-standing consensus surrounding these fundamental activities has resulted in the work of Fayol and his contemporaries being labelled as the 'classical' approach to management (for a detailed examination of this approach see, for example, Wren, 1979). However, depending on where a manager is located in the organizational hierarchy, the composition of these activities in their job may vary. Planning and organizing are the primary, but not exclusive, concern of senior managers. Leading and controlling are fundamental activities for first line managers, sometimes called supervisors, because these individuals have the most frequent direct contact with non-managerial personnel (those that are assumed to need leading and controlling). Middle managers act in all four areas to convert the policies and strategies created at a senior level into specific courses of action that can be implemented and monitored by first line managers. Hence, before we embark on an examination and explanation of some of the factors that cause management to be practised in different ways, it is worth remembering that underlying all this diversity there are some strands of commonality which hold the activity together.

Within the context of the hospitality industry the search for some of the common aspects of management practice has been far from easy. The professional body, the Hotel and Catering International Management Association (HCIMA) has played a central role in this quest. Since the mission of the HCIMA is to 'identify, promote and maintain the highest professional and ethical standards for management, education and training in the international hospitality industry' (HCIMA, 1988), it is easy to see why they are anxious to establish a common benchmark against which diverse management activities can be measured. Their first benchmark was created more than twenty years ago with the publication of *The Corpus of Professional Knowledge in*

Level	Main concerns	Major skill requirements
Senior management	Environment, goals, strategy and structure	Conceptual and human
Middle management (operational)	Co-ordination, tensions and conflicts, internal systems	Human
First line management (supervisory)	Operational processes, supervision and motivation of employees	Technical and human

Table 6.2 The levels of management

Hotel, Catering and Institutional Services (Johnson, 1977). More recently, in 1998, the *Corpus of Management Excellence* (HCIMA, 1988) was published and brought the original version up to date and attempted to create 'an international common currency' for management development within the hospitality industry. The current *Corpus* is interesting since in its search for benchmarks and common currencies, three levels of management and four clusters of knowledge are identified. The levels of management are 'supervisory', 'operational' and 'senior', and correspond to the HCIMA's own membership grades, the distinctions made earlier and in Table 6.2. Of the four clusters, two (core hospitality topics and key management themes) identify 'areas essential to the functioning of the hospitality industry' and 'generic management ideas and principles'. The remaining two clusters (sector topics and supporting hospitality topics) demonstrate 'the extent and breath of work activity within the hospitality sector'. Hence, the professional body is keen to strike a balance between generic practices, which have widespread applicability across the industry as a whole, and those activities which are necessary, but only in specific circumstances. Table 6.3 identifies some common challenges that hospitality managers face.

1 Maximizing/optimizing the opportunities presented by the World Wide Web and other aspects of information and communications technology.

2 Continuous, incremental improvements to both quantity and quality of product and service from a static (or reducing) resource base – doing more with the same or less resources.

3 Servicing increasingly sophisticated markets, ranging from a local to a global scale and composed of more demanding, better organized and more vocal customers.

4 Operating within changing legal, moral and ethical business frameworks.

5 Balancing the conflicting demands, which emanate from the full spectrum of organizational stakeholders.

6 Maintaining competitive advantage and staying ahead of the competition.

7 Building customer loyalty to retain, or develop, market share/brand image.

8 Integrating an increasingly diverse workforce.

9 Balancing short-term imperatives with longer-term objectives.

10 Continuous development of interpersonal, conceptual and diagnostic skills in an effort to maintain personal competence.

Table 6.3
Some common challenges for hospitality management

In some respects similar to the HCIMA, Mullins and Aldrich (1988: 30) have developed 'an integrated model of management and managerial behaviour, which balances generic practices and specialised attributes'. In the area labelled 'management activities' their model identifies common ground concerning the basic activities and processes of management. This common ground consists of three parts. First, there are the 'fundamental activities', which are identified as goal and objective setting, planning, organizing, motivating and measurement and control. This list is very similar to the activities identified previously as the 'classical' view of management. Second, there are the 'substantive activities', which are identified as communication, co-ordination, integration, responsibility and decision-making. Since they permeate the fundamental activities, these substantive activities are seen as no less important to the task of management. They are inherent in the process of management and are 'simply more descriptive of how the work of a manager is executed'. Whereas the fundamental activities identify what a manager does, the substantive activities begin to tackle the question of how a manager performs. Finally, 'related activities' are identified. These are broader activities, which constitute a backdrop against which the fundamental and substantive activities are performed. The personnel function is given as an example.

It is relatively easy to convert this area of the Mullins and Aldrich model into a must do (fundamental activities), should do (substantive activities) and could do (related activities) prescriptive list of management practice. Not surprisingly, it is in the must do category that the greatest level of consensus exists as to the common aspects of management.

Another useful three-stage model of managerial work is that developed by Stewart (1982). She identified:

1 The demands of managerial work, those tasks that anyone and everyone must do in the job.

2 The constraints on managerial work, those factors (both inside and outside the organization) which place limits on what the manager can do and achieve.

3 The choices associated with managerial work, those activities that a manager can undertake but is not forced to do so.

This third element, the one of choice, is a central characteristic of managerial work. Unlike some jobs, which are highly repetitive and are frequently determined by the needs of a specific production technology, managerial work often involves an element of choice over what is done and/or the manner in which it is done. Given that the managers are individuals, they therefore choose to exercise this freedom in various ways. Research by Stewart (1985) found that even where managers were involved in doing similar jobs they frequently chose to do them in different ways. Managers themselves vary according to age, gender, social, cultural and religious backgrounds and, hence, when a diverse set of individuals is given the opportunity to exercise an element of choice in their work, it would be unrealistic to expect a high level of uniformity in these choices. For example, an area in which managers differ significantly is in their reaction to, and hence use of, their powers of delegation. Some individuals seem comfortable in passing over responsibility for tasks to subordinates while others do so only with great reluctance.

Furthermore, managerial action is often problem driven. In other words, managers are confronted by organizational problems that need to be resolved. It is frequently impossible to identify a single solution to a particular problem that will work in all organizational settings. Managers make choices about how to solve problems in a variety of ways and, therefore, it is not surprising that the search for commonality in managerial work is difficult.

It may help to envisage management practice as a series of 'layers' of activity which are overlaid on each other (and therefore influence each other), rather like the structure of an onion. At the 'core' of the onion are the activities that are common to all managerial work and have been identified as classical activities. However, this core is hidden. Getting to it involves 'peeling away' at the layers of activity which surround and mask it. These layers of activity are often idiosyncratic to either individual managers and/or the specific organizations in which they work. Management practices are therefore a combination of generic and individual activities that are tightly wrapped together to produce a recognizable structure.

Clearly, then, despite the existence of some common, core activities, management is not homogenous. It is carried out in a variety of ways at different levels, in a variety of organizations. In truth, it is this variability which makes the study of management practices so absorbing. It is to an examination of this heterogeneity that our attention now turns.

This section has largely identified factors that tend to be common across the industry. We shall now move on to explore factors that tend to differ across industry sectors or, in some cases, even within industry sectors. While it is hard to make generalizations, we will try to examine management practice across industry sectors according to a number of variables which it has been suggested may account for these differences. Stewart (1985) argues that management activity differs according to a range of factors including size of the operation, nature of the industry, the rate of change in the environment and the competitive position of the organization. These fit into her second category of the constraints on managerial work, identified earlier (Stewart, 1982). Drucker (1974) stresses the importance of organizational goals. Fundamental questions such as, 'Does the organization aim to generate a profit?' 'Is it a stand alone unit or part of a wider operation?' are likely to be influential in the way in which managers operate. We shall now examine some of those goals across industry sectors and the way in which they influence the practice of management.

Financial goals

Clearly the overriding aim of the organization is likely to influence the practice of management. In other words, the things that are valued and/or considered important by the organization will influence the way in which it is managed. One such factor is whether or not the organization operates for profit. The profit sector of the industry is perhaps the one we are most familiar with, for example, most hotels and restaurants open to the public would fall into this category. In the not-for-profit sector hospitality operations would include parts of the public sector concerned with the provision of public sector services, for example, local authority run hostels or school meals services, catering and accommodation provided by charities and some industrial catering where employee feeding is subsidized by the employer.

Organizations that are in the profit sector, regardless of whether they actually make a profit, will be heavily influenced by this goal in the way in which the organization is managed. In this sector we have both private and public companies. For example, many owner-operated small hotels and restaurants will be private companies. By contrast, public companies are generally larger and employ managers who are accountable to the shareholders of the company. However, regardless of the type of company, in this sector survival depends on generating a profit and, in the longer term, increasing the value of the shareholders' investment. Sometimes investors will take the long-term view and may pursue a short-term loss position, because of a belief that there is future profit potential. However, if a profit is not generated and the investors do not see that there is potential for profit in the future, then there is little point in continuing in this business. In this type of environment revenue needs to exceed costs in order for value to be generated. As a result of this managers will seek ways of increasing revenue and/or reducing costs. Case 6.1 illustrates how powerful a driver of sustained managerial activity the search for profitability can be.

Case 6.1

(a) *McDonald's*

Harry J. Sonneborn was Ray Kroc's partner for ten years in the mid–1950s–1960s. Kroc was the colourful and amiable founder of the company who gave McDonald's its public image. He was a strong figure and took all the limelight. In contrast, Sonneborn had the impersonal style of a behind the scenes operator. Together they made a formidable combination.

'There was only one flaw in Kroc's plan – McDonald's had no way of making a profit. Kroc was romancing the fast-food business. The salesman in him was attracted to the volume potential and consumer appeal of a good 15-cent hamburger. The old-world thrift in him was fascinated with the efficiency of assembly-line food service ... He was not driven by acquiring money. He never analysed a business by its profit and loss statement, and he never took the time to understand his own company's balance sheet ...

Sonneborn's approach to business was totally financial. His principal interest in being in business was to make money ... His talents at financial negotiations ... could have been applied in any business, and Sonneborn would have been as content to apply them in the clothing business – his initial field – as in the hamburger business. In fact he viewed the food service business merely as a vehicle for making money in real estate. As such, he was the perfect counter-balance to Ray Kroc. He clearly had the motivation to make money that Kroc lacked.

"I never overlooked the aspects of finances with regard to the business," Sonneborn explains. "The name of the game was to make a profit."'

Source: Love, 1987: 151–6.

(b) *Accor*

A similar partnership lies behind the rise of Accor, the French hospitality company. Paul Dubrule and Gerard Pelisson are the central characters that sparked off 'an exceptional adventure and an entrepreneurial success the likes of which the World has seldom witnessed'. In Chapter 1 some observations were made about the possibility of comparing public houses and supermarkets. A similar comparison features in the following statement from Paul Dubrule:

'Let's face it money is a very important part of business. The earnings statement is our main judge. Having said that, one can always philosophise about how the money ought to be used. In the early days of our business, making money was very important, not just for our lifestyle, but also because it had symbolic value ... I could have gone into some other trade. At first, I wanted to set up supermarkets. But if someone had advised me to build windmills and I'd realised that there was a market for them, I would have made windmills. Again, let's be honest: I went into the hotel trade to do business.'

Source: Luc, 1999: 274–5.

In a not-for-profit situation, it is likely that there will be other drivers of managerial activity. Not-for-profit businesses may still make a profit or generate a surplus, but it is not their primary aim to do so. However, the drivers of managerial action may still be financially oriented. In some operations within this sector managers might be concerned with keeping to a pre-agreed budget, or contracted price. For example, in public sector catering, or contract catering where contracts are operated on a fixed cost basis, the main aim may be to keep food and labour costs within the budgeted figures.

Other objectives for organizations in this sector might include the provision of welfare or nutritional services. For example, where there is a 'captive' client base one of the objectives may be to promote healthy eating, or the provision of a balanced diet. Alternatively, in the context of airline catering, on-board meals are likely to be secondary to the main service, the transportation of the customer and may be used to distinguish the product offered from those of its competitors. Similarly, customers in a casino may be offered food and beverages free of charge or at low cost. Gaming is the main activity of the business, but the provision of food and drink may be one way of persuading customers to frequently visit this casino as opposed to one of the competitors. Hence the quality and attractiveness of the food and drink provision may make a substantial contribution to the specific advantage of the casino.

Management and ownership

How close the relationship is between ownership and management of the organization is likely to influence the practice of management. Where an establishment is owner-managed (e.g. a small hotel or restaurant), the financial success of the organization is likely to take on particular significance, because the success of the operation is closely related to the personal circumstances of the manager. Hence it is likely that the 'optimizing model' (Robbins, 1996) of decision-making will prevail. However, where an organization is managed by an employee(s) of the owners of the business, the goal of these managers may not be based on the optimization model, but rather the 'satisficing model' (Robbins, 1996) of decision-making. In other words, rather than profit maximization, managers may pursue a performance level that is 'good enough' to satisfy the investors. This may involve balancing the amount of effort required with achieving a result that will satisfy the shareholders. An employed manager might not see a small increase in profit as being worth a substantial increase in effort, since he or she may not personally benefit from this. By contrast, an owner-manager might be prepared to exercise a disproportionate amount of effort to bring about a small increase in profits. Some organizations have tried to encourage managers to use the optimizing model by linking their economic rewards to some measure of organizational performance. For example, if an employed manager is subject to performance-related pay (linked to the performance of the organization) this may alter the basis of his or her decision-making.

Contribution to organizational goals

Whether an operation is stand-alone or part of a wider organization will be likely to influence management practice. This factor will influence the extent to which a unit manager's goals are specific to the operation they are managing, or are subsumed under wider organizational goals. For example, where leisure facilities are incorporated into business hotels, this may be because market research has shown that the availability of these facilities is an important factor in influencing choice of hotel. The projected usage of these facilities might be quite low. Thus if you were to consider the feasibility of operating the leisure facilities in isolation from the broader business, it might appear a poor proposition. However, taking a wider organizational view, such facilities may be an important factor in influencing the occupancy levels and market share of the parent hotel. In these circumstances, the activities of the manager may have to be judged, not solely on the financial performance of the leisure facilities, but also on their contribution to the overall profitability of the hotel.

In a large multi-unit operation, contributions to the overall business also need to be considered. In the case of a chain of luxury hotels, it may be deemed necessary to have a presence in a prestige location, irrespective of the forecasted financial performance in this location. Equally, if a company wishes to project itself as being a global operator then it may need to be represented in a number of key locations, which may differ markedly in their economic/financial potential. Quite frequently in circumstances such as this a 'league table' or 'pecking order' emerges. This is based on the prestige of the individual operating units. The careers of general managers are often based on gradual, progressive movement up the league table. Good performance within one unit often leads to promotion to a higher-ranking unit. Hence career advancement is another driver of management activity, not only on a day-to-day basis, but over a more protracted timescale.

Managerial discretion

The extent to which the product is branded will also influence management practice. Where the product is branded there will be a high degree of product specification (e.g. Hilton Hotels, Pizza Hut, McDonald's) to ensure uniformity of customer experience. Where this is the case then managers will have a much lower level of discretion over the way in which they manage the product or service delivery process, since they will need to meet the brand specification. Control is important here since variability is often expensive and standardization may be associated not only with the brand, but may also yield economies of scale, as for example in low-cost pasta and pizza restaurants chains. By contrast in an establishment that focuses on a high level of customization or personalized service, managers are likely to have considerable discretion in their activities.

More generally, the level of centralization in larger organizations is also likely to be of relevance here, since if the organization is highly centralized, decisions will be made at head office and unit-level managers will have limited discretion available to them. Whereas, in a decentralized organization, managers are likely to have considerable decision-making power delegated to them in order to take account of local circumstances. However, research by Hales and Tamangani (1996), based on hospitality and retail managers, found that the level of centralization did not significantly influence managerial tasks, rather, the industry context was more important in determining the nature of managerial work. They suggest that unit management jobs in large organizations are essentially routine. Research by Goss-Turner (1999), examining the role of multi-unit managers in branded hospitality chains, found that even multi-unit managers were fundamentally implementers of policy, rather than creators of policy. He describes their role as being concerned with 'inspection, checking and control' (Goss-Turner, 1999: 53). He also found larger, more mature companies to be especially control oriented, while in more recently founded companies multi-unit managers had more autonomy.

Front of house/back of house

The immediate purpose of the manager's job may have an influence on the way in which they do their jobs. More specifically, the extent to which a manager's function is concerned with a process directly related to serving customers is likely to affect their approach. For example, a head chef or a front-office manager is managing a process that interacts directly with clients. By contrast, a human resource or purchasing manager is managing an activity which is not directly for clients, but tries to ensure that the organization is equipped and supported to meet its overall aims. Traditionally, in the hospitality industry we have tended to divide staff into 'back of house' or 'front of house'. For example, food-service staff will generally be front of house, whereas staff concerned with food production will tend to be seen as back of house. However, some problems arise here. For example, if a restaurant follows the trend of having a 'show kitchen', do chefs become front of house as a result? Housekeeping is normally viewed as being back of house, but housekeeping staff may have direct contact with guests and some of their work will take place in the public areas of a hotel. Alternatively, managerial work is sometimes divided into 'line' and 'staff' management. Line managers are those who are directly concerned with the production or service delivery process. Staff managers are concerned with performing an advisory or service function.

Another approach, and one which is perhaps more useful for our purposes, is to divide managers according to whether they deal with internal or external customers. In other words, finance or human resource managers essentially deal with internal customers; they provide services for elsewhere within the organization, whereas an executive chef or bars manager is directly concerned with managing provision for external customers. Those who are dealing directly with external customers are likely to have an immediacy about their role. In the kind of service environment within which the hospitality industry operates, the customer is frequently present while the service is performed. Hence, in order to deliver a quality service, there may be a need for flexibility to accommodate the particular set of circumstances, especially if things do not go to plan.

Managers concerned with servicing the needs of internal customers may also be under short-term pressure to provide the type and quality of service that the internal customer wants (especially if the internal customer has the option whether or not to 'buy' the service from the internal provider). However, managers who are away from the immediate concerns of the operation, may have a greater opportunity to examine the longer-term horizon and seek solutions for ongoing problems. Hence, these managers may do more planning (with a long-term focus) and controlling (see earlier discussion). This might, for example, involve planning for the future in terms of mounting a marketing campaign, or developing a new way of motivating staff.

The extent to which managerial activity is divided along these lines is likely to be a function of size. For example, most medium-sized restaurants would not have a separate personnel manager or a marketing manager, rather these would be subsumed into the general manager's role. Alternatively, a group of restaurants might well have people in these roles in order to support the work of the units. Also, in some areas we may see that these roles are increasingly blurred as a result of trends in management thinking. For example, the move towards HRM (instead of personnel management) is exemplified by the involvement of line managers in day-to-day HRM activities (Legge, 1995).

Outsourcing

Also as a result of trends in management, we may find that certain of an organization's activities are actually provided by another organization, which specializes in this kind of activity. Peters and Waterman (1982), in their study of the distinguishing features of the top-performing companies in the USA, identified what they termed 'sticking to the knitting' as one of the eight excellence characteristics. In other words, they argued organizations should do what they know and understand well and outsource their non-core activities to other organizations that specialize in those activities. Hospitality organizations may be involved at both ends of outsourcing – they may choose to outsource certain activities and are likely to have hospitality services outsourced to them by other organizations. An example of the first instance is where a hotel decides to outsource its laundry supply to a specialist company. Examples of the second case include catering firms that are contracted to provide an employee feeding service at a workplace, or school meals on behalf of a local authority. In the case of a contract catering company, the 'customer' is not then the consumer, but the contracting organization (e.g. an employer or a local authority). Such organizations are usually referred to as clients rather than customers.

Managerial activity may then be primarily geared towards fulfilling the contract, or meeting the needs of the client and only indirectly the needs of the actual consumer. Equally, for the hotel manager responsible for the provision of laundry, their job becomes focused on managing the contract, from the initial stages of selecting a contractor who is able to provide the appropriate nature and quality of service at the right price, to monitoring the performance of the contract on a day-to-day basis. Managing contracts involves a different emphasis and different managerial skills from more traditional approaches to management.

Conclusions

Despite similarities in the general concerns that confront managers, their jobs differ widely. The work of managers is varied and fragmented. This chapter has attempted to show how factors such as organizational goals, ownership, structure, size and the degree of customer contact influence the way in which management activity is discharged. Sometimes these factors combine in ways that produce only marginal differences in management practices. At other times they can combine to produce differences of kind rather than degree. The chapter has attempted to show that management practice is very much dependent upon the circumstances in which it occurs.

In a chapter of this length it is not possible to examine all the factors, in all their possible combinations, in all probable circumstances, which influence management practices. Our approach has, of necessity, been selective. There are drivers of managerial practice and activity which, while important, we have not been able to examine. However, as was pointed out in Chapter 1, the comparative approach is concerned with the discovery of similarities and differences among phenomena. We have attempted to provide a useful starting point for such an approach in the study of management practices. Clearly, this chapter is illustrative rather than comprehensive. We hope that readers are sufficiently enthused to continue with their journey of comparison. The remainder of the chapter provides some prompts for those who wish to do so.

At the beginning of this chapter the question 'what is it that makes some organizations appear to be well managed whilst others are less so?' was posed. In Chapter 1 an outline was given as to how one researcher (Nebel, 1991) had attempted to address a similar question from a practical standpoint. Now would seem an appropriate time to refresh your knowledge and understanding of this study before you proceed further in your own quest for enlightenment. You should then be in a better position to attempt an answer to this fundamental question. Without wishing to 'steer' you too much towards an answer, perhaps an examination of the relationship between the management practice and the setting in which it takes place would be worth while.

Summary

1 Management and its practice is a universal, but its manifestation is not.

2 Management per se involves certain core or generic activities, the relative importance of which might differ according to the level at which management is practised.

3 The organizational position occupied by a manager will have an influence on the specific focus and type of activities he or she has as a priority.

4 Management is an interpretative activity, which means that individual managers tend to impose their own preferences and personalities on management practice.

5 The nature of the organizational and competitive context within which management is practised will also influence how it is practised.

6 The visibility or invisibility, to the customer, of the management function has an impact on its practice.

Review questions

1 What sort of effects do managers have on our lives?

2 How do the job responsibilities of operative workers differ from those of managers?

3 Outline your reaction to the view that since there is no such thing as a typical organization or a management job it is pointless attempting to analyse them.

4 In what ways, if any, is a comparative approach to management of practical value to managers themselves?

5 As organizations downsize, the numbers and ranks of middle managers are reduced. How might this change impact upon the responsibilities of both senior and first line managers?

6 Is management in a large, profit-driven organization likely to be more similar to management within a within a large, not-for-profit organization or a small, profit driven organization?

7 How do customers influence hospitality management?

8 Make a more detailed comparison than that presented in Table 6.2, of the three levels of management presented in this chapter in terms of the activities involved in each level, their time horizons and the skills required for successful performance.

9 If you wanted to compare the roles and work undertaken of hotel general managers operating in UK and French hotels what additional issues would be involved?

10 What issues would you need to consider to make a valid comparison of the type of unit management practice found in a fast-food establishment with that in a retail supermarket?

Bibliography

Bedeian, A. G. (1986). *Management*. Dryden Press.

Brech, E. F. L. (1975). *The Principles and Practice of Management*. Longman.

Daft, R. L. (1995). *Understanding Management*. Harcourt Brace.

Deverell, C. S. (1985). *Business Administration and Management*. Van Nostrand Reinhold.

Drucker, P. F. (1954). *The Practice of Management*. Harper and Row.

Drucker, P. F. (1974). *Management Tasks, Responsibilities and Practices*. Harper Row.

Fayol, H (1916). *General and Industrial Management*. Trans. C. Storrs. Pitman.

Goss-Turner, S. (1999). The role of the multi-unit manager in branded hospitality chains. *Human Resource Management Journal*, **9** (4), 39–57.

Hales, C. and Tamangani, Z. (1996). An investigation of the relationship between organizational structure, managerial role expectations and managers' activities. *Journal of Management Studies*, **33** (6), 731–756.

Heller, R. (1990). *The Making of Managers*. Penguin.

Hotel and Catering International Management Association (HCIMA) (1988). *Corpus of Management Excellence*. HCIMA.

Johnson, P. (1977). *The Corpus of Professional Knowledge in Hotel, Catering and Institutional Services*. HCIMA.

Juran, J. M. (1964). *Managerial Breakthrough*. McGraw-Hill.

Legge, K. (1995). *Human Resource Management: Rhetorics and Reality*. Macmillan Business.

Love, J. F. (1987). *McDonald's: Behind the Arches*. Bantam Press

Luc, V. (1999). *Never Take No for an Answer*. Albin Michel

Martin, S. (1983). *Managing without Managers*. Sage.

Morris, M. J. (1988). *The First Time Manager*. Kogan Page.

Mullins, L. and Aldrich, P. (1988). An integrated model of management and managerial development. *Journal of Management Development*, **7** (3), 29–39.

Nebel, E. C. (1991). *Managing Hotels Effectively: Lessons from Outstanding General Managers*. Van Nostrand Reinhold.

Peters, T. and Waterman, R. (1982). *In Search of Excellence*. Harper and Row.

Robbins, S. P. (1996). *Organizational Behaviour*, 7th edn. Prentice-Hall.

Stewart, R. (1982). *Choices for the Manager*. McGraw-Hill.

Stewart, R. (1985). *The Reality of Management*. Pan Books.

Stoner, J. A. F., Freeman, R. E. and Gilbert, D. R. (1995). *Management*. Prentice Hall International.

Watson, T. J. (1994). *In Search of Management*. Routledge.

Wren, D. A. (1979). *The Evolution of Management Thought*. John Wiley.

Further reading

Drucker, P. F. (1999). *Management Challenges for the 21st Century*. Butterworth-Heinemann.

Knights, D. (1999). *Management Lives*. Sage.

Paton, R. et al. (eds) (1996). *The New Management Reader*. Routledge.

Preece, D. (1999). *Work, Change and Competition*. Routledge.

Watson, T. and Harris, P. (1999). *The Emergent Manager*. Sage.

Legal aspects of hospitality provision

Mike Boella

Objectives

This chapter sets out to look at how the law affects different sectors of the hospitality industry. The law referred to is the law of England and Wales and will be referred to as English law. The law of Scotland is not included because it varies in some important respects from English law. Some French law is included to provide a basis for comparison. When you have read this chapter you should be able to:

1 Explain the main rights and obligations that distinguish 'inns' from other types of business offering accommodation, food and drink.

2 Identify the different types of business which operate as a result of the regulation of the sale of alcoholic (intoxicating) beverages.

3 Identify the obligations created by legislation covering business activities such as gaming, performance of music.

4 State the obligations placed on all who offer food for human consumption.

5 Recognize that the law can vary considerably from one country to another. In this last case French hospitality law is used but it must be emphasized that French law is used as a way to illustrate the similarities and differences between different legal jurisdictions.

Introduction

At the outset it has to be emphasized that the law in general, applies equally to all hospitality businesses. The law of employment, for example, does not distinguish between employers in one industrial sector or another, although in the past it did by legislating different minimum rates of pay for different sectors and even for men and women. As a result several sectors, such as the contract catering sector, are not picked out specifically because the law does not distinguish this sector from businesses generally nor from most other hospitality businesses. In other cases however the law does vary. For historical reasons hotels or 'inns' occupy a special place in law which contrasts them with many other businesses. Licensing law, too, creates very specific conditions for different types of hospitality business.

The purpose of this chapter, in line with the overall objective of this book, is not to give a general description of law applying to the hospitality industry but to identify where the law varies between sectors. So, differences between 'inns', hotels and other hospitality businesses will be explored, as will the differences between licensing law of different sectors. Where there are specific requirements that distinguish some hospitality businesses from businesses generally, such as food safety laws, these will be referred to where appropriate.

Inns and other businesses offering accommodation, food and drink

The law covering innkeepers and others concerned with travellers has a long history which can be traced back to *Justinian's Institutes*, published in 533 BC (Atherton and Atherton, 1998). The law of England and Wales, and many other countries whose law is based on English common law such as the USA and Australia, draws a distinction between 'inns' and other establishments. In English law the term 'inn' is used to describe those hotels which fall within the scope of the Hotel Proprietors Act 1956.

The word 'inn', therefore, has a specific legal meaning and only those establishments that fall within the definition of an inn have the rights and obligations of inns. Those establishments that fall outside the scope of the definition are not subject to the duties imposed upon inns nor do they have the right of *lien* to which innkeepers are entitled.

Inns

The Hotel Proprietors Act 1956 (section 1.1) (HPA) states that only hotels within the meaning of the Act shall be deemed to be inns and that the rights and duties of an innkeeper shall apply only to such establishments. The definition of a hotel under the Act is to be found in section 1(3):

> In this Act the expression 'hotel' means an establishment held out by the proprietor as offering food, drink and, if so required, sleeping accommodation, without special contract, to any traveller presenting himself who appears able and willing to pay a reasonable sum for the services and facilities and who is in a fit state to be received.

This contrasts with most other businesses including hospitality businesses in which the owners have a right to refuse customers. A licensee of a bar, the manager of a leisure centre or public house has the right to refuse to serve anyone so long as the refusal does not fall within the scope of discrimination law (see Case 7.1).

Case 7.1

Discrimination

A West Indian cricketer was refused accommodation at the Imperial Hotel, London, on the basis that he was black. The Imperial had vacant rooms but directed the cricketer to another hotel owned by the same company. The cricketer brought an action against the Imperial Hotel. The Imperial argued that they had discharged their duty by offering alternative accommodation.

It was held that an innkeeper owes separate duties to travellers at each inn. A duty that was not discharged at one inn could not be discharged at another.

Source: Constantine v Imperial Hotels Ltd, 1944, 2 All ER 171.

It is not easy to define in a strict way what a hotel is within the meaning of section 1(3) HPA 1956. Obviously larger establishments, such as major hotels are clearly within the definition, as are many modest hotels, but where is the borderline to be drawn in legal terms? The hotel must be 'held out' as ready and willing to take travellers 'without special contract'. That is to say, innkeepers will not pick and choose between travellers to whom they will offer their services, provided such travellers are fit to be received and willing to pay a reasonable sum for the services rendered.

Any establishment that advertises it restricts its clientele is not within the definition, e.g. 'no children', 'no coaches'. Of course, hoteliers are able to restrict their clientele in certain ways, e.g. by having a rule that all men using the restaurant of a hotel must wear a jacket and tie. Such a restriction may be justifiable on the ground that those men not wearing a jacket and tie are not 'in a fit state to be received'. Hoteliers must not, of course, restrict their clientele on the basis of either sex, race or disability which, if racial discrimination law had been in place in 1944 would have applied to the case of *Constantine v Imperial Hotels Ltd* (Case 7.1).

It must not be assumed that if the words 'inn' or 'hotel' appear in the title of the establishment it is an inn under section 1(3) HPA 1956. Many establishments use the world 'hotel' for various reasons, one being that in earlier days it may have been a hotel but has since stopped offering accommodation. The safest course of action is to define an inn by stating what it is not! An inn is *not*:

1 Any establishment which offers food and drink but not accommodation, e.g. a public house or restaurant.

2 Any establishment which offers both food and drink and accommodation, but requires that accommodation be booked in advance, e.g. halls of residence, lodging houses.

3 Any establishment where the proprietor makes it known that it reserves the right to pick and choose between those who wish to use the accommodation available.

4 Membership clubs or such institutions where accommodation is available only to club members and their guests.

5 Youth hostels and similar organizations where membership of an organization is required of those seeking accommodation.

6 Establishments that take only long-term guests by prior arrangements, e.g. rest homes.

All these establishments are not bound by the duties, nor do they have the rights of 'innkeepers'. Some of these will be examined in more detail later.

In France, hotels are similarly obliged to accept customers but this arises from a very different legal principle. Article 30 of the *Ordonnance du 1er decembre 1986* 'forbids to refuse the sale of a product or service to a consumer, except for legitimate reason'. This forbids all businesses, once they have decided to offer goods or services for sale, to refuse a sale, except for a legitimate reason. The problem for the French is to determine what is a 'legitimate reason'. Two such reasons follow. The hotel is obliged to refuse entry to prostitutes and unaccompanied minors, and to people in an intoxicated state and those affected by the use of drugs.

Apart from this law the *Confederation Française des hoteliers, restaurateurs, cafetiers and discotheques,* in their article 2, state that the 'hotelier has the right to refuse entry to a client not dressed in a manner which corresponds to that of those habitually received'. This right to receive or not to receive customers however is limited by the *Ordonnance du 1er decembre 1986* and also by the law of 11 July 1975 that prevents all discrimination. Discrimination is defined as 'refusing to provide a good or service because of the origin, gender, lifestyle (*moeurs*), family situation, ethnicity, race, religion or nationality of the customer'. In English law discrimination is more narrowly defined and does not include lifestyle reasons or nationality, although it does include disability both from the customer's and the employee's viewpoint.

Duties of the innkeeper

The proprietor of a hotel within the HPA 1956 can be defined as an innkeeper, i.e. the proprietor of an inn. The innkeeper does not have to be an individual; in many cases the innkeeper will be a company. This is so even if the licence for the sale of intoxicating liquor is in the name of the manager. So, to whom does an innkeeper owe the duties? Section 1(3) HPA 1956 uses the words 'any traveller'; it is important to understand the meaning of the terms 'traveller' and 'guest' (see Case 7.2).

Case 7.2

What determines who is a traveller?

A farmer on his way home ... drove to an inn having passed his own home. The question arose of whether or not the farmer was a traveller and thus owed the duties afforded to travellers.

It was held that if a person came to an inn he or she should be afforded the protection given to travellers ... even if the person was a local resident and did not intend to use sleeping accommodation.

Source: Williams v Linnitt,
1951, All ER 278.

As Case 7.2 illustrates we can see that a traveller is not necessarily a guest. The term 'guest' is used to describe a traveller who has engaged sleeping accommodation at the inn. Hence a traveller becomes a guest upon taking one night's sleeping accommodation and any rights he or she has extend for twenty-four hours before a night's booking and for twenty-four hours afterwards. This provides a hotel guest with more rights than most other businesses' customers. The term 'traveller' is given a very broad definition: it includes any person en route from one place to another who calls at the inn to make use of the services available, i.e. food, drink and accommodation. Whether a person is a traveller is primarily a question of fact.

The duty to provide refreshment

The duty to provide refreshment for a traveller is outside the scope of the 1956 Act; it is a duty imposed upon innkeepers by common law (see Case 7.2). The duty of the innkeeper is to provide the traveller with reasonable refreshment at any hour of the day or night. However, innkeepers may refuse to provide food and drink if their excuse for doing so is reasonable. Failure to do so may, if it is without reasonable excuse, render the innkeeper liable to criminal prosecution.

The duty to provide accommodation

An innkeeper is under a duty to provide accommodation at the inn without prior contract to any traveller who seeks accommodation. See Cases 7.1 and 7.3.

Case 7.3

Who can be excluded from a hotel?

Rothfield a moneylender, who was otherwise of good character, sought business from other guests staying at the hotel and caused much disquiet and annoyance to the other guests ... Rothfield was asked to leave.

The court held that the innkeeper was fully justified in having Rothfield removed from the hotel.

Source: *Rothfield* v *North British Hotels*, 1920, SC 805.

The duty to receive guests therefore is not absolute and is qualified to the extent that the traveller must be in a fit state to be received (see Cases 7.3 and 7.4) and able to pay a reasonable sum. Payment may be required in advance of the use of the accommodation.

Case 7.4

If the inn is full is the innkeeper under a duty to provide the traveller with some form of shelter?

A traveller called at an inn after his vehicle broke down ... he was refused accommodation because all the rooms were occupied. The traveller asked if he could sleep in a public room. The innkeeper refused.

It was held that the innkeeper did not have to provide accommodation in a public room.

Source: *Browne* v *Brandt*, 1902, 1 KB 696.

Case 7.4 illustrates a situation that could be of importance where an innkeeper has to deal with stranded people, e.g. after the Aintree racecourse bomb scare. Once the hotel is full there is no further obligation to receive guests (travellers).

The innkeeper's right to refuse service

As shown above the innkeeper has a right to refuse service to the traveller in certain circumstances. These circumstances come from common law and section 1(3) HPA, 1956 which defines the meaning of the term 'inn', and thereby sets the parameters of the duty owed to travellers. Section 1(3) HPA 1956 requires that the traveller 'appears able and willing to pay a reasonable sum for the services and facilities provided' and furthermore that the traveller 'is in a fit state to be received'. These restrictions amount to a right on the part of the innkeeper to refuse service to certain travellers. This right allows the innkeeper a certain amount of latitude to pick and choose between those requiring service, and so enables the innkeeper to regulate his or her premises.

At this point it is important to keep in mind a fundamental principle in English civil law, namely freedom of contract. This is the right of any person to contract (or refuse to contract) with any other person, the terms of the agreement being negotiated between the parties. It can be argued that the innkeeper's duties towards travellers operate as an exception to freedom of contract. This point arises from the fact that, since innkeepers are under a duty to contract with travellers who seek refreshment or accommodation, they do not have freedom of contract, since they cannot refuse the traveller service.

The innkeeper's freedom of contract is limited in other ways too. The Race Relations Act 1976, the Sex Discrimination Act 1975 and the Disability Discrimination Act 1995 provide a right of action for persons who have been refused service on racial, gender or disability grounds. This restraint applies to inns and other establishments alike.

The innkeeper's duty towards the property of guests

Historically innkeepers were responsible under common law for the property of their guests. This was because it was thought that they were often in league with thieves who preyed on travellers (see Case 7.5).

Case 7.5

If a guest leaves property in the bedroom and the property is stolen is the innkeeper liable?

Mr and Mrs Carpenter checked in at an inn, went down for dinner leaving jewellery in their locked room. They did not ask to leave it with the reception for safe-keeping. Was the inn liable for the loss? The hotel argued that they owed no duty to Mrs Carpenter and that Mrs Carpenter had been negligent in leaving the jewellery in the room.

The court held that Mrs Carpenter had taken reasonable care of the jewellery, accordingly the innkeeper was liable.

Source: Carpenter v *Haymarket Hotel Ltd*, 1931, 1 KB 363 (QBD).

In many countries, including the UK, innkeepers have a strict duty to care for the property of their guests. This duty, it should be noted, is not owed to all visitors to a hotel, only to guests.

A guest is a person who has engaged a minimum of one night's accommodation. The innkeeper is an insurer of the property of guests that is lost or stolen within the *hospitium* of the inn. Hospitium covers more than the inn itself; it incorporates the precincts of the inn and those parts of the premises closely related with the operation of the inn, e.g. car parks, garages, leisure club. The test as to whether a particular area comes within the hospitium of the inn appears to be: 'Is the area in question intended and suitable for use in connection with the innkeeper's business?'

If, for instance, the innkeeper places guests' property or invites guests to leave their property by the entrance to the inn, e.g. while waiting for a taxi, the innkeeper will still be liable for the property since, although the property is outside the inn itself, it is still within the hospitium of the inn (*Watson* v. *People's Refreshment Association Ltd*, 1952, 1 KB 318).

In English law the innkeeper's liability for guests' property is strict, with some exceptions such as the guest's own misconduct or negligence (see Case 7.6). The innkeeper's duty is to keep the goods safe; this liability is not dependent on how the goods are lost or damaged, except where loss or damage is due to the fault of the guest.

Case 7.6

How can we define negligence on the part of the guest?

Ms Shacklock left her jewellery and about £600 in her bedroom locked in a suitcase. However she left her bedroom door open. The property was stolen.

It was held that because the hotel required guests to leave their rooms open for the room-maids to service the rooms the guest had not been negligent.

Source: Shacklock v Ethorpe Ltd
[1939] 3 All ER 372 (HL)

This strict liability for the loss of, or damage caused to, guests' property attaches only to *innkeepers*. In other cases of lost property customers would have to establish negligence on the part of the owners of the business in order to recover compensation.

Under the Hotel Proprietor's Act a hotel can limit its liability to £50 per item or £100 per guest by displaying a statutory notice in the reception area of the hotel, i.e. where the contract is entered into. In the USA the equivalent notice must be posted conspicuously. In many other countries the value of the limitation or liability is a multiple of the daily tariff. In France, for example, the multiple is 100 times the daily room rate, which is far in excess of the UK sum. In contrast other businesses such as restaurants, bars and guesthouses do not have a similar liability. In these cases the customer suffering damage or loss would have to prove in a civil court that the owner of the business had been negligent.

The rights of an innkeeper

Because an innkeeper is subject to certain duties to which other businesses are not, the innkeeper has certain rights which other businesses, including hotels not falling within the definition of an inn, do not possess. The most important right is the right of *lien*.

Where a guest or traveller refuses to pay, or cannot pay the hotel bill he or she may be guilty of a crime under section 3 of the Theft Act 1978. In addition the innkeeper has a right of lien over any property, other than that excluded by section 2(2) HPA 1956, i.e. the guest's vehicle or property left in the vehicle. The innkeeper is not, however, entitled to detain the guest (risk of an action for false imprisonment). The lien extends not only to the property of the guests; it also includes any property that they bring with them to the inn as their luggage, including property that may not belong to them. The innkeeper has the right, after a certain period of time, to sell the property, to settle any unpaid account, to deduct any associated expenses such as storage and cost of advertising. Any balance must then be paid to the guest.

In France, in similar vein, the Penal Code has created the criminal offence of fraud of food and accommodation. Two conditions are necessary. First, the customer must be unable (absolutely) to pay or he or she refuses to pay, and he or she should have ordered the food or reserved a room. No crime has been committed if the hotel has not presented the bill within ten days of the guest's arrival or if the hotel has continued to provide lodging despite the non-payment.

If a customer leaves the hotel without paying, the hotel has the legal right to retain the guest's property (article 2102 Code Civil). Property includes vehicles, which are excluded under English law. The hotel must make a request to the *Tribunal d'Instance* for an order to sell the goods by auction. The customer, should he be identifiable, should be given eight days' notice and can oppose the sale or settle his or her debt with the hotel. Any money realized from the auction will go to settling first the costs of the process and then the hotel. The hotel has to take care because if the costs are greater than any sum realized the hotel has to pay the expenses of the process. In England the only requirement is that the hotel advertises the intention to sell. It does not need a court authorization.

The guest's occupation of accommodation

An innkeeper may enter the room let to the guest at any time. The innkeeper retains control over the guests' rooms during their stay, and may bring their stay to an end, subject to the actual terms of the contract entered into. This contrasts with some other forms of contracts for accommodation such as leases which may grant the occupier an exclusive right to occupy the premises, in which cases eviction orders would be necessary, should the occupier refuse to leave.

Duties owed by all hospitality businesses including inns

As we have seen above, the rights and duties of an 'innkeeper' form a special category. No special obligations or rights attach to proprietors of establishments other than inns. They are instead covered by the same laws, which generally are common to all businesses. In effect this means that a business wishing to recover moneys owed would have to start proceedings through the civil courts. All hospitality businesses have certain duties imposed upon them by law. These include:

1 The duties imposed upon the occupier of premises towards visitors (e.g. guests, travellers, contractors, even trespassers!) to the premises, under the Occupiers' Liability Acts 1957 and 1984, and statutes such as the Health and Safety at Work Act 1974. It has to be emphasized that under this general heading are many different and specific regulations, too numerous to discuss here, but they can include regulations covering swimming pools, sun beds, solaria.

2 A civil duty to take reasonable care of guests' property brought to the premises under the tort of negligence, or as an implied term of the contract of booking.

3 The duty not to discriminate in the provision of services to the public, on the basis of a person's race or sex (section 20 Race Relations Act 1974; section 29 Sex Discrimination Act 1975; Disability Discrimination Act 1995).

4 Duties imposed by the Food Safety Act 1990, Weights and Measures Act 1985.

The rights of innkeepers and the proprietors of other hospitality businesses

The rights common to both innkeepers and the proprietors of other hospitality businesses are the right to control the premises and refuse service so as to maintain good order and decency. However, innkeepers have the following sole rights:

1 The right to demand payment in advance of service. This can be deemed to be evidence that the guest is 'willing and able to pay', as provided for in the Hotel Proprietors Act 1956. Other businesses may also ask for prepayment, but as a common law condition of the contract, not arising out of statute.

2 The innkeeper's lien over guest's property. Other businesses do not have a similar right excepting for businesses such as garages or repair shops in which cases they can ask for payment for work done or services rendered before releasing the property.

In addition, the innkeeper's sole duties are:

1 The duty to provide a traveller with refreshment and, if so required, accommodation.

2 The strict duty of responsibility for the property of guests at the inn.

The rights of the owners of businesses other than inns include:

1 The right to pick and choose between persons requesting service.

2 The right to refuse service (subject to statutory restraints as to race, disability and sex discrimination) to any person at the will of the proprietor.

Yield management is common practice, and has been, for many years. It takes many different forms in the hospitality industry. Refusing single customers a table in a restaurant is one example. Taking the table d'hôte menu off at a certain time, and happy hours are both examples of 'yield management'. In hotels it is a common practice to overbook the rooms available at the hotel expecting that some bookings will be cancelled. If a hotel overbooks accommodation and confirms to a guest that a room has been reserved for him or her, and on the date in question the hotel is full and the guest is provided with either no accommodation at all or substitute accommodation which does not have the facilities described, an offence has been committed under section 14(1) Trade Descriptions Act 1968. This applies to all businesses including hotels, restaurants, conference centres and the like.

Pricing

All hospitality businesses, excepting registered clubs, are covered by Part III of the Consumer Protection Act 1987 which creates a general criminal offence of giving a misleading price indication.

Additional charges are discouraged; the recommendation under the Act's code of practice being that if customers are to pay non-optional extra charges (e.g. a service charge) these should be incorporated within fully inclusive prices, where possible. This fact, along with any other charges such as cover charge or a minimum charge should be clearly displayed on menus, both inside and outside. Optional additional sums also are not to be suggested (e.g. service not included) in the menu or on the bill presented to customers. Registered (or members') clubs are not covered by this order because it is deemed that sales do not take place in a club. Members are exchanging assets, i.e. their own stock for their own money.

In the whole of the UK there is no statutory price control applied to hotel accommodation pricing. As a result of yield management practices hotel prices can vary by the season, time of week, and even by the time of day. However, the display of hotel accommodation prices is regulated specifically by the Tourism (Sleeping Accommodation Price Display) Order 1977. This order requires the display of overnight accommodation prices in residential establishments with four or more rooms. The display must include the following:

1 The prices must be clearly displayed by means of a notice at reception or in the hotel entrance.

2 Both maximum and minimum prices should be displayed.

Enforcement is by the local authority trading standards office. A fine may be imposed upon conviction for breach of the order.

In France, according to the *Ordonnance du 1er decembre 1986*, prices are not subject to control either. Hotels can therefore fix their prices as they wish, except that they are still subject to strict law concerning the advertising and the display of prices. For example, The *decret de 13 juin 1966*, requires a triple display of hotel room prices as follows:

1 Outside the hotel, maximum and minimum prices for the different categories of room, at reception a notice indicating the hotel category and room prices for one and two persons, with 'prix nets' or 'taxes et services compris', the number of rooms and accompanying bathroom/shower etc arrangements, as well as their prices.

2 In each room, a notice measuring 12 × 8 centimetres, must be attached to each entrance door with the same information as that displayed at the reception desk.

This has consequences for yield management practices because, while it is legal to offer rooms at lower than the displayed prices, it is not legal to offer them at higher than the displayed prices.

Under the Price Marking (Food and Drink on Premises) Order 1979, prices of both food and drink must be displayed in a clear and legible way in restaurants, cafés, bars, self-service cafeterias, etc. In the case of restaurants a menu must be displayed at the entrance so that it can be read from the street. In the case of bars it must be displayed so that it is visible to customers before they make a purchase at the bar. Where a restaurant is inside a building such as a hotel or public house the menu must be displayed at the entrance to the restaurant area. The main exceptions to this are:

1 Where the supply is only to members of a bona fide club or their guests.

2 At staff restaurants, works canteens and similar establishments.

3 At guesthouses or hotels where the supply is only to people staying there.

4 Any food which is not normally available but specially prepared at the request of the customers or food which is provided at a price agreed in advance is excluded from the Order.

In the case of self-service premises the price list must be at the place where the customer chooses his or her food and also at the entrance if the price list cannot be seen there.

Hotel guest registration

For the vast majority of businesses in the UK there is no need to keep a record of customers. However, hotels fall into a special category in that the Immigration (Hotel Records) Order 1972, requires all guests over the age of sixteen to register their full name and nationality, or have it registered for them. The hotel is required to keep a record of such information that is open to inspection by the police for a period of up to twelve months. British subjects and Commonwealth citizens need not give their address. Each guest must be entered separately in the register. 'Aliens', those who are neither British nor Commonwealth citizens, must give their passport details as well as their name and nationality. In addition they must state the date on which they intend to leave the hotel and their intended destination.

Because hotels have rights and duties towards their guests, i.e. those who have taken accommodation within a twenty-four hour period, registration is a valuable proof of such status. People staying in a guest's room, without registering, may not be deemed to be a guest. In fact they may be deemed to be a trespasser.

In France the *decret du 20 mai 1975* cancelled the need for the 'police register' of French travellers. However, there is still the need to register foreign guests. The exact requirement is specified in the Official Journal of 6 June 1976: hotel address, room number, the identity of the guest, the nationality, number of children under fifteen years of age, date of entry into France and probable date of leaving together with the guest's signature. These registration slips have to be delivered to the police.

Many other countries have similar registration requirements and in some cases, Switzerland for example, registration records may be collected and entered daily on to police computers as one way of controlling criminal activities.

Hotel classification

Hotel classification in the whole of the UK is a totally voluntary procedure – hotels can opt to be 'classified' by a number of different organizations including the National Tourist Boards, the Automobile Association or the Royal Automobile Club. There is no direct national or local government involvement. The only legal issue is that of trade description and possible misrepresentation by making false or misleading claims regarding classification.

In France hotel classification is made compulsory by the *decret du 13 juin 1966* and regulated by the *decret du 14 fevrier 1986*, amended by the *arreté du 27 avril 1988*. The classification system describes the different levels of services demanded by each classification. The object of such classification is to allow the consumer to have a certain guarantee of the level of comfort of the hotel.

Sale of intoxicating liquor

In the UK the sale of intoxicating liquor (or alcoholic beverages) is regulated principally by the Licensing Act 1964, as subsequently amended by a number of other Acts. This Act is currently under review and there are likely to be significant changes to English licensing laws in the near future. The licensing law reflects the needs of different sectors within the hospitality industry, with different licences for different sectors. In essence the different licences and sectors are as follows:

1 Public houses: full justices' on-licence.

2 Off-licences: justices' licences either for the sale of all intoxicating liquor or licences restricted to the sale of beer, cider and wine only.

3 Restaurants, cafés, etc.: justices' licence restricting sale of intoxicating liquor to those taking a bona fide meal

4 Residential: justices' licence restricting sale to residents and their guests (who are not to buy drinks themselves).

5 Proprietary clubs: one of the above justices' licences.

6 Members clubs: a registration certificate.

Apart from these, the main simple types of licence, some can also be found in various combinations such as restaurant and residential. In addition there are several variations on such licences which may add restrictive conditions (imposed by the local magistrates) or which may extend permitted hours. Other licences will permit public entertainment, music and dancing.

It is a criminal offence contrary to the Licensing Act 1964 to sell or expose for sale any intoxicating liquor without a justices' licence. However, and interestingly, not all businesses need justices' licences. The exceptions are:

1 The sale of liquor in a theatre.

2 The supply of liquor to a member of a registered club.

3 The sale of liquor on board a ship or aircraft which is en route, or its sale on a train to passengers who may, if they wish, be supplied with food.

4 Sale of liquor to service personnel in naval or military canteens.

The law and practice of liquor licensing in the UK is currently controlled by local licensing justices, i.e. magistrates, but this is under review and likely to be subject to quite significant change. The various types of justices' licence are as follows.

Full on-licence

A full on-licence enables the licensee to sell all intoxicating liquors including beers, cider, wines, fortified wines and spirits, for consumption either on or off the premises to any member of the public who is permitted by the law to consume it. This is the broadest form of justices' licence, and is the form of licence that applies to public houses and to many hotels. The justices have a complete discretion whether or not to grant a full on-licence that distinguishes it from other licences such as the restaurant licence over which magistrates have less discretion.

Off-licence

An off-licence permits the sale of liquor for consumption off the premises. These are held by what are commonly referred to as 'off-licences' and by supermarkets selling alcoholic beverages.

Restaurants

There are two kinds of licence that a restaurant may apply for in order to serve drinks with meals:

1 An ordinary justices' licence with a condition that a drink may be served only with a meal.

2 A restaurant licence.

The more common application is for a restaurant licence, because the licensing justices have very limited powers to refuse the granting of such a licence. Also there are likely to be fewer objections from local licensees to the grant of a restaurant licence.

A restaurant, for the purposes of the grant of a restaurant licence, is 'premises structurally adapted and bona fide used, or intended to be used, for the purpose of providing the customary main meal at midday or in the evening, or both, for the accommodation of persons frequenting the premises'. The justices, when granting a restaurant licence, may attach certain conditions. However, they must attach the following two conditions:

1 The restaurant must be able to serve both water and soft drinks as well as alcohol.

2 Alcohol can be served only to those taking table meals.

Hotels

A residential licence authorizes the sale of liquor to residents of a hotel, i.e. premises which are 'bona fide' used, or intended to be used, for the purpose of habitually providing for reward board and lodging, including breakfast and one other meal at least of the customary main meals'. This definition includes both 'inns' as defined by the Hotel Proprietors Act 1956 (section 1.3) and also private hotels, i.e. those not included by the HPA definition.

The justices must be satisfied that the premises are suitable for use as a licensed hotel. Two conditions are attached to the grant of a residential licence: other beverages (including water) must be available with meals; and adequate seating must be provided in a room at the hotel which is not used as sleeping accommodation or for the service of food, and in which there is neither supply nor consumption of intoxicating liquor.

These licenses are largely mirrored in French law, although a hotel, which does not sell alcoholic beverages (e.g. a bed and breakfast hotel), does need a category one licence. This allows the service of breakfast and non-alcoholic beverages. In the UK such a hotel would not need a licence. The only statutory requirement would be that, as a food premises, it would have to register with the local authority (Food Premises [Registration] Regulations 1991).

However, in France, if the hotel has a restaurant it has to have a *licence de restaurant*, i.e. a licence allowing the sale of either the first two categories of intoxicating beverages (fermented, i.e. beers and wine) or a full licence (allowing the sale of all intoxicating beverages including distilled spirits). If the hotel has a bar it will need a licence of the second category (fermented drinks; beers and wines) or of the third category (fortified wines and liqueurs) or of the fourth category (includes distilled spirits), dependent upon what the owner wants to offer his or her customers.

Thus, we see that in France a distinction is made between fermented drinks (beers and wines) and distilled drinks (i.e. spirits). In the UK the distinction is similar excepting that licences can be for the sale of beer only (rare), or for wine and beer only (e.g. wine bars, fairly common) or for a full licence.

Combined licences

It is possible to combine a residential licence with a restaurant licence. This enables liquor to be sold to residents and to members of the general public who are dining in the restaurant of a hotel. This form of licence is most useful to small and medium-sized hotels which have a restaurant which is open to the public, but to which other licencees might object to a full on licence or to which licensing magistrates might refuse the grant of a 'full' on-licence.

Occasional licences

An occasional licence is granted to a person who already holds an on-licence for one set of premises and who wishes to sell liquor at some event which is to be held at premises that are normally unlicensed. This includes parties and balls, fetes, wedding breakfasts and twenty-first birthday parties. Such a licence can be a valuable asset to those licensees wishing to do business off their own premises.

Charitable organizations and occasional permissions

The Licensing (Occasional Permissions) Act 1983 empowers licensing justices in England and Wales to grant to representatives of organizations not carried on for private gain occasional permissions authorizing the sale of intoxicating liquor at functions connected with the activities of such organizations.

Clubs: proprietary and members'

For the purposes of the licensing laws there are two kinds of clubs: proprietory or licensed clubs and members' or registered clubs. A licensed club, unlike a registered club, is a business set up to make a profit. In order to sell drink legally, such clubs must have a justices' licence. In most respects such clubs are subject to the same laws as those applying to premises with a full on-licence.

A registered club, on the other hand, is owned by its members. Examples include many different sports clubs and can also include organizations such as student union bars. The main aim of such clubs is not to make a profit but is one where the profits go to the members and where club property is owned in equal shares by the members. Technically when members pay for any goods such as drinks at the bar, this constitutes a 'transfer of assets' not a 'sale' because the goods are already the property of the members. In order to offer liquor to members the club must have a registration certificate, which is obtainable from an ordinary session of the magistrates' court.

In order to be a registered club, a club must have a registration certificate, which will be granted only if the club complies with certain requirements:

1 The club must be established and conducted in good faith as a club.

2 There must be at least twenty-five members.

3 At least two days must elapse between a new member applying for membership and his or her using the club as a member.

4 No one must gain any financial benefit from the supply of alcohol by the club.

5 The purchase and supply of drink must be supervised by the club's committee, or by a sub-committee whose members serve between one and five years.

6 Alcohol can be supplied only on behalf of the club.

The rules regarding children in registered clubs are less strict than for normal licensed premises, i.e. children are allowed in the areas where the service and consumption of alcohol takes place. Likewise in clubs it is permitted to practice sex discrimination. Many members' clubs restrict membership to one sex or the other. In many clubs also some areas of the club premises are 'out of bounds' to members of the opposite sex (usually women). This situation is currently under review and we may see a change to the law in the future.

Permitted hours

For most businesses the opening hours are a matter of the owner's own wishes and the local authority which may choose to restrict opening hours of some types of business. In the case of the sale and consumption of alcohol the hours during which intoxicating drinks can be sold are regulated by the Licensing Acts 1964 and as subsequently amended. The hours vary dependent upon the type of business and often its location. Public houses, for example, are normally restricted to selling intoxicating liquor between 1100 and 2300 hours with an additional twenty minutes for 'drinking up'. Hotels can sell liquor to residents for twenty-four hours a day, should they choose. There is no obligation on licensed premises to open their doors or to sell during the permitted hours. It is a criminal offence under section 59 Licensing Act 1964 for any person to sell or supply intoxicating liquor except during permitted hours. A customer who consumes liquor outside permitted hours is also committing a separate, though related, offence.

Public houses and bars

The permitted hours for licensed premises on weekdays other than Christmas Day or Good Friday are from 1100 hours to 2300 hours. On Sundays, (other than when Christmas Day falls on a Sunday) and Good Friday, the permitted hours are 1200 hours to 2230 hours. On Christmas Day, the permitted hours are 1200 hours to 1500, and 1900 to 2230 hours.

Licensing justices have the power to vary the weekday hours for their area by fixing an earlier opening hour but not earlier than 1000 hours. Where the justices vary the permitted hours in this way they may do so for different weekdays and for different periods of not less than eight consecutive weeks.

Off-licences

The permitted hours on weekdays, other than Christmas Day, are from 0800 hours until the evening closing time which will be either 2230 hours or 2300. The permitted hours on Sundays, other than Christmas Day, shall begin at 1000 hours. On Christmas Day the hours are the same as for on-licensed premises.

On-licensed premises that have a separate off-licence department can obtain permission from the licensing justices to have the full off-licence hours for that part.

Registered clubs

The permitted hours for registered clubs on normal weekdays are the same as the general licensing hours, i.e. the same as local public houses. On Sundays, Christmas Day and Good Friday special rules apply.

Restaurants and proprietary clubs

Such businesses may obtain extensions to the normally permitted hours. These include:

1 Supper hour certificate (section 68 Licensing Act 1964): this permits restaurants selling bona fide meals to extend the normal permitted hours by one hour. Drinking-up time is an additional half-hour.

2 Extended hours orders (section 70 Licensing Act 1964): such an order extends the permitted hours for a further hour on weekdays (except Good Friday, Maundy Thursday and Easter eve) in any part of licensed premises where there is a supper hour certificate in force and where substantial refreshment and live entertainment are provided to which the sale of intoxicating liquor is ancillary.

3 Special hours certificates (section 77 Licensing Act 1964): this form of extension exists for the benefit of restaurants, etc., where the sale of liquor accompanies, and is ancillary to, the service of substantial refreshment, and where music and dancing are provided.

The protection of people under eighteen (likely to be reduced to sixteen in the future)

A licensee is not permitted knowingly to sell liquor to a person under eighteen, nor to allow a person under eighteen to consume liquor in a bar, nor to allow anyone else to make such a sale. A person under eighteen is not permitted to buy liquor in licensed premises, nor to consume liquor in a bar. No person is allowed to buy liquor for consumption in a bar in licensed premises for a person under eighteen.

One feature that distinguishes licensed premises from many other sectors of the economy is the employment of young persons. This is because, for cultural reasons, it was felt that young people could be adversely affected by witnessing the consumption of alcohol by adults. Section 170 Licensing Act 1964 prohibits people under the age of eighteen from being employed, whether for wages or otherwise, during those hours when the bar is being used for the sale of liquor. Employees under eighteen may, however, work in licensed premises if they are engaged on an approved apprenticeship scheme.

Gambling

The Gaming Act 1968, with very limited exceptions, bans gaming without a licence or certificate. However, the playing of dominoes and cribbage for money is allowed in public houses, but the licensing justices may restrict this by imposing limits on the stakes played for. Furthermore, gaming must not be the main attraction of the premises. Casinos, are obviously an exception, but have to meet certain very strict licensing requirements.

Weights and measures

All catering businesses, with the exception of registered clubs, are subject to similar weights and measures legislation. The law does, however, create a little flexibility so that businesses may have some choice of which measure to use. The choice may be determined by the degree to which customers are price sensitive so public houses may use the 25 ml spirit measure and up-market hotels and restaurants will use the larger, 35 ml measure. Similar considerations may influence wine measure choice.

The Weights and Measures Act 1963, Schedule 4, requires the following:

1 Draught beer or cider may be sold only by retail in quantities of one-third pint, one-half pint, or multiples of one-half pint.

2 Gin, rum, vodka and whisky must sold in measures of 25 or 35 mls or multiples thereof. The same measure must be used throughout the same business.

3 Wine sold by the glass must be sold in measures of 125 mls or 175 mls or multiples of these. When sold in a carafe wine must be sold in measures of 250 mls, 500 mls, 750 mls or one litre except when sold in pre-sealed containers, e.g. bottles.

Registered clubs are an exception because, technically speaking, sales do not take place in clubs as the members (the owners) of the club are consuming their own assets. However, most clubs use the above measures.

Miscellaneous licences

There are a number of different forms of entertainments, etc. where a licence of some sort or another is required by law. Examples include music, dancing, billiards, gaming, gaming machines and videos. The more common are discussed below.

Performing copyright music: the need for two licences

Under the Copyright, Designs and Patents Act 1988 music is the personal property of the composer. The copyright lasts for the lifetime of the composer and for a further fifty years. Copyright music can only be played in places open to the public, which can include supermarkets, shopping centres, public houses, restaurants, staff canteens, discos, etc., if a licence has been granted by the owner of the copyright. Effectively, this means the Performing Rights Society that acts on behalf of the composers of music. This licence is required for both live and recorded music. In the case of recorded music another licence, this time for the benefit of the recording company is required. This is obtained from Phonographic Performance Limited.

Television

Many businesses such as public houses and hotels offer television to their customers. A special licence has to be obtained. A domestic television licence does not permit the public performance of copyright material.

Music, dancing and theatre

In addition to the above licence concerned with copyright, a licence may be required for the public performance of music. Certain local authorities operate a licensing system, whereas others do not. Some large public houses provide serious theatrical entertainment; such theatres require a licence under the Theatres Act 1968. In addition, restrictions as to the service of liquor, etc. may be imposed by the licensing authority.

Food safety and hygiene

All catering businesses are subject to the Food Safety Act 1990 that regulates the standard and quality of food. The Act does not distinguish between different sectors of the hospitality industry, although through secondary legislation (i.e. regulations) various specific activities are regulated, e.g. the Materials and Articles in Contact with Food Regulations 1987. Such specific regulations will have very significant effects on some sectors and perhaps none at all on other sectors. The 1987 Regulations (above) are of great significance to take-away businesses but may be of no importance to up-market restaurants.

How operators comply with the law, however, can vary. Large companies and sectors, where risk of serious consequences are high (e.g. multinational fast food operators and flight caterers) tend to pay very strict attention to the law, frequently surpassing any legal requirements.

The main aims and objectives of the Food Safety Act 1990 may be summarized as being to:

- include an umbrella offence of supplying food that fails to comply with 'food safety requirements';

- provide powers of enforcement, including the detention and seizure of food and in-factory enforcement;

- enable detailed legislation to be made adapting the law to new technical developments, and regulating novel foods;

- provide power to require registration of food premises, allow the issue of improvement notices, and enable premises to be closed down more quickly if the public health is at risk;

- allow government ministers to tackle potentially serious problems immediately by the use of emergency control orders;

- strengthen controls over contaminants and residues;

- enable government ministers to require hygiene training for food handlers.

It should be remembered that the 1990 Act applies to every business involved in the food chain, from farmers and grocers, primary food-processing establishments, e.g. dairies, food manufacturers, companies transporting, distributing and storing food, through to retailers, restaurants and cafés. This incorporates those organizations and individuals running small catering businesses (often from their own home) and non-profit-making organizations, e.g. the Women's Royal Voluntary Service and the Women's Institute, who may process and sell food at bazaars, fetes, etc.

Food Safety Regulations 1995

The main food hygiene regulations of importance to the caterer are the Food Safety (General Food Hygiene) Regulations 1995 and the Food Safety (Temperature Control) Regulations 1995. The former regulations apply to all food retailers, caterers, processors, manufacturers and distributors, including non-profit-making concerns such as voluntary markets. These 1995 Regulations place a strong onus on owners and managers to identify food safety risks and to design and implement appropriate preventive measures which may include management techniques such as Hazard Analysis and Critical Control Points (HACCP).

The Food Safety (Temperature Control) Regulations 1995 replaced earlier and quite complex regulations. There are now only three important temperatures 8°C, 63°C (and 82°C in Scotland). Manufacturers can vary upward the 8°C ceiling if there is a scientific basis to do so. Food that is to be served hot should be held at over 63°C. In Scotland food that is to be reheated must attain a temperature of 82°C unless this will adversely affect the food.

Conclusion

This chapter has set out to identify those areas where the law differs between sectors and where it is similar. Some comparisons between French and English law have also been made. In most cases the law does not distinguish between different industry sectors or types of hospitality operation. Employment law, as just one example, is the same in principle for all employers and employees, although there are very specific regulations associated with industry-specific risks and the employment of young persons on licensed premises.

However, this chapter has also shown that within the UK hospitality industry there are some specific and important differences between some types of business. For example, we have seen that:

1 'Inns' occupy a special place in UK law. They have rights and obligations that set them apart from virtually all other businesses.

2 The sale of intoxicating drink is very strictly regulated through the law that provides licences for a range of different industry sectors, operations and businesses.

3 French and English law is very similar in some respects and different in others, the control of the sale of alcohol being one example. On the other hand there are differences such as the voluntary system of hotel classification in the UK and the statutory system in France.

4 A range of activities that may be specific to particular types of hospitality business, or which may just constitute some of the services of many such businesses (e.g. music), are strictly regulated through law.

Summary

1 Hospitality enterprises may be distinguished in a number of different ways. These can include establishments that provide: *accommodation*, such as hotels or inns; *food*, such as restaurants; *alcoholic beverages*, such as public houses and bars; *various forms of leisure activities*, such as leisure centres and night clubs.

2 The law governing the sale of alcohol regulates a number of different categories of hospitality business including clubs, businesses with full on licences, residential licences, restaurant licences, off licences.

3 Hospitality businesses may also be distinguished by the way in which activities including gaming, the performance of music and certain other activities are regulated.

4 All hospitality businesses providing food for human consumption are regulated in certain ways.

5 The law regulating hospitality businesses has distinct similarities but there are also important differences in different countries.

Review questions

1 How do the rights and duties of innkeepers and other types of hospitality business differ in respect of:
   (a) Offering or refusing to provide food, drink and accommodation?
   (b) Responsibility for guests' property?
   (c) Securing payment?

2 How does pricing legislation affect businesses generally and the different sectors of the hospitality industry?

3 Distinguish between guest registration legislation affecting businesses generally and the different sectors of the hospitality industry.

4 In what ways do the hotel classification systems operated in the UK and in France differ?

5 What are the differences between a full on-licence and the other principal types of alcohol licence?

6 What are the key similarities and differences between proprietary clubs and members' clubs?

7 What is the main difference affecting the employment of young persons in businesses generally and in the licensed sectors of the hospitality industry?

8 How does the weights and measures legislation affect most hospitality businesses and registered (members') clubs?

9 To what extent do differences in legislation affect the ability to compare different types of hospitality activity?

10 What are the implications for making international comparisons of hospitality operations of legal differences in different countries?

Bibliography

Atherton T. and Atherton T. (1998). *Tourism, Travel and Hospitality Law*. LBC Information Services.

Further reading

Boella M. and Pannett. A. (1999). *Principles of Hospitality Law*. 4th edn. Capsules.

Boella M. J. (ed.) (up-dated six times a year). *Croner's Catering Reference Book*. Croner Publications.

Boella M. J. (ed.) (up-dated four times a year). *Croner's Catering A– Z Reference Book*. Croner Publications.

Poustie, M. and Geddes, N. (1999). *Hospitality and Tourism Law*. Thomson Business Press.

Financial structures and practices

Cathy Burgess

Objectives

Within this chapter an attempt will be made to compare the value of the various techniques in the different sectors, although given the variety of features evident across the sectors some comparisons have little meaning. By the end of the chapter, therefore, you should be able to:

1 Explain the importance of the 'bottom-line' to the manager.

2 Describe some of the main techniques used in hospitality to effectively control the business – ratio analysis, cost control, pricing and budgeting.

3 Compare the characteristics of the various sectors from a financial perspective.

Introduction

Many of the techniques used in financial management in the hospitality business are similar to those found in other industries. There are three main criteria that are important to the successful management of any business:

- the maximization of revenue
- the minimization of costs
- the safeguarding of assets.

Within the various sectors of hospitality, likewise, the basic principles of management are found in all areas, but their individual characteristics require different approaches from a control perspective. You have already read about many of these characteristics in previous chapters. For instance, in-flight catering and fast food are strongly oriented towards mass production and hence the strict control of stock and materials used is crucial, but in a five-star restaurant this is less important and, in a leisure centre, may be minimal.

In terms of financial management there are a range of techniques useful to managers, and the aim of this chapter is to help you understand those that are relevant within the different sectors. There have been very few comparisons of the different hospitality sectors from a financial perspective, with researchers tending to restrict themselves to practices within a specific sector. For example, Maher (1995) has concentrated on labour costs in hotels whereas Mason and Opperman (1996) have looked at theme parks. Comparisons may be made between countries (Schmidgall, Borchgrevnik and Zahl-Begnum, 1996) or different types of hotel (BDO Hospitality Consulting, 1998). Hospitality accounting textbooks offer a range of techniques for the manager but tend not to make direct comparisons between sectors (Coltman, 1997; Harris and Hazzard, 1992). Some limited contrasts have been shown by deFranco and Schmidgall (1998) and Burgess (1999a) but unfortunately the areas researched (cash management and financial responsibilities, respectively) are outside the remit of this chapter.

The types of comparisons that can be made between businesses are those that have a standard format applicable to different areas. Ratios are used to evaluate the performance of all businesses, regardless of the industry that they serve. Comparison of some of these (e.g. return on equity or gearing) are applied at corporate level (when, for instance, a hotel group will be compared to a brewer or a restaurant company), and hence are outside the remit of this chapter. Within each individual sector, however, comparisons against standards are frequent, and some of these are discussed below. Ratios such as profitability or wage cost may be applied to a leisure centre, a tour operator or a guesthouse although as their staffing needs are totally different the wage percentages will vary according to sector. The most common comparisons are made of actual results against budget and also prior year results but others are made against other businesses in the sector, against published industry averages (e.g. BDO Hospitality Consulting, 1998) or established benchmarks, should they exist. Companies will also review the performance of one unit against another in a division and perhaps one division to another in order to gauge the effectiveness of the various divisional managers. Other, non-financial, comparisons such as size of company, market-share or level of environmental management may also be made at corporate or unit level, but again these are not discussed here.

Before we consider some of the individual techniques practised in hospitality we need to look at the importance of control to a business. If we can effectively manage the different elements of the unit – revenues, expenses and assets – then we can maximize profit (or, in the case of the non-profit sectors, break even or minimize subsidies).

The fundamental principles of controlling a business are (Davis, Lockwood and Stone, 1998: 98):

Planning

1 Operations:
 (a) purchasing
 (b) receiving
 (c) storage and issue
 (d) preparation
 (e) selling.

2 Management:
 (a) costs
 (b) assessment
 (c) correction.

The realities are that these are all very people oriented and hence are subject to their behaviour – in terms of their efficiency of work, their honesty or their purchasing power. As a result there is:

• a lack of consistency of materials and product

• a lack of efficiency of people and equipment

• inconsistency of sales mix (Davis, Lockwood and Stone, 1998: 101).

All these functions need to work together and we will be looking at some of these key elements – planning (budgeting and pricing), standard setting and measurement (ratios and variance analysis) and implementation (cost control) – in this chapter.

First, however, we need to consider the different types of report available to help managers understand their area of business and the bottom line.

The profit and loss (P&L) report

In order to make comparisons it is important to produce reports that will enable managers to review the performance of their areas against standards. Within most units the main emphasis tends to be on revenues (sales) and expenses (costs) – and therefore profit. This is not true of all sectors; some such as private members clubs or hospitals are in business for the purposes of breaking even (no profit or loss) and others to actively run on subsidies – e.g. a staff restaurant which is providing a benefit to employees.

Management reports

These are produced within almost all businesses to provide financial information to help the managers run their areas. The P&L may be produced either for an individual department or for the unit as a whole. A business such as an independent public house might need only one statement to show their results each month (Figure 8.1). This shows only actual results here but the statement should also include both budget and variance columns for comparison.

For many businesses, however, this type of statement is not adequate. Where a unit comprises many different departments each should have its own separate statement. As an example, even a small hotel may include rooms, restaurant, bar, room and lounge service, leisure centre, kitchen, administration, telephones, repairs and maintenance, and so on – nine departments at least. A leisure centre could have a pool, health club, beauty

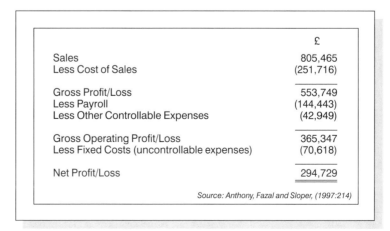

Figure 8.1
Simple layout profit and loss report for the Dog and Duck
Source: Anthony, Fazal, and Sloper, 1997: 214.

	£
Sales	805,465
Less Cost of Sales	(251,716)
Gross Profit/Loss	553,749
Less Payroll	(144,443)
Less Other Controllable Expenses	(42,949)
Gross Operating Profit/Loss	365,347
Less Fixed Costs (uncontrollable expenses)	(70,618)
Net Profit/Loss	294,729

Source: Anthony, Fazal and Sloper, (1997:214)

therapy, membership, fitness classes, retail and catering departments – all with different characteristics and hence different potential control problems. Having separate financial statements helps the manager identify problem areas and take corrective action. Also, many managers are appraised on their financial performance and so the bottom line can be important to them in terms of bonuses and/or promotion.

Within hospitality there are several standard published layouts for departmental and total reports, which many businesses have adopted. The Uniform System of Accounts for Lodging (USAL – Hotel Association of New York City, 1996) is an international standard now in common use in hotels, and there are similar reports for clubs and restaurants (e.g. National Restaurant Association, 1996). Figure 8.2 shows a typical departmental report for a hotel.

This month					Year to date			
Actual	Budget	Variance	Last year		Actual	Budget	Variance	Last year
				Sales				
				Cost of sales				
				Gross Profit				
				Payroll				
				Expenses				
				Departmental profit				

(Adapted from USAL, 1996)

Figure 8.2 Departmental profit centre report: hotels
Source: adapted from Hotel Association of New York City, 1996.

These columns each show both monetary and percentage figures. Similar statements may also be used for departments without sales, e.g. administration or kitchen. Where the hotel is very large some departmental statements may be subdivided into smaller ones. For instance, one large London hotel has a food and beverage (F&B) statement which consolidated separate reports for three restaurants, two bars, a nightclub, lounge, room service, kitchen, stewarding, banqueting, private meeting rooms and F&B management.

Performance analysis

Financial statements have little value unless they are used for the better management of the business. Comparison of actual to budgeted results may be performed either in monetary figures or by ratios and gives an indication of where action needs to be taken. Different sectors are interested in different types of ratio according to the key features of their businesses. Comparisons may also be made between different units in a company (for instance, budget hotels or pasta restaurants where a standard product is offered in all units) or against published international standards (e.g. BDO Hospitality Consulting, 1998).

Customers

All sectors, however, are interested in the number of customers they have served (in whatever capacity) as this reflects on how efficiently the business is operating. These may be stated in different ways:

1 Hotels look at room occupancy – the number of rooms sold as a proportion of those available for sale. This may be sub-divided by business segment and day of the week, depending on the size and variety of the clientele.

2 Residential accommodation also looks at occupancy although over a longer timescale

3 Theme parks and leisure attractions are interested in the actual number of customers, by age group (and hence different entrance fees), who have passed through the turnstiles.

4 High-volume restaurants may look at 'seat turnover' – how many customers have been served in a day compared with seats available whereas a small restaurant may be delighted if all their seats are filled just once in a single day.

5 Fast-food restaurants look at customers on an hourly basis which assists in planning cooking and staffing levels.

6 In-flight caterers are paid per passenger, and so for them the number of customers is crucial to the fee they are able to charge the airline.

Revenue ratios

Sales achieved per customer are also important. For the hotel the most common ratio quoted is the *average room rate* (ARR – rooms revenue divided by rooms sold). They should also pay equal attention – but often do not – to the amount of food and beverage revenue that each guest generates. The room rate is the average *achieved*, after all discounts, and may be considerably less than the published ('rack') rate – an example is a £43.00 ARR but a rack rate of £59.95 (Guild, 1999). Restaurants look at the average spend per cover for both food and beverage, and by meal period. A theme park will calculate not just the entrance receipts, but

F&B and retail revenue for each customer. Some contract caterers receive a subsidy per paying customer, based on the difference between actual spend and the costs of providing the service, and hence the average spend per customer is also important to them.

Costs

All businesses look at some general costs – individual and total costs as a percentage of sales, cost per customer and so on. The most popular food-based ratio is the food cost percentage, which is a measure by which many chefs are assessed. It is calculated by taking the cost of raw materials (food) as a percentage of the sales of those products. It takes no account of seasonal variations in the cost of raw materials and so, for instance, in a fish restaurant the cost percentage may go up and down daily according to the price of raw fish supplied. This ratio is of far more value where food is supplied preprepared (frozen, for instance) or prices have been contracted with suppliers. Here any variation in cost is the responsibility of the kitchen staff as it is based on their efficient use of the materials.

However, there are occasions where the food cost percentage is meaningless. On a cruise ship the cost of meals is included within the fare the passenger pays, and so there are no food sales figures to use (Carnival Cruise Lines, 1999). Here the chef is more likely to have a budget of food cost per passenger per day. Even a small pub may pay little attention to food cost if they exclusively use fresh food according to what is available to purchase locally, and if the quality of the product is more important than its profitability.

Some sectors focus on specific cost ratios for various reasons. For instance, in-flight catering concentrates on the cost per passenger mile, which is an essential factor in the charge made for the service to the airline. Part of this is 'worked value points' (McCool, 1996) based on the number of minutes taken to produce a passenger meal. Other service costs, such as packing, cutlery, storage and transportation are added. In-flight catering contracts are very tightly controlled and managed because, as the volumes are high, there is potential for a small mistake to escalate and seriously affect profits.

Productivity

For some sectors productivity is crucial to the effective management of labour costs. Fast-food restaurants typically organize their staffing schedules according to the level of business anticipated at a particular time of day – so lunchtime may have the highest staffing levels, with early morning having only a minimal level. Productivity is less important in a five-star hotel where managers may have a large number of full-time staff employed in order to maintain the quality of service, but more important in a budget hotel which may only employ room-cleaning staff when there are dirty rooms available to clean. Productivity may also be calculated and expressed as a percentage, minutes taken to clean a room, rooms cleaned per staff member per day or a cost per customer.

Bottom line percentages

Certain types of business rely heavily on the profit percentage achieved at gross operating profit (GOP) level. Hotels that are operated via management contract are often subject to a fee based on the achieved GOP, and a franchised restaurant may operate in a similar way. Other restaurants, e.g. at an airport or in a shopping complex, may pay rent based on a percentage of sales and, occasionally, on profits. This encourages the operator to maximize sales and to be efficient in their control of costs.

Case 8.1

Types of published hotel statistics

Table 8.1 shows examples of the type of statistics published within the hotel sector that may be used for comparison between types of hotel.

	Your hotel	Composite hotels	Variance
Room occupancy	81.3%	83.3%	−2.0%
Average room rate	£173.72	£174.16	− £0.44
Room yield	£141.27	£145.05	− £3.78
F&B spend per cover	£21.66	£19.25	£2.41
Room hire per square m	£35.77	£64.98	− £29.21
Employees per occupied room night	1.5	1.2	0.4

Source: Tim Steel, Arthur Andersen, 1999.

Table 8.1 London Luxury Hotel Performance Survey (Arthur Andersen)

Question:
how might a manager use these types of statistics to compare with hotels that are not luxury hotels, or located in London? Could they be used for different sectors, or are they only appropriate for hotels?

After looking at some of the financial information available to managers, and the type of comparisons that can be made, we can now look at the control of costs in the different sectors.

Cost control

The effective control of costs is essential to the bottom line for many types of business. Again, standards may be set as to the cost levels achievable and it is against these that the actual performance needs to be assessed. Relatively minor actions can cause significant effects and we need to know how costs behave so that we can understand the effectiveness of management actions.

Types of costs

Fixed costs do not change with the level of business and tend to remain relatively stable all year. It is difficult to manage these once established. Some examples are rent, rates, salaries, mortgage payments. *Variable costs* change in proportion to the level of business – if you sell something then you incur a cost. Examples of these are cost of food or wine, bed linen, packaging for fast food. *Semi-variable costs* have partly fixed and partly variable elements. Two examples are wages, where there is a fixed basic wage but overtime is variable, or telephone bills, where the line rental is fixed, but cost of calls is variable.

Different sectors have different proportions of these types of costs – and hence different needs. In general, the higher the status of the business, the greater the proportion of fixed to variable costs. For example, staff in an up-market restaurant will tend to be full-time, highly skilled employees (fixed cost) whereas the majority of staff in fast-food establishments are part time and unskilled (a variable cost). Cost structures may also be different dependent on location. For instance, if you have to transport all staff, goods and services to a remote island or jungle site, transport will form a large proportion of fixed costs. Similarly, if there are established working practices (e.g. in school meals) then all staff and perhaps utility costs may be fixed.

If we look first at the two most important costs – raw materials and labour – we will then be able to compare the relevance of these in the different sectors. Other costs are generally not as significant as these but still need to be effectively managed.

Raw materials

These are variable costs and directly related to the volume of meals sold – if you sell a pizza you will incur the cost of the ingredients. Food in particular is characterized by the number of procedures it has to go through before it may be sold – ordering, receiving, storage, issue, storage again, manufacture and then service (Schillaci, 1993) – all of which have potential problems. Much food is perishable although some sectors have converted to longer-life products (packaged or frozen) to reduce loss. Given the range of foodstuffs, even in a limited-menu outlet, there can be a high embodied value in stocks. Beverages are also problematic with high values held in wines and spirits making them desirable to would-be thieves. Careful management of draught beer can minimize losses due to wastage to as low as 1 per cent whereas bad management can result in 4 per cent of sales being lost (Anthony, Fazal and Sloper, 1997: 167).

Labour

Labour is the other major cost of the hospitality business and, depending on the sector, may be incurred through varying proportions of fixed and variable cost elements. It is one area where managers often try to cut corners in order to reduce their overall costs. For some sectors this is the dominant expense – e.g. in hospital cleaning labour forms 90 per cent of the total costs (Brown, 1996).

For many businesses, particularly those where traditional labour patterns still feature, salaried staff costs, which are fixed in nature, form a large proportion of the total labour cost. However, this may be appropriate where the volume of business is fairly constant and effective rostering (if business patterns allow this) can minimize the impact of overstaffing. There is also a perception that full-time staff are more stable employees so potential gains in terms of staff turnover and customer service may outweigh financial considerations (Wood, 1997).

Increasingly there is a trend towards greater flexibility in employment. The variability of hours worked allows managers to match staff levels to potential business volumes, hence keeping an equitable payroll percentage. Some areas of the country also have lower pay rates than others, which affect the payroll costs. For example, two very similar properties, such as budget hotels in different regions, may have different payroll percentages despite equivalent productivity levels.

Different sectors

Sectors which traditionally have very strong controls – and narrow margins – are those where the business is contracted to provide a service for other operators – such as contract and in-flight catering. These businesses are constantly under pressure to provide a better service at a cheaper rate. Due to this they have utilized technology to maximize their efficiency by (e.g. in-flight catering) generating accurate calculations of passenger numbers in order to optimize levels of ordering, production, costing and billing (Broome, Clark and Ramis, 1997).

Branded restaurants and hotels form two types – hard or soft (Mullen, 1998). Soft brands allow local variety of décor, pricing and menus and so may react to local control issues (e.g. if labour costs are high then materials may be bought in rather than made on site to compensate). Hard brands have everything standar-dized and so a customer will expect the same menu and service style whatever part of the country they visit. These tend to have national standard suppliers who guarantee prices of raw materi-als (and some other goods) to all outlets. Some of these materials may be preprepared to minimize wastage and reduce the need for experienced kitchen staff. Branded hotels are designed for low maintenance and cleaning to minimize costs, whereas older individual hotels may have higher wage costs due to labour-intensive furniture and fittings.

Case 8.2

Cruise ship costs

One of the key benefits to cruise ship passengers is the number and variety of meals and facilities that are all included in the price. The *Carnival Cruise Lines* (1999: 5) brochure shows:

Flights and transfers
Twin-bedded (and upward) cabin
Eight meals and snacks per day, including a Captains Dinner and a Cocktail Party
24-hour cabin service
Entertainment – night-club, disco, 3 bands and an orchestra, movies
Library and games room
3 pools
Children's activities and 'dozens' of other activities
Gratuities up to £80 per couple per trip

Question: which of these costs may be con-sidered fixed, variable or semi-variable? Are there other sectors where this structure might appear?

Some businesses are highly seasonal and this affects their cost structures. Traditionally many seaside hotels used to close in winter due to low occupancies but now tend to remain open and look for new markets that will generate some revenue to cover their fixed operating costs. Apartment complexes and large hotels in resort areas can offer economies of scale in that a relatively small management team can operate a large number of room blocks and other facilities. Operative staff may be hired on a flexible, perhaps seasonal, basis so the opportunity is available to open and close different areas according to demand.

Other businesses are totally dependent on the weather for high volumes of customers – e.g. outdoor wedding receptions and sports events such as cricket fixtures, golf and tennis tournaments. Here all but the core staff are employed purely for specific events, which ensures the matching of labour cost to business levels. All equipment and materials may have to be transported to the event, which incurs additional costs such as van hire, refrigeration, electrical generators and storage containers (Payne, 1990).

Case 8.3

Large-scale sports event

One example of a large-scale sports event is the Olympic Games in Sydney in 2000 (Mitchell, 1999) where the potential control issues for the provision of catering are huge. The catering budget for a total of fifty-five days (including the subsequent Paralympic Games) is estimated at A$100 million (around £40 million). Over five million meals require around 17 000 staff in forty venues to serve not just athletes and spectators but officials, media and corporate hospitality suites. At the end it all has to be dismantled and taken away.

Question: How do you cope with the logistics of assembling the equipment, staff and raw materials if you are to provide an efficient service without costs spiralling out of control? Do other sectors have similar features (albeit on a smaller scale)?

A few businesses have very simple cost structures. A guesthouse offers just two or three products – a room, breakfast and perhaps dinner. As these are often owner-managed (Poorani and Smith, 1995) costs may be carefully controlled, again often by the use of flexible labour and purchase of food only when needed. Residential hostels, although larger in scale, often also offer a minimum number of products, to a fairly stable clientele, and so costs may be easily managed.

As you should be able to see by now diverse types of business have different needs in terms of cost control, although the basic principles remain the same. The base standards against which actual results are measured may be different – it is the variance against these that is important. Managers need to be aware of the effect of their actions on the different costs, whatever sector they operate in.

Pricing strategies

The pricing of products is key to the profitability of the establishment (or at least achievement of a breakeven point). It is, therefore, crucial for the manager to understand all the factors influencing the establishment of a price. Different sectors use different approaches depending on their customers and also the availability of information to them. There are two main types of pricing used in hospitality – cost-plus (where the costs and desired profit are added to give a price) and market pricing (where the customer 'decides' the price to be charged).

Cost-plus pricing

For this method the manager looks at all the costs that are incurred in producing the product and the desired profit is added to give a selling price. There are two types of cost-plus pricing. The gross profit approach uses only the cost of raw materials, to which is added a mark-up to cover all other costs and the profit required. This may be shown graphically (see Figure 8.3).

Cost base	Mark-up		
Direct Materials	All other costs	Profit	= selling price

Figure 8.3
Gross profit

This method is most common when pricing food and beverage in restaurants. It is called the gross profit (GP) method because the mark-up is equivalent to the GP achieved and is normally expressed as a percentage of the selling price. For example, different types of restaurant use different cost percentages which, in turn, result in different prices (see Table 8.2). Here the contract caterer column shows a situation where prices are set at just above food cost, to allow for wastage

Hence an identical food item may be sold at different prices depending on where it is consumed. You should also be aware that the selling price does not included value added tax, which needs to be added on afterwards to give a menu price (or any other type of 'price charged to customer').

This type of pricing is very simplistic and does not take into account any variations in other costs, which could include wages,

	Luxury restaurant	**Pub**	**Contract caterer**
Fillet steak			
Cost of raw materials	£3.00	£3.00	£3.00
Cost percentage	29.0%	42.0%	95.0%
Selling price	£10.34	£7.14	£3.16
Salmon fillet			
Cost of raw materials	£1.62	£1.62	£1.62
Cost percentage	29.0%	42.0%	95.0%
Selling price	£6.99	£3.86	£1.70

Source: *Caterer and Hotelkeeper*, 1999; Tim Steel, Arthur Andersen.

Table 8.2 Example of differences resulting from the gross profit method

linen, cutlery, rent, electricity, and so on. If the price remains stable, and the costs vary, then the profit will inevitably change on a daily basis. It is, therefore, only really suited to situations where accurate pricing is not a concern, e.g. a hotel restaurant that is providing a service for guests and profitability is not essential.

A more complex – and hence more accurate – type of cost-plus pricing is contribution pricing, where more of the costs are taken into account (see Figure 8.4).

| Cost base | Contribution | | |
| Variable costs | Fixed costs | Profit | = selling price |

Figure 8.4
Contribution pricing

With contribution pricing all the variable costs incurred in making the product are identified, and used as the cost base. This includes not just raw materials but also labour cost, packaging, fuel, bed linen, paper and so on. The mark-up here relates to the fixed costs and profit. This method is far more appropriate for fast-food type operations, or a bed and breakfast establishment.

Case 8.4

Contribution pricing for a guesthouse

The owner of a guesthouse can identify all the likely costs as the type of operation is fairly simple and may have only one or two products – the room plus breakfast, and possibly dinner in the evening. For the room rate, the variable costs might be bed linen, food for breakfast, labour to clean the room, shampoo and soap, totalling £7.50. The total amount of fixed costs, calculated per room, are £15.00 and the desired profit £10.00.

Question: Could the same method be used to price, for instance, café meals, visitor attractions or a package holiday?

	£
Variable costs	7.50
Fixed costs	15.00
Profit required	10.00
Minimal selling price for room	32.50

Table 8.3 Guesthouse costs and pricing

Where the business has a wide range of products this method is still feasible. A theme park, for example, may have lots of rides, retail shops, food outlets and vending machines but should still be able to identify all the different costs associated with each type.

Market-based pricing

It is all very well for accounting people to calculate a price to be charged – but will the customer pay it? Market-based pricing looks at what the customer will be willing to pay for the product, given the local economy, competition, and so on. Market-based pricing tends to ignore costs – or at least ignore the profit margin. For instance, a holiday village will charge an accommodation fee, which will need to be competitive with other similar villages. They will not necessarily decide to be cheaper, but will need to market themselves as a superior product if they are going to charge superior prices. Use of facilities such as a swimming pool will normally be included in the accommodation charge, but the exact cost of this will not always be taken into consideration.

Another example might be a pizza restaurant. An independent restaurant would look at the prices being charged by other, similar businesses in the area and then price themselves at either the same level or marginally cheaper. However, big chains look at their competition nationally rather than locally – hence the similarity of prices between the major competitors all around the country. Their prices, therefore, have a national influence rather than local one. Costs do matter – they are 'trimmed to fit' (Kotas, 1999: 107) – but the price is key.

Some establishments can charge a price far greater than needed to cover costs, due to the market demand. A five-star hotel or restaurant, or first-class travel on a train or aeroplane, can be priced at a far higher level than the cost + profit equation would normally suggest. Here price is an indication of quality and the challenge for management is to ensure that the quality of this first-class product or service matches the expectation of the customer. If you look at the rate charged for the same journey on the same train, you will see vastly different ticket prices available – for a return journey from Oxford to Edinburgh you can pay anything from £32 to £300 (Virgin trains, 1999). Those passengers paying the highest prices need to be assured that they will get value for money as well as those paying the least.

Prices may also be used to smooth demand for a product in some sectors, e.g. in offering off-season package holidays or Apex fares on trains or aeroplanes. Airfares are typically much lower if the passenger can stay over a Saturday night, and business hotels offer cut-price weekend leisure breaks. These prices may result in a minimal profit to the business (or may not even cover costs) but are a market-based decision taken to generate some contribution towards paying the fixed costs of an establishment. Hotel weekend-break guests, for example, may pay a minimal room rate but then spend money in the restaurant, bar and leisure centre which will increase overall revenues. As an example the London Hilton has a published rate (November 1999) of £270 for a double room but their midweek-break rate (*Hilton Hotels Leisure Breaks*, 1999) quotes £229 for two people, including breakfast. Similar lower-priced, packages are also available for conference delegates. For example, the Forte reservations office (29 October 1999) quoted prices for the Posthouse at Reading as £129 full rate but you could have a full twenty-four hour conference delegate rate for £155.

Businesses that have many different products may use a mixture of methods for pricing, and should also look at the relationship of different products to each other so that the profit for the entire operation may be optimized. This is called price integration (Schmidgall, 1997). Examples are the provision of a free leisure centre to hotel guests which may result in a higher room rate or offering a discounted meal and/or a free gift to a child in a road-side restaurant to encourage parents to eat there too.

All the above implies that profit is key but this may not be the prime motivator. Contract catering businesses typically work with 'cost-plus contracts' which means that they invoice clients for all costs plus a fee for profit and further expenses (Payne, 1990). Another method used in this sector is the fixed price contract in which both parties agree a price based on all the costs likely to be incurred, plus a profit to the contractor. For the client, the objective is often to minimize the cost to themselves while keeping their staff on site and accessible while eating their meals. Prices may also be determined by the client where other factors need to be considered – a student facility is one example.

Private members' clubs are typically run on a 'not-for-profit' basis, all facilities being provided for members at cost price or just above. Members, all of whom own a share of the club, pay an annual membership fee that funds the upkeep of the facilities including clubhouse, maintenance of sports or other facilities and staffing. Other facilities, such as meals, are then charged at a price that covers the cost of raw materials, labour and makes a contribution towards the fixed costs of the establishment. It is seen as a benefit that prices are kept as low as possible and may also have been written into the club rules that it runs on a breakeven basis only (deFranco and Schmidgall, 1998). The danger is that insufficient money is available to reinvest in new facilities, such as upgrading tennis courts or the kitchen, and so it is important that some small surpluses are made for future needs.

Pricing is undoubtedly a key feature for the profitability of a business. Some types of business can charge comparatively high prices and hence the cost control issue is less important. For others, such as in-flight catering, pricing is very competitive and so profit margins are minimal. The financial calculations are often overwritten by market considerations and the effective manager needs to be aware of the relationship between the two viewpoints.

Budgeting and forecasting

Budgets

Budgets are plans of action for the future that allow the unit to set standards and establish responsibilities. They then allow managers to review actual results and take corrective action if required. As shown earlier, ratio analysis is meaningless unless there is something with which to make a comparison. Budgets may be long term (strategic planning), medium term (the annual budget) or short term (a forecast) (Burgess, 1999b: 107). These processes then allow planning to take place in relation to:

- selling strategy (e.g. is there a need for a marketing campaign to attract new customers?)

- staffing (full time and part time)

- maximization of room occupancy and average spend

- open/closure policy (additional retail or food outlets)

- purchasing and storage (particularly perishable products).

What is budgeted for is dependent on the key drivers of the particular business:

1 Accommodation areas are interested in room occupancy and average room rate

2 Bars and restaurants need to know the numbers of guests and how much they will spend on food and beverage.

3 Cruise lines and in-flight caterers need exact passenger details, residential, hospital and welfare caterers the numbers of patients/residents.

4 A casino needs to know not just the number of potential players but also, on average, how long they will play at a particular game (Patterson, 1999).

5 Theme parks and attractions need to know the numbers of customers and estimate how many will purchase meals, ice creams, souvenirs and so on.

6 All need to estimate the peaks and troughs in customer demand.

In turn, once customer numbers are established then the costs of raw materials and other supplies can be planned, as can staffing levels and other costs.

All these are estimated on either the results of prior years and/or the experience of managers in their departments, though in some circumstances it may also be necessary to calculate a new figure entirely, e.g. if a new product is to be sold. Here the base costs and price (determined according to the pricing strategy adopted) are used, to which a 'best-guess' of the number of customers who may purchase the product is added. Again, the experience of managers in the sector is crucial for producing an accurate estimation of demand.

Other costs or revenues may be specific to the particular sector. For instance, a casino guest may be offered free accommodation as part of their 'package' to attract them to gamble at a specific resort. This needs to be budgeted for as it will still incur costs (Patterson, 1999). The chef on a cruise ship normally has a budget related to the notion of a food cost per passenger per day but the logistical problems of supplying perishable items mean that high stocks of everything have to be carried, stored effectively and used efficiently to minimize wastage. Ships also have costs which are not found elsewhere such as dry-dock maintenance and port charges (Less and Mager, 1999). Sports facilities could receive a subsidy from a local authority, rent from concessionaires (retail, catering, parking, and vending), sponsorship for events and advertising as well as income from membership and entrance fees (Farmer, Mulrooney and Amman, 1996).

It is evident, therefore, that the manager needs to be fully aware of the key characteristics of their particular, individual business, and also knowledgeable about cost behaviour, ratio analysis and pricing strategies. All these techniques are used in budgeting, to a greater or lesser degree in each sector of the hospitality industry.

Forecasting

Forecasting is done on a daily, weekly or monthly basis particularly where business volumes are very volatile. It may not be necessary where demand is stable and constant – guests in a residential home stay for a long time, labour tends to be stable and food and other costs predictable. Prison catering has similar characteristics.

The features of fast-food restaurants have already been discussed. Here there is a need to be able to forecast the peaks and troughs on an hourly basis that assists with the planning of food production and staffing so as to be able to minimize costs, and hence keep prices low to attract customers in a competitive market. Theme parks and other multi-unit sites also forecast variations in demand, which allows them to open or close units to satisfy demand while optimizing costs. With in-flight catering the profit margins are very small, and with the high volume of production even a small error on forecasting can cause an immense financial impact. Hospital catering also operates on very tight margins and so accurate forecasting is essential – but if your clientele are children who will not decide until the point of service what they want to eat (Gledhill, 1999) then the forecasting methods need to be flexible.

If a hotel can forecast gaps in occupancy it can take action – for instance, in selling more rooms (see Case 8.5). If additional sales are not possible then cost controls can be implemented – the housekeeper can schedule less room attendants and the chef can order fewer croissants for breakfast.

Case 8.5

Corus Hotels forecasting

Corus Hotels (formerly Regal) (Stokes, 1999) look up to three months in advance in forecasting terms and consider it an 'ongoing short-term review process to manage and monitor the business'.

Some of the items they forecast are:

1 Rooms: rooms on books, pick-up/fall-out factor, market segments and achievable rates.

2 F&B: covers from breakfast, day and twenty-four hour conference guests, dinner take-up percentage, wedding numbers, special events. Average spends per outlet, external bar guests.

3 Other income: per room or cover spends, leisure club members and spend, golf club members, spend and weather.

4 Payroll: fixed and variable headcount, turnover and shortages, training time, holidays.

5 Operating costs: fixed and variable.

Question:
Are these suitable for other sectors? How do revenues and costs inter-relate in the different sectors? Do similar businesses in the same sector have the same features?

Budgeting and forecasting are processes that allow managers to plan their business strategies and set standards against which actual performance may be measured. Similar techniques are used in all sectors; it is only the individual characteristics that may alter the emphasis within a particular area.

Conclusions

This chapter has explored some of the techniques that may be used to improve the financial performance of businesses operating in various hospitality sectors. Examples have been quoted from a range of types of business and, where possible, comparisons made. As has been shown it is often difficult to directly compare financial practices where the key drivers of the business type are so varied. However, within each sector budgets should be established which then allow direct comparisons to be made by managers. Benchmarks and industry averages may also be used for this purpose. The specific techniques discussed have been aimed at unit level but these may also be used by companies to compare corporate performance either within the company or against others.

The different characteristics of the various sectors mean that whereas complex cost control procedures are crucial to in-flight catering they are less important to a guesthouse. Similarly, although accurate cost-based pricing is a key issue for contract caterers it is less so for a five-star hotel and restaurant where market demand allows higher pricing than the costs suggest.

Hospitality businesses in some sectors are very production oriented, with others more geared to service. Hence the relative importance of the cost of raw materials to labour varies according to the primary focus of the business. However, the key support tool for the effective control of all hospitality businesses and functions is accurate and reliable information on both past results and for planning the future. However, effective controls are only achievable if managers have a thorough knowledge of the business and the desire to operate at the highest levels of efficiency, whatever the sector the business is in.

All businesses tend to be either cost-centred or profit-centred and in order to operate effectively a manager needs to be able to:

- know how costs behave for individual products and services and, as a result

- know which costs (and revenues) are controllable

- forecast revenues and costs for their area based on informed planning processes

- price the products and services to ensure optimum return

- analyse and interpret results using ratios and take corrective action when required.

For the future certain issues will continue to grow in importance – the profit sector will be increasingly pressured to improve profits and the cost sector to minimize costs – although not at the expense of product and service quality. As a result managers will need to constantly investigate new ways of managing their businesses with particular emphasis on using technology to improve all processes, depending on the key features of the individual sector.

Summary

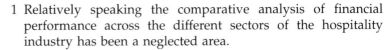

1 Relatively speaking the comparative analysis of financial performance across the different sectors of the hospitality industry has been a neglected area.

2 Within individual sectors comparisons made between similar types of hospitality businesses and against established standards are quite common.

3 The financial reports produced by different types of hospitality business do vary. This can make direct comparisons difficult.

4 Companies operating in the different sectors of the industry tend to focus on different types of financial ratios according to their importance to the nature of the hospitality business.

5 Business and financial practices vary across the sectors of the industry, which is reflected in the adoption of different pricing and costing strategies.

6 The business mix and cost structures of different types of hospitality company varies within, and across, the sectors.

Review questions

1 Are fixed costs essentially the same across the different sectors of the hospitality industry or do they differ in nature and scale?

2 Can fixed costs such as salaries be converted to variable costs and, if so, what are the implications of this for making financial comparisons?

3 What other types of ratios might be important to individual sectors of the hospitality industry?

4 To what extent is it important for marketers in different types of hospitality businesses to know about cost behaviour when pricing products?

5 What considerations would you need to take into account when trying to compare the financial performance of a hospitality company over a number of years?

6 What problems are likely to be encountered in trying to compare the financial performance of hotel companies operating in different countries?

7 How could the use of standard financial ratios help you to compare the financial performance of different types of hospitality company?

8 What are the comparative implications of different financial norms and/or goals in different sectors of the hospitality industry?

9 Why is a knowledge of the definitions used for a particular term, i.e. productivity, important when you are making comparisons between different sectors of the hospitality industry?

10 Financial control is a common feature of all hospitality businesses, but does this mean that how this is put into practice is the same across the sectors of the industry?

Bibliography

Anthony, G., Fazal, Z. and Sloper, T. (1997). *Pubs and Restaurants: An Industry Accounting and Auditing Guide.* Accountancy Books.

BDO Hospitality Consulting (1998). *United Kingdom Hotel Industry 1998.* BDO Hospitality Consulting

Broome, S., Clark, J. and Ramis, M. (1997). The airline catering management challenge Hospitality. *Industry International*, **16**, 22–23.

Brown, J. (1996). Hospital hotel services and residential care. in *Introduction to Hospitality Operations* (P. Jones, ed.), Cassell.

Burgess, C. (1999a). *Continuing Professional Education: Financial Educational Needs of Controllers, Consultants and General Managers.* On behalf of British Association of Hospitality Accountants/Oxford Brookes University.

Burgess, C (1999b). Forecasting and budgeting. In *Profit Planning* (P. Harris, ed.), 2nd edn, Butterworth-Heinemann.

Carnival Cruise Lines (1999) brochure. Airtours.

Caterer and Hotelkeeper (1999) Fresh food prices, 28 October, 72–73.

Coltman, M. M. (1997). *Hospitality Management Accounting.* 6th edn. Van Nostrand Reinhold.

deFranco, A. and Schmidgall, R. (1998). Hotels and clubs: how is cash handled? *Bottomline*, **13** (8), December–January, 11–13.

Farmer, P., Mulrooney, A. and Amman, R. (1996). *Sport Facility Planning and Management.* Fitness Information Technical Inc.

Gledhill, B. (1999). Jelly in their bellies. *Caterer and Hotelkeeper*, 29 July, 35.

Guild, S. (1999). Lodge logistics. *Caterer and Hotelkeeper*, 25 September, 40–41.

Harris, P. J. and Hazzard, P. A. (1992). *Managerial Accounting in the Hospitality Industry.* 5th edn. Stanley Thornes.

Hilton Hotels Leisure Breaks (1999). Brochure, Hotel Association of New York City (1996). *Uniform System of Accounts for the Lodging Industry.* 9th edn. Hotel Association of New York City.

Kotas, R. (1999). *Management Accounting for Hospitality and Tourism.* 3rd edn. International Thomson Business Press.

Less, M. and Mager, S. (1999). A cruise ship is not just a floating hotel. *Bottomline*, vol. **14** (3), April–May, 15–18, 20.

Maher, A. (1995). Labour recruitment and turnover costs in hotels. in *Accounting and Finance for the International Hospitality Industry* (P. Harris, ed.), Butterworth-Heinemann.

Mason, D. and Opperman, J. (1996). The business of theme park accounting. *Bottomline*, **11** (7), October–November, 11, 12, 24.

McCool, A. (1996). Pricing and cost management for in-flight food service industry. *Bottomline*, **11** (7), October–November, 14–16.

Mitchell, J. (1999). Feeding the flame. *Caterer and Hotelkeeper*, 19 September, 27, 28.

Mullen, R. (1998). Brand finale? *Caterer and Hotelkeeper*, 20 August, 52–53.

National Restaurant Association (1996). *The Uniform System of Accounts for Restaurants.* 7th edn. National Restaurant Association

Patterson, D. (1999). Forecasting casino revenues. *Bottomline*, **14** (2), March, 7–14.

Payne, R. (1990). The big event. *Leisure Management*, **10** (8), 68–70.

Poorani, A. and Smith, D. (1995). Financial characteristics of bed-and-breakfast inns. *Cornell Hotel and Restaurant Administration Quarterly*, **36** (5), October, 57–63.

Schillaci, J. (1993). The secret of success. *Bottomline*, **8** (5), October–November, 15–19.

Schmidgall, R. S. (1997). *Hospitality Industry Managerial Accounting.* 4th edn. Educational Institute of the American Hotel and Motel Association.

Schmidgall, R., Borchgrevnik C. and Zahl-Begnum, D. (1996). Operational budgeting practices of lodging firms in the US and Scandinavia. *International Journal of Hospitality Management*, **15** (2), 189–203.

Stokes, J. (1999). Forecasting, Presentation made at BAHA Accounting Conference, Birmingham, February.

Wood, R. (1997). *Working in Hotels and Catering.* International Thomson Business Press.

Virgin trains (1999). Fare details on 1 November at www.virgintrains.co.uk

Further reading

Coltman, M. M. (1997). *Hospitality Management Accounting*. 6th edn. Van Nostrand Reinhold.

Davis, B., Lockwood, A. and Stone, S. (1998). *Food and Beverage Management*. 3rd edn. Butterworth-Heinemann.

Harris, P. (1999). *Profit Planning*. 2nd edn. Butterworth-Heinemann.

Harris, P. J. and Hazzard, P. A. (1992). *Managerial Accounting in the Hospitality Industry*. 5th edn. Stanley Thornes.

Schmidgall, R. S. (1997). *Hospitality Industry Managerial Accounting*. 4th edn. Educational Institute of the American Hotel and Motel Association.

Hospitality information technology

Andy Frew

Objectives

The general objectives of this chapter are to provide an overview of the rapidly changing information technology (IT) landscape within hospitality in the UK, to offer illustrations of the shift in both vendor and client business models and to explain the information and communications technology context. In keeping with the overall theme of the text you will be invited to consider and draw comparisons in system type and business approach catalysed by current and emerging technologies. At the end of the chapter you should be able to:

1 Identify important IT systems and applications within the sector.

2 Compare systems on the basis of core technology concepts.

3 Identify some of the major technology influences on the hospitality industry.

4 Recognize the impact of these influences through specific applications.

Introduction

The explosive growth and adoption of new technologies within hospitality makes writing on the subject a necessarily selective and incomplete process, there will always be technologies, applications and indeed sectors which cannot be covered even in a dedicated text. This chapter therefore offers an introductory taste of hospitality information technology and, for those wishing to further explore this area, some simple comparative tools for the journey into this vast and stimulating domain.

The need for selection has led to the hotel sector being used as the central focus; this is arguably the largest sector and often drives the development of many new applications and systems. I would ask your indulgence in this choice since the points of significance that are brought out here may be most easily illustrated through this specific sector and applied throughout the industry.

Two main approaches to comparing technologies and their application are proposed:

- the nature of the processing and application environments and associated communication channel

- Internet-enabled application.

New technologies have made their mark and the Internet has already, and will continue to, fundamentally transform the hospitality industry and hospitality IT, sometimes in unexpected directions. So, instead of presenting a catalogue of system types and detailed functionality the approach will look at systems from a largely generic perspective and at vendors and users through the eyes of this (Internet) agent of change and its web client-server paradigm. For good or ill the Internet, especially when wearing its web-browsing party dress, is changing everything from daily operations to fundamental business models.

We shall undoubtedly look back on the early part of the twenty-first century as the time when global hyperlinking became an everyday reality and the rules changed for ever. Certainly, we are entering an immediate period of significant change, and there are many technological bottlenecks and attitudinal pain barriers to be overcome, but be certain, these barriers will come down. They are already falling as we can see around us with the ubiquitous advances in computer processing, storage capabilities and the global telecommunications infra-structure being relentlessly developed with faster and more robust components as Moore's Law (data density on integrated circuits doubles every eighteen months) marches on unchal-lenged. High-speed Internet access will become fact in less than a decade – if you do not agree then look at the upsurge in interest in integrated services digital networks (ISDN), asynchronous digital subscriber line (ADSL) and asynchronous transfer mode (ATM) and check out the Internet2 site (http://www.Internet2.edu) where trials are being undertaken at speeds almost 50 000 times faster than today's fastest modems.

The hyperlinked universe is really about to grow up and even now we are implementing interesting and constructive uses of the still clunky, immature, yet nonetheless powerful technologies; the Java applets, the cookies, the plug-ins and the download limbo that today represent the web. So am I then just an unashamed golly-gee-whizz technophile, the sort we are warned of by some authors (Peacock and Shaw, 1996; Peacock and Kubler, 1999)? Perhaps, though I would like to think otherwise. However, my point is simple – after two decades of watching technology in the sector both as observer and participant-observer it is evident that a sea change is under way. Other writers (Dehler, 1997; Kolodny, 1996) have been signalling the organizational impacts of new technologies for some years and we are now about to witness the impact on our industry. Two or three years ago trying to find a hospitality IT vendor with an e-mail address, never mind a website, was an almost futile search. The situation has completely reversed today and an industry, which almost boasts of its conservatism, is undergoing a radical transformation.

It is this shift that I will seek to use as the basis for comparisons in approach for both vendor and client. To begin with I will look at how we got here and the conventional perception of hospitality IT, then the focus will move to a consideration of where the new technologies may take us. The first phase of this shift – the first couple of decades – saw new technologies improving operations and management but, although this process of improvement is bound to continue, we are now on the threshold of a quantum shift where the new technologies will change what we actually do and, indeed, may redefine the hospitality industry.

An industry that had to be dragged screaming and kicking to adopt a graphical user interface has latterly seen the light and the pace of conversion is as exciting as it is astonishing. New products are beginning to appear, new solutions, and new approaches – in short new business models are being offered and all this before the tidal e-commerce and e-business waves wash over the industry!

The legacy

The hospitality industry, as was noted earlier, has a conservative reputation in relation to computing so we should perhaps start with acknowledging that this was not always the case, a landmark in commercial computing – the Lyons Electronic Office (LEO), was implemented in our industry in the early 1950s! Forty years ago you could have any kind of computer you liked as long as it was large, expensive, temperamental and required an expert team of nursemaids twenty-four hours a day. In almost all of our industry using these machines meant sending batches of data off to be processed and returned, a process that has survived until recent times in the form of payroll processing. Although these large mainframe computers evolved to become less expensive and more reliable, albeit still complex and more likely to occupy a room than a desktop, their model of centralized expertise and distributed, remote access through 'dumb' terminals became the norm.

Despite the costs involved, many hotel groups in the UK embraced this technology in the 1960s and 1970s and while the cost and complexity still put computerization beyond the reach of most hospitality businesses – the benefits of computerization were becoming evident to management and customers alike. The progressive introduction brought wider access to computing power in desk-sized if not desktop packages and it was even possible to have such systems brought in-house under the wing of a 'systems manager'. This internal solution produced a dramatic shift in turnaround time and it became possible to supplement 'batch-processing' with 'real time' operations such as checking-in guests and posting charges. The model, however, remained one of centralized processing and distributed access through terminals. This computer solution was still very expensive and limited in application, with both hardware and software being proprietary and systems provided by so-called 'turnkey', or one-stop-shop vendors. In fact the support and maintenance of these systems along with even the provision of system consumables was usually completely in the hands of the system vendor.

The late 1970s and early 1980s witnessed the first wave of real hotel computerization as systems became more widespread, staff expertise and customer awareness broadened and, through increasing user feedback, vendors refined their software. They also incorporated the common improvements in technology development – better processing, more robust components, and so forth. A real critical mass of users was building and there was even the establishment of the system managers association as those at the sharp end of implementation sought to share experience and influence vendors. If you entered a computerized UK hotel during this period you would certainly encounter dumb terminals connected with an on-site minicomputer or an off-site mainframe computer.

This situation began to change in the 1980s with the introduction of microcomputers – these novel beasts with their own processor (microprocessor) could actually sit on a desktop and do really useful things such as spreadsheet calculation *and* do them in real time. Suddenly, those who wrote the cheques could see the benefits of computerization and it is no accident that early spreadsheets such as VisiCalc were heralded as the primary drivers of microcomputer adoption with hotel back offices being among the first beneficiaries. Other general purpose (or horizontal) software applications such as word processing and databases quickly followed, and thus began a very rapid expansion in desktop computing – the prospect of an interactive processor, however limited, was enormously alluring and hospitality, like industry elsewhere, began to engage in serious microcomputer adoption.

Microcomputers were not, for the most part, any kind of substitute for minicomputers – they were either supplementary to these systems in the larger hospitality businesses or they represented the first foray into computing. They were much smaller, much more robust, cheaper and, although much less powerful, they could, it was claimed, be usefully operated by someone with little or no computer expertise. These machines were single user or stand-alone machines in the first instance and again almost universally dealt with spreadsheet or accounting functions with occasional word-processing or database applications.

It was not long, however, before two significant things happened: industry-specific (or vertical) software began to be written for these microcomputers either derived from the minicomputer environment or actually written from scratch; and users began to think about networking these microcomputers to share resources. The age of microcomputer dominance had begun.

Today most of us are familiar with the key attributes of a microcomputer – the processor (the faster the better), memory (the more the better), peripheral devices (keyboards, mice, printers, scanners etc.), application software (horizontal, vertical and bespoke) and, of course, the suite of programs that makes it all hang together – the operating system (OS). In the world of mainframes and minicomputers OSs were based on the premise that there would be a central processor and many users, each of which would (rapidly) share its time, i.e. – a multi-user, time-sharing environment. Such OSs were not entirely inappropriate for the new one-to-one interaction of the microprocessor and so began a period of rapid proliferation of new OSs. Users were presented now with multiple vendor offerings incorporating a huge array of proprietary hardware and software (written in a bewildering range of programming languages) now embedded in an assortment of OSs.

On the surface, this unhelpful diversity could have constrained the adoption rate of microcomputer-based systems, however, such was the perceived (and very real) benefit of relatively inexpensive computing power and its ability to deliver enhanced management efficiency and service quality, that systems were bought in unheard of quantities and new vendors emerged almost every other month! One text (Braham, 1988) stated that in the UK there were thirty-eight companies offering micro-computer-based solutions and described the situation as 'one of the most hotly contested in the world'. A decade or so later and you could easily find almost 200 companies offering micro-computer-based applications to the UK hospitality industry – draw your own conclusions! The most recent of the few texts tackling hospitality it (O'Connor, 2000) makes commendable efforts at covering the now vast field at an introductory level.

Thankfully this growth has not been mirrored in a profusion and confusion of programming languages and operating systems. The advent of the Intel-based IBM personal computer (PC) with its DOS operating system and the subsequent successors and clones produced an almost de facto standard for micro-computer use. As we have moved through the 1990s, the influence of OSs and their underlying standards have begun to be understood and this standardization has matured to the point where the hardware and operating systems (stand-alone, net-worked and inter-networked) are now almost seen as a straight-forward commodity. As we shall also see, the days of proprietary vendor tie-ins and their traditional business approaches appear to be numbered. Underlying standards are beginning to play an even greater role in hospitality IT as the Internet protocols are ever more widely adopted and, while this heralds some good news for hard-pressed hospitality businesses, it presents acute challenges to vendors.

It should be remembered that although the very powerful high-end microcomputers and workstations have progressively eroded the original domains of mainframe and minicomputers, they still very much have a role in rapid high-volume processing environments. The 1990s could be characterized as the decade when the benefits of this standardization began to really hit home. The real cost of purchasing microcomputers fell while their capability continued to improve and, although the adoption rate of computers in small to medium-sized enterprises (SMEs) has been disappointingly low, we are now in a position where even the smallest of SMEs can cost-effectively consider com-puterization. The importance of SMEs and their relative uptake of information and communication technologies (ICT) offer some interesting lessons for our industry (Evans and Peacock, 1999). However, before getting too far ahead of the story let us take a look at the current scene.

A vanishing inheritance

The most common encounter users have with computer-based systems is with a single standalone machine, which may be connected to a small internal or local area network (LAN) with a variety of other devices, or perhaps even to a more complex set of networks and internetworks. However, we can reduce the apparent complexity somewhat if we adopt the logic of the schematic in Figure 9.1.

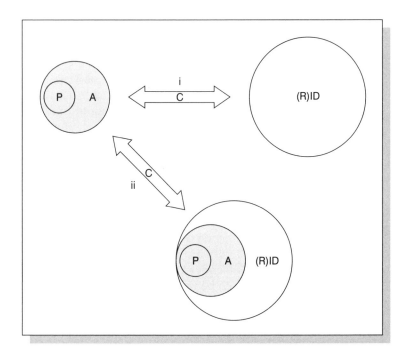

Figure 9.1
Generalized schematic for computer-based systems

In Figure 9.1, *P* is the core processing environment and *A* represents the application or software environment, *C* is the communications channel or medium to the interaction device(s), *ID*. Interaction devices may be physically local to the machine or may be remote, *RID* and any machine or interaction device may be static (workstation, electronic point of sale [EPOS] terminal, minibar) or portable (e.g. laptop, smart card, mobile phone, personal digital assistant [PDA], etc.).

One scenario for *i*, is where the *P* is a microprocessor such as an Intel Pentium III embedded in a microcomputer. *A* may be, for example, energy management software running under Windows NT, *C* encompasses hard-wiring to local microcomputer ports, port concentrators etc. and links to the interaction devices employed by the user, e.g. screen, keyboard, mouse, printer, etc., or perhaps remote interaction device(s) such as temperature sensors or valve controllers.

In *ii*, we can imagine the same scenario this time extended to include communication with an interaction device which itself contains processing capability and hence a potential application environment, i.e. the remote device has become 'smart' – perhaps remote sensors with onboard processing – such as intelligent room thermostats. Or, we could describe the situation where one microcomputer is communicating with another on a network, perhaps the first is running front office software and is passing guest history information to a second machine used for marketing purposes, the communication channel is the LAN and in each case the processor is a microprocessor embedded in a microcomputer running, for example, Windows applications. And so on.

Of course microcomputers do not represent the set of all hardware, and all software need not be based on Windows applications; the generalized conceptual model can be applied to any computer-based system or combination of computer-based systems. Before elaborating on this, a few more words about networks.

Networks

In the above examples, we can readily see that each micro-computer contains its own processing environment; the application environment is constructed through a combination of locally accessed software and that called from the fileserver. The workstations communicate with local interaction devices with no

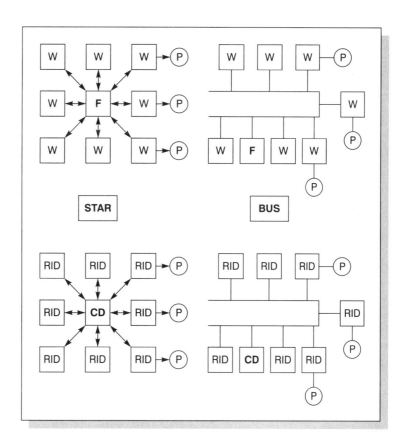

Figure 9.2
Specific and generic network topologies

embedded processing environment, e.g. screen, keyboard, mouse, printer, etc, and also with remote interaction devices which do have embedded processing such as the fileserver. It is worth while to think about how networks are laid out, the most common configuration for LANs are star and bus networks (Figure 9.2) although other topologies such as ring and wireless are possible.

Perhaps the best way of interpreting Figure 9.2 is to regard the top pair of topologies as a typical LAN whereas the bottom pair refer to the generic case of any networked computer based devices. Thus, the arrangement, which sees a fileserver (*F*) with a variety of workstations (*W*) some of which having attached printers (*P*), can easily be generalized whereby *F* can be seen as a central controlling or co-ordinating device (*CD*), W can be any kind of remote interaction device (*RID*) and *P* is now a peripheral attached to this *RID*. Thus, what may be a simple means of considering the layout of a microcomputer-based LAN, such as may be used for a property management system (PMS), can now also be used to consider *any* combination of devices and systems, e.g. a minibar configuration. Therefore it may provide a comparative basis for examining *any* system.

A basic LAN will be composed of several microcomputers, at least one of which will be significantly more powerful (faster processor, more RAM, greater disk storage and so forth), and be used to handle network traffic and store most of the programs and most of the data – the fileserver or server. The individual microcomputers on the network, sometimes called workstations, are generally used for input and output but rarely for any significant levels of program or data storage.

Networks are conceptually simple enough comprising *servers, clients, communication media* and *protocols*:

1 Any computer capable of sharing resources with other computers is a *server* with the most obvious examples of shared resources being files, printers, email distribution, and web documents.

2 A *client* is a computer that uses resources shared by servers. General-purpose clients may let computers access file- and printer-sharing services, while e-mail servers require their clients to have specialized e-mail client software. Computers may be clients for many types of service and also simultaneously function as a server and as a client, e.g. turning on the file- and printer-sharing feature of a Windows 98 computer leads it to appear on the network as a server but it can also continue to work as a network client.

3 Servers and clients need to communicate in order to exchange data and this communication takes place through a communication channel or *medium.* Computer networks use many

types of media with the most common being copper cable, but optical fibre, microwave and light media are not unusual.

4 The languages of network communication are called *protocols* – the vocabulary and grammar necessary for digital co-operation.

Local and wide area networks

With microcomputers, the most common form of network solution is to use a LAN with a cable linking the various computers and other devices. A LAN may be simply defined as a network within a limited geographical area usually no more than a single room or perhaps a single building. In addition to simply cabling the computers together, each computer must have on board a network card. Wide area networks (WANs) cover larger geographical distances and may even be global. The national telecommunications infrastructure is a WAN. Wide area networks are typically slower than LANs and can be very expensive (putting communications satellites and microwave stations and laying miles of fibre optic cable). You do not have to look very far for a WAN; you probably use one almost every day – the Internet, the world's biggest WAN.

With this background it is now useful to peruse some of the systems in use in hotels (Figure 9.3) and then consider placing these in the context of the schematics outlined in Figures 9.1 and 9.2. The left-hand box in Figure 9.3 encompasses a range of internal systems and, depending on size, the hotel may have some or indeed all of these systems. The right-hand box

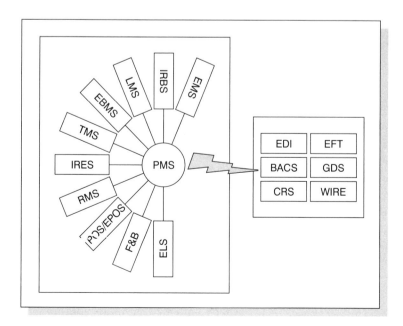

Figure 9.3
Indicative hotel systems

encompasses typical external communications and systems where data and information may be passed from the external to the internal business environment, and vice versa.

The figure is laid out such that the PMS is viewed as a kind of 'hub' through which other 'peripheral' systems may communicate. Around this central system are arrayed the internal peripheral systems and a range of potential external systems. This is, of course, an entirely artificial device since very few businesses actually have this range of systems in place and in some the PMS itself may be absent, but nonetheless it does serve to indicate the possibilities. Certainly the concept of PMS as the key guest and information interface is a powerful one.

The following represent some of the internal systems adopted by hotels:

- EBMS – electronic bar management system

- ELS – electronic locking system

- EMS – energy management system

- EPOS – electronic point of sale system

- F&B – food and beverage system

- IRBS – in-room business system

- IRES – in-room entertainment system

- LMS – leisure management system

- RMS – restaurant management system

- TMS – telephone management system.

In addition some or all of the systems may be connected directly or through the LAN to external systems such as:

- BACS – bank automated clearing service

- CRS – central reservations system

- EDI – electronic data interchange

- EFT – electronic funds transfer

- GDS – global distribution system

- Wire – wire services (e.g. Reuters).

Thus, any of these systems may be viewed in terms of the earlier conceptual approaches (Figure 9.4).

Some examples of internal systems will now be given. However, you may find it useful to use this basis of comparison to explore the full range of systems and the vendor offerings for each category. A more comprehensive selection of systems is

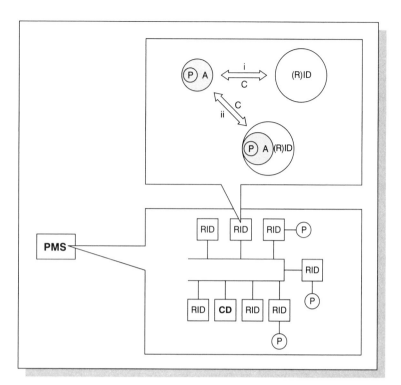

Figure 9.4
Generalized schematic and topology illustrating PMS

offered on a variety of exhibition and professional association websites (see the 'Further reading' section at the end of the chapter). So, let us start with the most common hotel system of all – the property management system.

Property management systems

In a typical hotel the PMS will comprise a suite of software handling the core front and back office operations, loaded on to a fileserver that in turn is networked with several micro-computers or workstations. It is a feature of local area networking that the system may be configured such that all software may be accessible from any workstation, but in practice some functions are usually dedicated to specific workstations or groups of workstations. There may be, perhaps, three workstations at reception each capable of accessing the software suite, although these workstations could also be networked to a single printer, usually it is more convenient (consider busy check-in/out periods) to have a local printer attached to each.

The network will often have a separate workstation handling advanced reservations, and others picking up the accounting functions and so forth. Using the conceptual approach of Figure 9.1 as a comparison, we can see that the processing environment is clear, several processing and applications environments, physically distributed and with (usually) hard-wired connections between each workstation as the communications channel. In addition to each workstation with its processing and application environment, one of the processing environments (the fileserver) has network operating system software loaded as part of its application environment to handle the flow of traffic across the network. It is possible to classify components on the basis suggested earlier, i.e. the processing environment(s), application environment(s), communication media and the interaction devices. Leading UK suppliers of such systems include Innsite (http://www.innsite.co.uk) and AremisSoft (http://www.aremissoft.com).

Energy management systems

These systems are commonly employed to handle, heating, lighting and so on, and may be viewed from the perspective of guest comfort and control of their environment or from the system management perspective in controlling costs. Such systems, in order to function, will typically have components in rooms to enable guest selection of room temperature or lighting, these in-room devices will send signals to the devices which in turn activate lighting control or heat control. From the management perspective there is a requirement to monitor and control the use of systems which demand energy within a building – this may be the power supplied to lift systems, heating systems, lighting systems and so on and this requirement produces a demand for sensors to indicate the status of systems and actuators to implement a change in the status of the systems. In short, management wish to examine current usage and take decisions to improve the overall operation, e.g. reducing or raising heating levels in rooms, floors, areas of the building as appropriate to use, perhaps reducing energy use at critical thresholds to avoid punitive tariffs on use etc.

Any energy management system will therefore comprise a variety of remote devices and a means of monitoring the status of the physical environment's key attributes: temperature, light, power and so on. There is a very simple division between what the guest can effect (simple local change) and what management may effect: monitoring and control of all systems. All changes to the status of attributes are recorded to provide historical analysis and a basis for future action – ultimately aimed at facilitating the lowest cost of operation consistent with optimum guest satisfaction.

Energy management systems may, on the surface, appear to be fiendishly complex systems but closer inspection using our comparative approach reveals that they resolve themselves into relatively simple configurations. Typically a stand-alone microcomputer will be loaded with a suite of software with extensive functionality including the capacity to send and receive signals from an array of remote devices – some are sensors and some are actuators. In any event there is usually a significant amount of cable running around the building between the computer and these remote devices. If control is desired down to room level, then clearly these RIDs must be placed in each room and physically connected in some way back to the controlling device – the energy management computer. A diagram describing the arrangement would look much like Figure 9.1 but with perhaps hundreds of communication channels and a mixture of interaction devices local and remote, intelligent and dumb.

Restaurant management systems

Restaurant management systems follow the same pattern. While they may appear to be superficially complex they can be analysed through the same kind of comparative analysis as above. Restaurant operations are often tremendously involved and may comprise very large numbers of widely differing transactions – tracking and ordering stock, menu planning/engineering, order processing and so on. A typical environment may comprise several restaurants, bars, dozens of staff and operate on many levels. In the final analysis what is required is the appropriate functionality to be embedded in the software (the application environment), a means of processing (the processing environment), devices for taking orders and communicating these to kitchens, bars etc., server tracking, bill generation, etc.

So we usually have a central microcomputer on to which is loaded the restaurant management software. This computer is connected to the remote interaction devices such as, point of sale (POS)/electronic funds transfer at point of sale (EFTPOS), printers, handheld devices in some kind of network – so, again, usually lots of cabling (and perhaps wireless or infrared for the handheld devices. Again the configuration will typically be a star or bus arrangement with the interaction devices a mixture of dumb and intelligent (think about what the interaction devices look like in each case).

Electronic locking systems

By now I am sure you have the idea – an ELS may comprise hundreds of remote interaction devices (the door locks) that may be programmed centrally from a single microcomputer that has been loaded with the ELS software. This software is usually no more sophisticated than providing the ability to generate a unique code for the door and produce a unique guest key in the form of a punched card or magnetic stripe card for example (well not unique exactly since the system will be capable of generating staff access keys at various levels and also capable of tracking usage). Suppliers of electronic locking systems include Saflok (http://www.saflok.com) and Vingcard (http://www.vingcard.com).

Electronic bar management systems

The most common type is the in-room minibar system and these machines have onboard sensors (and sometimes processors) to log usage types, rates, price and so on. These data must be communicated to the PMS so that appropriate charges appear on the guest bill and stocking levels are properly controlled. The devices themselves may be very sophisticated but in terms of our comparative context we can again see that they may be regarded as remote interaction devices connected via a communication medium (usually hard-wired) to a controlling device, i.e. a microcomputer hosting the software. As with electronic locking systems there may be hundreds of cable runs from the remote devices back to the controlling device. There are many suppliers of these systems, e.g. Minibar (http://www.minibar.ch/) or Bartech (http://www.bartech.fr).

Telephone management systems

Call-accounting and telephone systems are a crucial part of any hotel system set-up. In this case the controlling device and processing environment is the switchboard or private automatic branch exchange (PABX), loaded with appropriate software to handle all the usual telephone functions plus hotel specific applications such as alarm calls, baby-listening and so forth. The communication medium is usually hard-wired copper cable running to each remote interaction device: handsets, fax machines, Internet access terminals and so on and even the handsets nowadays may well have onboard processing themselves.

It is immediately apparent how different the remote interaction devices can be and how similar the controlling device in each case – usually a microcomputer loaded with software with the appropriate functionality. Would it not be nice if these systems could intercommunicate and would it not be even nicer if I did not have to buy new hardware for every new system? In a hotel of any size, there may be many of these systems around (a London hotel I regularly stay in at one time boasted of having seventeen separate systems!) and approaching the controlling computers is often an exercise in spaghetti cable avoidance!

There is a clear imperative to link systems together. A PMS which records a guest check-in could usefully instruct the TMS to open the room lines, log calls and post charges; it could link to the RMS to provide immediate name validation and posting of charges when the guest has a drink in the bar, or to POS at any other revenue outlet, or to the EMS to provide the guest temperature preference recorded in guest history and so on. The effective linking systems, or system interfacing, is much sought after in the industry. All that is required for this to occur is not really much more complicated than the set of standards that let you connect any old printer to your computer – a physical connection, a set of protocols and a bit of software – the interface software.

Unfortunately the reality is far from simple. As we have already seen the range of vendors is vast, even in the UK, and despite the great strides forward in standardizing, they do not all use the same operating system. Even where they do, they do not necessarily implement their software in the same manner. While there is much talk of open systems and the search for compatibility, the reality is that many vendors adopt a proprietary approach to implementation. However, the news is not all bad. If you use systems from the larger vendors in each category then the likelihood is that the interface software will already exist, provided you are happy to pay for the privilege! Of course, if you adopt a system from a smaller or a newer vendor then the chances are that an interface does not yet exist and may have to be (expensively) put together for you.

Although there have been many initiatives over the years to seek to bring vendors together to adopt a common standard, until recently, unlike the counterparts in for example the travel technology world, this has met with dismal failure. However, the new technologies and changing business models brought about through this have led to the Hospitality Information Technology Interface Standards initiative – HITIS more of which later (http://www.hitis.org).

In addition to the above drives to interface more fully, there is an equally reasonable demand to implement systems on the minimum hardware configuration and avoid duplication and redundancy. While most systems require a basic controlling device or even a powerful server, there is often a good case for simply mounting the system-specific software on an existing LAN. Thus instead of a PMS and EMS being quite distinct systems (perhaps even interfaced), it is reasonable to suppose that EMS software could in fact be mounted on the PMS LAN and one of the workstations then function as the physical interface to the EMS communication media. In other words, although our conceptual approach in Figure 9.3 is useful, in reality many of those shaded system boxes could be laid on top of the PMS box reflecting a growing network with growing software functionality.

New technologies: new networks

Hospitality system vendors at one time could look forward to earning respectable margins on hardware and software sales, while installation, training, support and maintenance provided equally healthy revenue streams. Although there remain a few exceptions, it is now possible to consider the vertical software functionality and application environment as being separable from the hardware and horizontal software needs. The boxes and general purpose software have become commodities.

Even worse news for vendors is that with each passing month more and more software is being made available in an open, portable format and proprietary control is further shrinking. With third party installation and maintenance now becoming commonplace for hardware, the remaining traditional territory open to system vendors is training and software support, but even here third party support companies, on-line training and training organizations are being increasingly used and, for vendors keen to survive, a changing customer relationship has been inevitable.

Just as it has taken twenty years for computerization and in particular microcomputerization to permeate the industry, with the various stakeholders only now seriously reconciling them-selves to the importance of system standards, the conceptual and business models in this conventional wisdom may now be swept aside by the new wave of technological innovation fuelled by the Internet. We shall now try to make some sense of the existing position by seeking to identify consistent aspects of systems and, through this, lead into illustrating the Internet as an agent of change.

The Internet

During the 1960s and 1970s, although LANs and WANs made it easier to share information within organizations, the exchange of data stopped at the boundaries of the network. Each networking technology passed information in a different way, depending on the design of its hardware. Certain LAN technologies would only work with specific computers and most LAN and WAN technologies were incompatible with each other.

The Internet was designed to interconnect the different types of networks and allow information to move freely among users, regardless of which computer workstations, operating systems or networks they used. The connected network then needed a common *protocol* – and this new protocol was called *transmission control protocol/Internet protocol* (TCP/IP). The Internet is a global network of many different computers that communicate using a common language. There are countless numbers of server computers in use on the Internet, each providing some type of information or service. The number of users (currently estimated at over 200 million) and services on the Internet continues to grow each year, as the variety of available services increases.

What is available?

Perhaps the most ubiquitous Internet service, *e-mail* is the postal system of the Internet. It lets you exchange text messages and computer files with anyone on the Internet who has an e-mail address. Modern e-mail programs support richly formatted text, embedded sound files, video clips and background pictures. Using a *chat* program, two or more people connected to the Internet at the same time can enjoy a real-time conversation by sending and receiving instant text messages. Popular Internet chat programs have additional features, such as the ability to instantly exchange pictures, sounds and other files.

File-transfer protocol (FTP) is an Internet service that lets users transfer files from one computer to another. Files on FTP servers can be accessed with FTP client programs or through a web browser. *Usenet* is a worldwide network of UNIX systems that is used as a bulletin board system by special-interest discussion groups. Client software known as a newsreader is required to read articles in a newsgroup.

Still the fastest growing Internet service today, the *web* is the global set of interconnected hypertext files residing on web servers all over the world. With a browser, users can click on hyperlinks to browse through pages that combine text, graphics, animations, sound, and video clips into interactive documents.

Intranets and extranets

The Internet's ability to cross technological and geographical boundaries has not gone unnoticed in the business world, and e-mail, for example, is now common in most businesses. Even so, companies are vigorously examining ways to extend the Internet, and particularly the World Wide Web, within their organizations. In this way intranets and extranets have been born. An *intranet* is a computer network designed for exclusive access *within* a company or organization typically to:

- provide database access

- distribute software

- distribute electronic documents.

- provide training.

An *extranet* is an extension of an intranet, using web technology to allow vendors and customers of a company or organization to share resources and communicate with each other, and can be set up to allow limited access to corporate resources on a company's intranet. One of the main advantages of an extranet lies in the enhanced efficiency it lends to important business relationships such as purchasing – e-procurement.

New solutions

There is already considerable fusion of computing and communications technologies whether web-enabled or interactive digital television, cellular and Internet telephony, geographical information systems (GIS) and global positioning systems (GPS) etc. The importance of technological alliances and mergers is now being reflected in the business world, an example being the merger of Time Warner with AOL; a wedding of vast multimedia content and global web-oriented delivery systems. Let us now look at the impact on systems available to hotels (Figure 9.5).

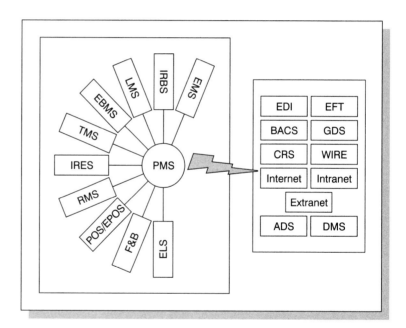

Figure 9.5
Indicative hotel systems: extended

The hotel of today is faced with a very different scenario to that of even a few short years ago. It is no longer a case of selecting systems and striving for good interfacing and good integration. Vendors are metamorphosing and consumers are becoming more sophisticated and more demanding. As a consequence hotel solutions are becoming more adventurous. For example, The Bonham Hotel (see Case 9.1) was recently given the Hospitality Solutions Show award for best use of technology.

Case 9.1

The Internet has changed much in terms of how businesses adapt and employ the technology. This example, like others cited in this chapter, has been drawn from the Hospitality Solutions Show 1990 Technology Awards, where the property was voted best for use of technology in an individual outlet. The owners of the three Edinburgh luxury hotels in the Town House Company; The Bonham, Channings and The Howard, introduced a complete digital communication and entertainment system (Mediamax) in each of The Bonham's forty-eight bedrooms claiming to be the first hotel in Europe to offer this service. The aim, according to Marco Truffelli, Head of IT for the group was to provide a solution giving all guests (of whom 65 per cent are high-profile business travellers) a complete information, communication and entertainment system offering a 'virtual office environment' combined with the latest in-home entertainment technology.

The system consists of a box in each bedroom under the guest's television connected by a SCART cable. Using an infrared keyboard and on-screen menu, the guests can:

- access full PC capability
- send or receive e-mail
- surf the Internet
- watch digital video disc (DVD) movies
- listen to compact discs (CDs)
- play 3-dimensional games.

The in-room system is linked to the extensive hotel LAN, supported by fibre-optic infrastructure providing always-on 128 kbps Internet access. When guests enter their room and switch on the system they are automatically presented with a menu including:

- word processing
- spreadsheet
- Internet access
- e-mail
- printing
- information services.

They simply choose an option from the infrared keyboard and use the television as a PC. The system allows not only the use of generic and corporate e-mail but also enables guests to exchange documents with other guests should they choose. The information service provides both information and links to travel and tourism information as well as an on-line selection of international newspapers. These information services are also replicated on an Internet-enabled kiosk the reception area. The benefits include guests being able to access up-to-the-minute information from their room, business travellers have access to a 'virtual office', can leave their laptops at home and can exchange documents on the hotel LAN.

An example of a vendor shifting in response to changing technology and market demand is Innsite – for long associated with one of the most popular PMS solutions and a flagship for the 'traditional' solutions. In the last year or so there has been a constructive and high profile move towards a different sort of solution (see Case 9.2).

Case 9.2

In a keynote paper, Tony Ferrari, managing director of Innsite one of the UK's largest hotel system vendors, sums up this shift in policy:

> PMS systems that operated independently have been superseded by a second generation which link the elements of PMS, CRS and Data Warehouse. These still cannot provide the flexibility that is critical to contemporary group operations. Only the arrival of a third generation of application software based on Intranet technology provides solutions that map onto hotel requirements rather than forcing business practice to follow systems.
>
> (Ferrari, 1999)

This view reflects the changing business model of hotel groups with greater and greater centralization of function. Innsite have adopted the client-server approach to enable clients to access functionality as it is needed. Centralized group servers can hold all data on an Intranet and remote users such as hotel workstations may be 'thin clients' being configured as required. This centralization of data differs markedly from the traditional consolidation approach and offers enormous flexibility in how data and information are accessed and distributed – much greater control. Innsite call this evolution Chain Management Solutions (CMS).

At the other end of the spectrum, the SMEs, Innsite are again using the new technologies to pilot a bureau style system whereby Innsite (not the hotel group in this case) host the server and make the functionality available through the Internet. This solution, again client-server, perhaps underscores the earlier comments about vendor survival options and sees the SME having an extremely low cost of ownership as they are not involved in system purchase as such at all!

In addition to the new technologies offering opportunities and challenges to existing stakeholders, hoteliers rethinking their operations and vendors repositioning themselves, etc., they also provide a stimulus to new entrants to the marketplace with new models and new formats. A good example of this is HotelView (see Case 9.3), a company that, without the Internet, would have no infrastructure to deliver its services.

Case 9.3

Hotelview describes itself as the 'Video Jukebox of the travel industry' and is an example of a vendor that is a new entrant to a new marketplace – website streaming video. They have created a website enhancement tool that produces a full-motion multimedia tour, two to four minute television-like advertisements as mini-tours of properties, attractions and destinations. 'Advertising even on the Internet is usually frustrating for hotel marketing directors because they can't tell the entire story of their property with just still photos and catchy slogans' explains David Chestler, HotelView's General Manager, 'with HotelView, the viewer, either travel agent or consumer can experience the hotel in the comfort of their own home or office and have a close-up look at the property'.

HotelView is accessed through the hotel's own website. Once the viewer selects the video option they are taken to the HotelView website which is a typical example of an active distribution site, seductively populated with useful portals and tools and returned transparently. The company will either translate and edit existing footage or produce original high-quality video – the video material is accessed via the hotel site or may be accessed through www.hotelview-.com, through the travel channel on www.broadcast.com, by travel agents, tour operators, car rental companies, destinations and so forth. To access the user need only use a browser with RealPlayer installed and, although T1 lines or ISDN are recommended, modem access is nonetheless very effective.

However, like many new players in the new distribution arena, the site suffers from a less than comprehensive database of hotels, destinations and attractions.

As you can see, the benefits of the Internet are having a real impact on distribution in the hotel sector. The traditional hotel electronic distribution world of GDS and CRS has now been shaken up by the so-called alternative distribution systems (ADSs). In response to this the GDS have been seeking to reposition, and realign themselves. For example, to the web presence of SABRE with its Travelocity site (http://www.travelocity.com) or as booking engines for others, e.g. Worldspan, as the key inventory behind the dramatic rise of Microsoft's virtual travel agency Expedia (http://www.expedia.com). The ADSs are making significant inroads and in particular SMEs now find themselves with affordable global distribution outlets either through their local destination management systems or through data aggregator ADS such as WorldRes.com (see Case 9.4).

Case 9.4

WorldRes.com

WorldRes.com is one of the new breed of ADSs offering hotel electronic distribution – information and reservations – through their global website http://www.PlacesToStay-.com, recently named Travel Site of the Year by Hotel Interactive. It is claimed that 'any property – from a single B&B to an international chain of resorts' can participate. Unlike the GDS, for example, there is no upfront subscription but simply a small transaction fee per reservation. These reservations may come directly from WorldRes or through their partner network (it is an increasingly common feature for distribution intermediaries to forge extensive links, alliances and portals offering multiple channels and routes to market).

Hotel inventory and information can be updated from the property simply through a microcomputer and Internet access. Member content is stored in a central database and thus any changes are automatically transmitted to all partners simultaneously. The company also claim 'The WorldRes system is completely Internet based and independent of older, mainframe-based airline CRS or intermediary systems. And in contrast to most major travel websites, hotels are not required to participate in those proprietary systems to receive real-time reservations through WorldRes.'

The system is designed to handle millions of simultaneous transactions, has full transaction security and extensive fault tolerance and backup.

Conclusions

The history of hospitality computerization can be represented simply by two waves: twenty years of mainframe and mini-computer introduction into a very small proportion of hospitality businesses, followed by twenty years of microcomputer adoption culminating in significant penetration of microcomputer-based systems, substantial maturity and moves towards standardization and standards. Now we are at the dawn of a third wave that promises to transform much of the industry. Only time will tell if this transformation will take two more decades to complete, but the process has undeniably begun.

In looking at the spread and use of information and communication technologies in hospitality we can rationalize the multitude of systems that confront us and make comparisons between them using the two approaches offered in this chapter. This we can do, first, by identifying core processing and application environments along with the communication media and interaction devices and, second, by examining the degree to which the systems have become 'web-enabled'. We have briefly touched upon technological convergence and fusion and, as we move into the new technological era, our concepts and constructs may become less useful as processing environment, application environment, communication media and interaction devices coalesce in a seamless web of intelligent systems and agents.

In the final analysis, we are neither in the information technology business nor the Internet business, we are in the hospitality business and while the new technologies offer tremendous support and opportunities, and indeed help redefine hospitality, if our hospitality focus is lost we will become just another commodity-based retail business. We may even see room nights being traded on the global markets!

I will leave the final word to Clifford Stoll (Stoll, 1995), perhaps one of the most respected, and influential commentators on the future of the Internet; the reader may ponder his view:

> Me, an Internet addict? Hey – I'm leading a full life with family and friends, and a job. Computers are a sideline, not my life. Jupiter is rising in the east, looking down on

the Connecticut farm where I am vacationing. On one side, a forest, on the other, a cornfield . . . But I don't care. Fingers on the keyboard I'm bathed in the cold glow of my cathode ray tube, answering email. Tonight twenty letters want replies, three people have invited me to chat over the network, there's a dozen newsgroups to read and a volley of files to download . . . Even on vacation I can't escape the computer networks. I take a deep breath and pull the plug.

Summary

So, we have undertaken a whirlwind tour of hospitality IT, or at least a section of it. The central points for you to think about include the following:

1 Information and communication technologies are becoming an increasingly important part of the industry and in many areas are fundamentally transforming its nature.

2 The installed technology base. The legacy systems contribute to inertia in new system adoption but increasing standardisation in systems, operating systems and communication protocols is catalysing change.

3 It is possible to reduce almost any kind of computer-based system or network found in the hospitality industry to simple conceptual components and this can be a useful technique in both analysing existing or configuring potential systems.

4 The Internet is already being extensively employed to extend the scope of the installed system base within the industry, in particular in electronic distribution. It is also significantly changing many existing business models precipitating the appearance of energetic new entrants unencumbered by neither legacy systems nor relationships.

5 The power of many new technologies is now increasingly accessible for SMEs, global distribution is becoming a realistic option for this group for the first time and the rise of application service provision may also make affordable functionality available on a pay per use basis.

6 All stakeholders in the value chain, including vendors, are finding that they have to adapt their strategies in the light of incipient ubiquitous high bandwidth and an inexpensive, functionality-rich cyberspace.

Review questions

1 Consider the ways in which a small hospitality enterprise might take advantage of the Internet. Where might the priorities lie? Distribution? Back Office?

2 How might the application service providers approach offer front or back office functionality to SMEs?

3 To what extent are traditional hotel central reservations systems similar to the new infomediaries or alternative distribution system providers such as WorldRes.com?

4 What challenges are posed for brand or image management by the new distribution channels?

5 How might a hotel chain make use of Internet chat facilities?

6 What might be the advantages in all devices having an IP address? Think about the practical implications such as cabling or reduced telephony charges for POS polling etc.

7 On what basis could you make valid comparisons between the types of reservation system used by hotels and those used by cinemas, leisure centres or airlines?

8 Are the reservation systems used by restaurants essentially the same as those used by hotels, or not?

9 Do the more generic types of system, i.e. EPOS, stock control, food and beverage management, etc., operate in the same way in whatever type of hospitality business they are installed?

10 If you wanted to compare the operation of a property management system installed in all the hotels within a company, how would you go about this and what factors do you think you would need to take into consideration?

Bibliography

Braham, B. (1988). *Computer Systems in the Hotel and Catering Industry*. Cassell.

Dehler, G. (1997). The T-form organisation: using technology to design organizations for the 21st century and waves of change: business evolution through information technology, *Journal of Engineering and Technology Management*, **13**, 315–319.

Evans, G. and Peacock, M. (1999). A comparative study of ICT in tourism and hospitality SMEs in Europe.In *Information and Communications Technologies in Tourism* (D. Buhalis and W. Schertler, eds) pp. 247–258, Springer-Verlag.

Ferrari, T. (1999). Company Information Sheet issued at The HITEC Conference, Atlanta, USA.

Kolodny, H. (1996). New technology and the emerging organisational paradigm, *Human Relations*, **49** (12).

O'Connor, P. (2000) *Using Computers in Hospitality.* Cassell.

Peacock, M. and Kubler, M. (1999). Time-space novelties; information technology and workplace communication within the hospitality industry. In *Hospitality Information Technology* (A. Frew, ed.) pp. 97–104, HITA.

Peacock, M. and Shaw, H. (1996). Bytes and bias: technophilia in technology writing. In *Hospitality Information Technology* (A. Frew, ed.) pp. 134–140, HITA.

Stoll, C. (1995). *Silicon Snake Oil, Second Thoughts on the Information Highway.* Pan Books.

Further reading and useful websites

Collins, G. and Malik, T. (1997), *Hospitality Information Technology.* Kendall Hunt.

http://www.eurhotec.com

http://www.hita.co.uk

http://www.hitecshow.org/vendors

http://www.hospitality-net.com

http://www.hosp-solutions.co.uk

http://www.updateplus.com

O'Connor, P. (1999). *Electronic Information Distribution in Tourism and Hospitality.* CAB International.

Werthner, H. and Klein, S. (1999). *Information Technology and Tourism: A Challenging Relationship.* Springer-Verlag.

Conclusions and further thoughts

Bob Brotherton

Now you have experienced the comparative approach to analysing the hospitality industry you should be in a position to judge the extent to which this approach can enhance your understanding of the nature, characteristics and operational features prevailing in the industry. Hopefully you will concur with my contention that this approach enables you to gain a fuller understanding of these aspects. The alternative, studying different aspects/sectors in isolation from one another, often appears to be superficially attractive because in many senses it is easier in the first instance. However, it becomes less so as you realize that the real world does not operate within such convenient little boxes and this means you have to go on to make your own comparisons with little, or no, help. Though this can be a valuable learning exercise, being left entirely to your own devices may well lead to the adoption of quite ad hoc and superficial approaches to making these comparisons. Having read this book there can now be no excuse for such sloppiness!

The chapters in this book provide you with key information relating to the theme each has adopted. In addition, they have also suggested a series of possible perspectives, models, criteria and thoughts to help you think about useful and valid ways of comparing the particular set of issues you are interested in. Beyond this they have also alerted you to issues, questions and problems you are likely to encounter in trying to do this. The combination of these elements should not only help you to establish a rounded and critical view of the contemporary hospitality industry but also give you a basic framework that can be used to further your understanding of the industry as it evolves and changes over time.

Let me illustrate this briefly for you. The 'hotel industry development' models used by Litteljohn in Chapter 2 clearly have value in helping you to understand how the hotel sector of the industry has evolved over time and under different societal conditions. Indeed, to understand what we have today it is often fruitful to examine what we had in the past and how we have moved from then to now. However, this does not mean that the value of such models lies solely in their ability to help us understand the past and the present. The thinking underlying these models could be extended into the future. For example, you might want to explore how a range of possible future changes may impact on the structure and operation of the hotel, or another, sector over the next five to ten years. To try and do this without any clear base, or reference point, may well mean it becomes an exercise reduced to one constituting a best guess, based on your individual and subjective interpretation of the possibilities. By contrast, adoption of the model approach that Litteljohn advocates would, at the very least, give you a foundation to work from in trying to predict the future, and a framework within which to place the possible future options. This may not be perfect, as trying to predict the future on the basis of the past can be problematic, but it would be preferable to the alternative!

In a similar, but slightly different way, the systems thinking and modelling approach discussed by Jones and Lockwood in Chapter 3 is also transportable to other contexts. Although Chapter 3 applies this approach to investigate the nature of operating systems and products, you will have noticed a similar approach being used by Frew in Chapter 9 to explore hospitality information technology applications. Indeed, the word 'systems', not surprisingly, is used extensively in this IT chapter. Given a moment's reflection I am sure that you will see the value in adopting such an approach to analysing a wide range of hospitality activities. If you need help with this just think about all the elements of hospitality that we routinely refer to as 'systems' – e.g. food production and service systems, front office systems, reservation systems, accounting systems, personnel or human resource management systems, purchasing systems, distribution systems, etc. On a wider scale we also commonly refer to the economic system, the political system, the legal system, etc. Are you convinced yet?

This should not only suggest that the hospitality industry needs to be viewed as a system existing within the context of wider systems, but also that its systems can be compared with similar systems existing in other industries and/or countries. I have suggested earlier that there is value in the hospitality manager adopting less 'tunnel vision' in relation to his or her job and becoming more of an outward-looking manager. To both enhance current practice and introduce new, innovative practices it is vital that tomorrow's hospitality manager becomes more comparative in his or her thinking. Comparing systems used in the hospitality industry with those in other industries can be beneficial as this activity will introduce new ideas and practices into the industry.

On the other hand, I would not want to give you the impression that the rich variety and complexity of the hospitality industry can always be reduced to a simple model or system. Although there is little doubt that the use of models and systems thinking can help to reduce some of the complexity of the real world to make it more readily understandable there is a danger in this approach. As you know, most things are not as simple and straightforward as they may initially appear. This is particularly the case when people, and all their individual idiosyncrasies, are added to the equation. Such complications are highlighted by Lucas and Wood and Kelliher and Johnson in Chapters 5 and 6 respectively.

The authors of these chapters suggest that any attempt to understand management and work practices through a simple 'reductionist' approach is likely to fail. But, is this not a contradiction of what I have been advocating above? The short answer is no. It is possible to strip away much of the surface complexity surrounding these types of practice in order to identify their fundamental aspects. For example, the core functions of management and basic patterns/systems of work organization can be identified as a basis for making comparisons. In this sense the generic 'essence' can be isolated from the specific 'idiosyncratic' influences that impinge on such practices in different contexts.

However, what is different here is the central role that people play in these practices. Of course people are involved, frequently inextricably, with the other aspects of hospitality activity dealt with in this book but their involvement, and its significance, in these respects is invariably mediated by other factors. In the areas of management and work practices it is the intensity and inherent variability of people-to-people interaction that makes it more difficult to reduce to it a simple prescriptive model. Clearly this indicates that these aspects can be more problematic to analyse and understand than others that may have more of a universal reference point. Conversely, it also suggests that these aspects of hospitality constitute an interesting and fertile field for further comparative investigation.

At an international level the opportunities for comparative study are immense, as some of the chapters have indicated.

Furthermore, as the hospitality industry becomes increasingly international, if not global, in its structure and operations, this comparative focus will cease to be one of a potentially desirable option for the busy hospitality manager and constitute a necessary task. Hospitality managers will increasingly work for the same company in different countries and face a bewildering variety of customs, cultures and practices. They will also be operating under different legal systems and financial practices and conventions. Some of the issues relating to the former are raised by Boella in Chapter 7. Although Burgess (Chapter 8) does not systematically explore the international dimension relating to the latter, as this was not part of her brief, this chapter does contain a number of underlying issues relating to this dimension. For example, how do international hospitality companies reconcile their company-wide financial practices with the financial norms and requirements existing within the different countries they operate in? How do they deal with different tax regimes and invoicing/payment methods or the attitudes to pricing and cost control adopted in different cultures?

In conclusion there is no doubt that the hospitality industry, with all its myriad manifestations and practices, is an exciting and rewarding industry to study, especially when this is undertaken on a comparative basis. The industry is constantly evolving and changing. Its structure, who owns whom, how companies organize themselves, what brands, products and services endure or die, how managers' view their role, and the external influences/constraints it faces are changing all the time. Such a dynamic picture can not be adequately understood by simply taking a snapshot of a specific production/service style or the present characteristics of a particular sector. A knowledge of the characteristics of the hotel sector today is valuable today, but of relatively limited value if that is all it remains. In five years' time the sector will not look, or operate, as it does now. Therefore, the mere description of current structures/practices is of limited value to tomorrow's hospitality manager. What you really require is an enquiring mind that can understand the structures and practices underlying the surface picture we see on an everyday basis. Hopefully this book will have gone some way to developing this type of mindset for you.

Index